THE COMPLETE
golf
MANUAL

STEVE NEWELL

DK

**LONDON, NEW YORK, MUNICH,
MELBOURNE, DELHI**

Project Editor Bob Bridle
Senior Art Editor Gillian Andrews
Production Editor Joanna Byrne
Production Controller Mandy Inness
Managing Editor Stephanie Farrow
Senior Managing Art Editor Lee Griffiths

Senior Designer Phil Gamble
Senior Editor Richard Gilbert
Designers Brian Flynn, Hugh Schermuly,
Mandy Earey, Susan St. Louis
Jacket Designer Mark Cavanagh

Photographer Gerard Brown
Photoshoot Art Director Nigel Wright

First published in Great Britain in 2010
by Dorling Kindersley Limited,
80 Strand, London WC2 0RL

A Penguin Company

Based on content previously published in
The Golf Instruction Manual

2 4 6 8 10 9 7 5 3 1

A CIP catalogue record of this book is available from the
British Library.

ISBN 978-1-4053-5523-0

Printed and bound in Singapore by Star Standard

Discover more at **www.dk.com**

CONTENTS

Foreword 7
Introduction 8
How to Use This Book 12

CHAPTER ONE:
ASSESSING AND IMPROVING
YOUR GAME   16
Checking The Fundamentals 18

OFF THE TEE 28
Level One 30
Level Two 42
Level Three 54
The Perfect Tee Shot 64

IRON PLAY 66
Level One 68
Level Two 82
Level Three 95
The Perfect Iron Shot 104

PITCHING 106
Level One 108
Level Two 122
Level Three 136
The Perfect Pitch Shot 146

CHIPPING 148
Level One 150
Level Two 162
Level Three 174
The Perfect Chip Shot 184

BUNKER PLAY 186
Level One 188
Level Two 204
Level Three 218
The Perfect Bunker Shot 230

PUTTING 232
Level One 234
Level Two 248
Level Three 270
The Perfect Putt 278

CHAPTER TWO:
FAULTS AND FIXES   280
The Slice 282
The Hook 283
The "Heavy-contact" Chip 284
The Shanked Iron Shot 285
The Skied Drive 286
The Top 287
Loss of Power 288
Weak Shot from Rough 289
The Push Shot 290
The Pull Shot 291

CHAPTER THREE:
THE ART OF SHOTMAKING   292
Sloping Lies 294
Tackling Problem Shots 298
Conjuring Effective Escape Shots ... 300
Better Wind Play 302
How to Hit High and Low Shots 304
Two Simple Ways to Shape Your Shots .. 306

CHAPTER FOUR:
PLAYING THE GAME   308
Warming up Before a Round 310
The Value of a Pre-shot Routine 312
Strategy Off the Tee 314
On the Fairway and in the Rough .. 316
Improving Your Mental Approach ... 318
Simplifying Winter Golf 320
Monitor Your Performance 322

CHAPTER FIVE:
REFERENCE SECTION   324
Buying the Right Equipment 326
Types of Play and Handicaps 332
The Importance of Good Etiquette ... 334
The Golden Rules of Golf 338

Glossary 346
Index 348
Acknowledgments 352

FOREWORD

GOLF HAS BEEN A PART OF MY LIFE from an early age. I caddied for my dad when I was about eight years old, started playing soon after that, and managed to get down to scratch by the time I was 14. A year later I was world junior champion, by which time I was pretty certain I wanted golf to be my profession. I was lucky when I was growing up to have the right influences and some wonderful role models, which together instilled in me the importance of practising good fundamentals and developing a sound swing with good rhythm. *The Complete Golf Manual* constantly reinforces these same virtues while giving you a clear and easy-to-follow route to a lower handicap.

I know from playing pro-ams that a lot of amateurs receive little constructive tuition and therefore have no real idea how to develop their game. This is a shame, because there is so much enjoyment to be gained from improving and shooting lower scores. To me, striving to improve is part and parcel of the game's challenge, even at professional level. And anyone who works through this book is bound to end up playing better golf.

I think the golf swing is like a chain reaction. If you adopt a good address position it is easier to make a better takeaway. If you make a good takeaway you are more likely to get to the top of the backswing in good shape, and so on. The format of *The Complete Golf Manual* reflects this philosophy. The book contains all the important building blocks of a successful game – it revisits the fundamentals (which are essential to long-term success) and takes you step-by-step through to the advanced stages of each department of the game.

Steve Newell is an experienced instruction writer, and we have worked together on many projects over the last seven or eight years. Steve has put together excellent books for me, and he has produced another superb guide in *The Complete Golf Manual*. I hope you enjoy the book as much as I did – it is your passport to better golf.

ERNIE ELS

INTRODUCTION

T HE FACT THAT THIS BOOK is now in your hands suggests that you are well aware of golf's addictive nature. Virtually everyone who seriously embarks upon the game is destined for a life-long affair. Once ensnared in golf's irresistible grip, it is hard to imagine ever not playing, even if everyday commitments make the gaps between rounds painfully long at times.

While it may be rather clichéd to boast of golf's varied playing arena (it's true, every course is different in its own special way) or to highlight the manner in which golfers of unequal ability can compete on even terms due to the handicapping system, these are undeniably two of the attributes that make golf special. They are part of the game's challenge and charm.

Only part, however, because ultimately it is the physical act of playing the game that is so compelling. Stripped bare, golf may appear to be little more than a stick-and-ball game, but surely no other sport asks more telling questions of your mind and body. The scenario involving you, a club, a little white ball, and a 10-cm (4-in) target far in the distance – often out of sight – presents a demanding physical challenge. And there is no under-estimating the skills required to swing a club with accuracy at speeds sometimes in excess of

GRAND OLD MAN
Old Tom Morris was the finest golfer in the world during the late 19th century, winning the Open Championship four times. He is buried at the "Home of Golf": St Andrews.

160 kph (100 mph). This is why a great shot, in which the ball sails towards your chosen target, produces such excitement.

The mental side of the game is equally important, of course. Compared with most other sports, you have an age between shots to contemplate opposite ends of the emotional spectrum. Even during the few seconds in which you stand over the ball, golf's psychological "swingometer" remains hard at work. When you win these mind games – when your swing is on song and you produce a good score at the end of a round – it is a wonderful feeling. When you fail, it can be soul-destroying because you have no one to blame but yourself. Nevertheless, even on the bad days there is nearly always at least one glimpse of magic – the experience of hitting a great shot or holing a long putt – that lifts your spirits and keeps you coming back for more. This "high" is essentially the catalyst that fuels the desire to become a better player, to experience that feeling not just for one shot, or one hole, but for as much of your playing time as possible.

STUNNING SURROUNDINGS
Golf is a game played amid breathtaking scenery. The Cypress Point course on the Monterey Peninsula, California, is a classic example. Here the ocean very much comes into consideration.

THE EARLY DAYS

Ever since the first ball was struck (which may have been as early as the 16th century), people have striven to find a way of getting from a teeing ground to a hole with as few strokes as possible. In golf's early days, swing technique was shaped mainly out of circumstance rather than choice. The earliest proper courses (which probably date from the 17th century) were almost certainly the coastal links in Scotland. There, it was soon discovered that a rounded swing, whereby the hands and arms swing the club on a flat plane around the body, produced a low ball-flight and plenty of run. This suited the windswept landscape of the Scottish coast.

As photographs of the great players of the late 19th century confirm, playing in a tweed jacket and tie (as was the tradition in the early years) would have restricted arm movement, hampering a free, up-and-down swing of the hands and arms. Also, even up until the late 19th century, the likes of Mungo Park, Old Tom Morris, and Allen Robertson – all great players – would stand with their feet nearly twice as far apart as today's top golfers, with their knees bent more than is usual nowadays, and with the ball way back in the stance (even for the driving clubs).

HOME-CRAFTED EQUIPMENT

Equipment-making has always been a highly-skilled art, and many of the top players of the 19th and early 20th century crafted with their own hands the tools that they wielded to such great effect. But, by today's standards, the clubs and balls that were used appear rather primitive. Clubs were wooden-shafted, and the fat, leather-wrapped handles called for a grip totally unlike the overlapping and interlocking methods mostly employed today. Indeed, the club was held in the palm of each hand, very much like the grip for holding a baseball bat.

Up until the mid-19th century, golf balls were made of stitched leather stuffed tightly with feathers, hence the name "feathery ball". These balls were not only expensive, but their playability was horrendous. Once wet, they would deform and not fly in a straight line. By the latter part of the 19th century, balls were being made of gutta-percha, a rubber-like substance secreted from percha trees. These "gutties" were cheaper and more uniform in shape. They also flew better and lasted longer. Nevertheless, it was impossible to spin them in the way of today's high-tech balls, and gutties tended to fly on a low trajectory with plenty of run on landing.

THE MODERN GAME

By the early part of the 20th century, the golf swing was rapidly becoming more athletic, efficient, and powerful – not to mention elegant. Harry Vardon popularized the grip that to this day bears his name (also known as the overlapping grip), where the little finger of the right hand overlaps the index finger of the left. Vardon was also one of the first golfers to recommend fanning the left foot out at address to encourage a clearing of the left hip through impact. Bobby Jones was among the first to advocate a more narrow stance, as he felt that if the feet were too wide apart, the lower body became locked in place, reducing mobility in the swing. Golfers soon started to stand a little more upright, slightly nearer to the ball, and with their feet closer together.

All of these subtle changes added up to a much more upright golf swing. Byron Nelson, perhaps the first great player with a distinctly upright swing (which suited his tall stature), won 11 tournaments in a row during the 1945 season, a record that will probably never be matched. Byron's style of play was perfectly suited to the new

TALENTED AMATEUR
Even though Bobby Jones never turned professional, he was the dominant golfer of the 1920s, winning four US Opens, three Open Championships, five US Amateurs, and one British Amateur.

steel-shafted clubs, which had only just replaced the inferior hickory-shafted clubs (which were much whippier and therefore necessitated an "around-the-body" swing).

The legendary Ben Hogan, who is still regarded by some as the greatest golfer ever, shaped the game not so much in the way it was played but in the manner in which it was practised. He would hit balls until his hands bled, striving for, and achieving, a level of near-perfection that is still unsurpassed. Many now emulate his selfless work ethic on the practice ranges at professional tour events all over the world. Although he was nearly killed in a terrible car accident in 1949, he fought back to become an even more accomplished golfer than before, winning the three major championships he played in 1953.

Jack Nicklaus, winner of more major championships than any other golfer, has been one of the greatest influences on the game for much of the latter part of the 20th century. When he burst on to the scene in the early 1960s, the great Bobby Jones remarked that "he plays a game with which I am

INSPIRATIONAL PLAYER
Jack Nicklaus is probably the greatest golfer who ever lived. He is certainly the smartest thinker and course strategist, which is why his major record is unlikely to be surpassed.

not familiar". But soon everyone wanted to play like Nicklaus – his style spawned a generation of upright swingers with elegant, high-hands finishes (and an arched back in the followthrough). In such a technique, the club travels up and down in more of a straight line, which means that the hands are higher, both in the backswing and followthrough.

One of the most influential modern-day figures in the game is not a player, but a coach: David Leadbetter. His associations in the mid-to-late 1980s with multiple major winners Nick Faldo and Nick Price popularized a swing less upright than the one employed by Nicklaus. This newer swing is a more rotary action that synchronizes the body-turn and arm-swing more effectively. Today, therefore, most golfers finish their swing in a much more rounded position, with the spine less arched, and the club more across the back of the neck (in an upright swing, the shaft points more towards the ground). This latest swing is more consistent, more sustainable, and places less strain on the lower back than an upright swing.

THE ROLE OF THE COACH
Teaching philosophies have also evolved over the years and become less polarized. Today's great teachers – such as David Leadbetter, Butch Harmon, and John Jacobs – work on essentially the same principles, but each applies individuality and different communication methods to the coaching role. While the standard of golf teaching has improved and become more uniform, golfers of all standards have grown increasingly receptive to tuition. This is partly because golfers have become familiar with the player/coach culture that exists in sport today and have been inspired by the success of partnerships such as David Leadbetter and Nick Faldo or Tiger Woods and Butch Harmon. Consequently, golfers are keen to harness the expertise of great players and coaches. Thousands of teaching books are bought every year, and research shows that at least 70 per cent of all golf magazines are purchased primarily for the game-improvement articles featuring top players and teachers. Golfers wishing to improve can now benefit from high-speed photography that freeze-frames the golf swing in motion, capturing every detail of an incredibly dynamic

movement. This technique emphasizes the athletic nature of the game and adds to the aspirational element of striving for a better swing.

YOUR PERSONAL COACH

Today, there is surely not a golfer in the world who does not want to shoot lower scores. Alas, most do not have a personal swing guru to turn to in times of need. But, in a variety of significant ways, this book intends to fulfil that role.

Modern golf instruction is based on wisdom passed down from inspirational teachers over the years – from Harry Vardon to Butch Harmon. The exercises in this book – the largest number of practice drills ever compiled in one book – take and expand upon this wealth of golfing knowledge. The drills are designed to cure faults and promote all the right moves, helping to ensure that your practice sessions have a constructive focus and clearly defined goals. Each department of the game is covered – from tee shots to putting; from shotmaking to etiquette – and hundreds of

WORLD NUMBER ONE
Lorena Ochoa has emerged as the dominant player in the women's game in the second decade of the 21st century. Like former World No. 1 Annika Sorenstam, Ochoa has no apparent weaknesses, only an arsenal of strengths – among them, an exquisite short game.

specially commissioned photographs bring into focus every detail of the movements required for a perfect technique. We can sometimes forget that much of what we learn is influenced by imitation, and that is why the images of golfers with superb swings play such a prominent role in this book.

The structure of the book encourages you to assess your ability in each department of the game before you embark on a programme of self-improvement. Through a series of tests you will gain an accurate and honest assessment of your game from the tee to the green. Whatever standard you play to, this book offers a way to improve while also explaining how to remedy faults that may creep into your game.

In my view, golf tuition should be inspirational and aspirational. Playing better golf is not just about the practicalities of producing good shots, it is also about the sensations and emotions that the game evokes. I believe this book will inspire you to enjoy the game, as well as teach you how to achieve your goals. The book is designed to educate you about the way you play, to help you understand how the golf swing works, and to make perfectly clear what you have to do to improve. A tremendous amount of work has gone into ensuring that the overall flow and content of the book is logical, and that every page works as hard as possible so that you will gain maximum benefit from all the advice given. I hope you enjoy the book and what it does for your game, and that you will continue to refer to it in years to come. The greatest satisfaction in golf comes from self-improvement, and I am confident that this book will show you the way to fully realize your golfing potential.

SUCCESSFUL DUO
Tiger Woods worked with Butch Harmon for the first 10 years of his professional career, and with considerable success, but then turned to another experienced and proven coach – Hank Haney.

HOW TO USE THIS BOOK

THIS BOOK HAS BEEN STRUCTURED in such a way that using it is like having a personal tutor guide you systematically through every area of the game. Once you have completed all the exercises and learned about almost every other aspect of golf – from shaping shots to etiquette – you will properly understand your swing and what action is required to sustain long-term progress down the handicap ladder.

CHAPTER ONE: ASSESSING AND IMPROVING YOUR GAME

Chapter One shows you how to assess and improve your game, beginning with an examination of the fundamentals. Six sections, from "Off the Tee" to "Putting", follow. For each, you take a test, work through a set of drills appropriate to your ability, re-take the test, and move up to the next level if you have improved sufficiently.

LEFT-HANDED PLAYERS
Although the instructions in this book are for right-handed players, left-handed players need only reverse the directions. For example: "the little finger of your right hand overlaps the left forefinger" becomes, "the little finger of your left hand overlaps the right forefinger".

THE FUNDAMENTALS
Before beginning the drills, it is important to assess your fundamentals – grip, aim, stance, and posture.

LOGICAL ADVICE
Step-by-step instructions aid understanding

TESTS
The simple test at the beginning of each section provides an assessment of your ability and determines which of the three levels is most appropriate to you. All six tests (Off the Tee, Iron Play, Pitching, Chipping, Bunker Play, and Putting) are based around hitting 15 balls to a predetermined target.

LEVEL ONE
The drills in this level are for beginners and less-proficient golfers.

LEVEL TWO
Intermediate golfers will benefit most from the drills in this level.

LEVEL THREE
The Level Three drills are geared towards more accomplished players.

TEST IN PROGRESS
One large image clearly shows you how to perform the test

SUMMARY BOX
This succinct text gives you a key thought to take with you as you work through the drills

PERFORMANCE CHART
Once you have your test results, use this chart to work out which level to start at

LEVEL ONE

Although the drills and key checkpoints in this level are tailored to less-accomplished players, every golfer would benefit from working through this section.

SEQUENCES

Many drills feature sequential images that show how to perform the exercise

LEVEL TWO

It is likely that many club players will start at this level. However, even highly skilled golfers will find plenty of interest in Level Two.

GRAPHICS

Throughout the book, special lines and arrows illustrate ball-flight, alignment, swing path, and so on

LEVEL THREE

Proficient players will find these drills, which are mostly concerned with fine-tuning, challenging and rewarding.

DRILLS

Each drill begins with an introduction that explains the purpose of the exercise. Numbered instructions clearly describe how to perform the drill. An "end paragraph" summarizes what has been learned and sometimes offers extra information

KEY CHECKPOINTS

These short pieces of expert advice offer hints and swing thoughts that will be of enormous benefit to your game

THE PERFECT SHOT

These spreads, which appear at the end of each section, show you exactly how the shot in question should be done, as demonstrated by a leading tour professional. The key elements of the swing are broken down and explained, providing an inspirational guide to the perfect shot.

STEP-BY-STEP SEQUENCE

Images of the swing in action show you how your swing links together

FINAL REMINDERS

Before you move to the next section, there is a list of the most vital points to remember

"DOWN THE LINE"

The most important points in the swing, seen from behind the golfer ("down the line"), are carefully examined

CHAPTER TWO: **FAULTS AND FIXES**

No matter how good you are, there are times when faults will creep into your game. Do not despair though: this chapter presents the ten most common faults and shows you how to fix them quickly and efficiently.

FAULTS
Before you can correct a problem in your game, it is essential to understand what is creating the fault. The text and image here do just that

CAUSES
A detailed, annotated diagram provides a close-up examination of the factors at impact that are causing the fault

FINAL THOUGHT
This block of text offers extra advice, cross-referenced to a relevant section in Chapter One, for those who wish to try an alternative "fix"

FIXES
An instructive image, graphics, text, and annotation combine to present a clear and straightforward way to fix the fault for good

CHAPTER THREE: **THE ART OF SHOTMAKING**

There are many situations when it is necessary to adapt your swing. Whether you want to play from a sloping lie, escape from a divot-mark, combat a fierce wind, or shape a draw, this chapter gives you all the shotmaking skills you will ever need.

HELPFUL INTRODUCTION
Each section begins with introductory text that provides general information about the shotmaking situation, such as "sloping lies", being discussed

DETAILED ANALYSIS
The technical adjustments required to play from different types of sloping lies (for example) are closely examined using text, freeze-frame images, graphics, and annotation

SWING SHAPE
Layered images not only provide a dynamic element to the page but also show you how your club and body should move as you swing

EXTRA INFORMATION
Feature boxes are used if a particular point requires further expansion or explanation

CHAPTER FOUR:
PLAYING THE GAME

Golf is so much more than just hitting a ball and hoping for the best. For example, what you do before you strike the ball can be just as important as the swing you make. This chapter covers the areas of the game that go beyond striking the ball, such as pre-shot routines, psychological factors, and winter golf.

INSTRUCTIVE IMAGES
At every possible opportunity, a photograph is used to illustrate the subject in question

VITAL PHOTOGRAPHS
To aid understanding, each portion of text is accompanied by an image that helps illustrate the salient point or points that are being discussed

SPECIAL SKILLS
Whenever a particular technical adjustment is required, this is fully illustrated and explained, leaving no room for confusion

LOGICAL GROUPINGS
Each aspect of playing the game is broken down into a series of smaller categories

KEY CHECKPOINT
Although most key checkpoints are situated in Chapter One, these pertinent slices of advice also appear in later chapters

CHAPTER FIVE:
REFERENCE SECTION

What happens if a crow flies off with your ball? What is the difference between a bladed iron and an iron that is peripherally weighted? How is the order of play determined on the tee and on the green? These and many other questions are answered in this concluding section of the book, which covers everything from buying the right equipment to golf's most important rules.

FEATURE PULL-OUTS
Close-up photographs zoom in on key areas of interest

DESCRIPTIVE TEXT
Every aspect of the subject in question is described clearly and fully

CHAPTER ONE

ASSESSING AND IMPROVING YOUR GAME

CHAPTER ONE has more than twice the number of pages of all the other chapters combined. This reflects the intentions of the book: to give you the foundations of an effective golf game and to build on these to transform you into a more complete golfer. The key concepts throughout are self-assessment and self-improvement. After a discussion of golf's fundamentals, the chapter moves systematically through every department of the game – from tee shots to putting – each starting with a test to establish your level of ability. Then comes a series of progressively more advanced drills, designed to develop your game slowly but surely. Armed with the knowledge and techniques gained from this chapter, you will soon be playing better golf.

CHECKING THE FUNDAMENTALS: GRIP

THE GRIP IS ALMOST CERTAINLY THE MOST IMPORTANT of the four fundamentals. Given that your hands are the only point of contact with the club, it is amazing how little attention is given to this aspect of the game. Many golfers take their grip for granted simply because it feels comfortable. The trouble is, comfortable doesn't necessarily mean correct: you may well have a fault in your grip and not realize it. If this is the case, it is highly likely that your game is being seriously hindered. It is therefore fair to say that no golfer is too experienced or too skilled to re-evaluate the grip. An improved grip can very swiftly hand you a passport to better golf. However, developing a better grip is not as easy as you might think – perseverance is required. It is perhaps helpful to bear in mind the words of Ben Hogan: "If you don't feel like you've made a grip change, then you haven't made a grip change at all". Although a change of grip is bound to feel uncomfortable for a while, this period need not last long if you rehearse your perfect grip as often as possible, even if only for a few minutes each day. Waggle the club around to familiarize yourself with the new feelings: you will be amazed how quickly the different hand positions start to feel comfortable. The dedication you show in these initial stages will stand you in good stead for many years to come. A sound grip promotes a neutral clubface position throughout your swing, eliminating the need to make compensations as you swing.

Right hand
Hold the butt-end of the club steady

Left-handed players

If you are a left-handed player, you should form your grip in the same way as described in the three steps to "Forming the Perfect Grip", except that your hands are swapped.

Grip variations

Over the last 100 years or so there have been three accepted grips. The baseball grip is ideal for young golfers or those who have arthritic problems in their hands. By far the most popular style is the overlapping grip, where the little finger of the right hand literally rides "piggyback" on the forefinger of the left hand. This method is favoured by players such as Nick Faldo and Ernie Els. A variation on the overlapping method is the interlocking grip, where the little finger of the right hand is entwined with the forefinger of the left.

Baseball grip

Overlapping grip

Interlocking grip

Left hand
Lay the club diagonally across the palm of your left hand

KEY CHECKPOINT
Grip pressure

If your grip is too tight, this can restrict the free-flowing motion of your swing. If it is too loose, your hands may slip as you swing. This simple exercise will ensure that you have the correct grip pressure. Take a club and grip it as hard as you can (100 per cent). Then relax your grip so that you are barely holding the club (0 per cent). Now hold the club with a pressure halfway between these two extremes (50 per cent). This is the perfect grip pressure, although it may vary slightly according to personal preference.

Left-hand "V"
Make sure that the left-hand "V" points towards your chin

Right-hand "V"
Make sure that the right-hand "V" points towards your right shoulder

1 **FORMING THE PERFECT GRIP**
Rest the club on the ground so that the clubface looks straight at the target. Bring your left hand forward from its natural hanging position, and place the club handle diagonally across your palm, running from the base of your index finger through the middle of your palm. Close your fingers around the club, making sure that your thumb sits fractionally to the right of centre on the handle. You should be able to see two and a half of the knuckles of your left hand.

2 The palm of your right hand should mirror the position of the clubface, in other words it should face the target. Start by holding your right hand flat against the club's grip. Then feed the club into your hand, along the base of your middle two fingers.

3 Close the fingers of your right hand around the grip. Your forefinger should adopt a "trigger position". Since this is an overlapping grip (left), the little finger of your right hand overlaps the left forefinger. Your right thumb should run diagonally down the side of the club's grip. You should be able to see two of the knuckles of your right hand.

CHECKING THE FUNDAMENTALS: AIM

IF YOU WERE FIRING A GUN you would naturally take great care to aim correctly. Otherwise you would, it is safe to assume, miss your target. Yet when it comes to hitting a ball, many golfers pay little attention to their aim, while others simply do not know how to aim correctly. If your aim is poor, this will affect not only each shot you play but also your long-term golfing prospects. This is because if you aim incorrectly, it takes a bad swing to hit the ball towards your target, which means that you will be constantly (unwittingly) making poor swings in an attempt to strike the ball in the right direction. Before you know it, you will have rehearsed a poor swing so often that you will not know any other way. And the longer you swing badly, the harder it is to correct your faults. More alarming is the fact that if you do make a good swing, you will miss your target. If you habitually practise perfect aim, however, no compensations or corrections in your swing are necessary to hit the target consistently. This means that your swing will prosper and the game will seem much easier. And the good news is that aiming is extremely simple, but it does require constant checking. Therefore, the principles demonstrated here should be applied to every shot you hit, whether you are practising or playing a proper round.

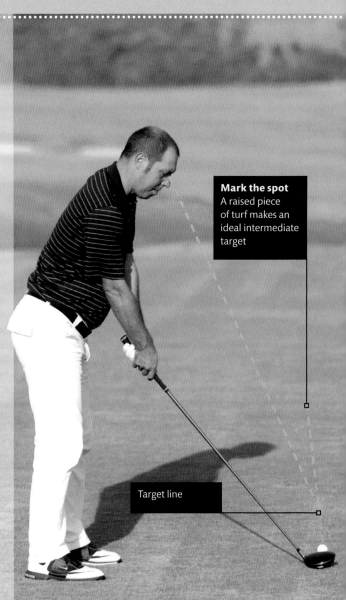

Mark the spot
A raised piece of turf makes an ideal intermediate target

Target line

KEY CHECKPOINT

Grip first, then take aim

Good clubface aim can easily be ruined in the process of forming your grip on the club. This means that placing the club behind the ball one-handed and then froming your grip is not a good idea - it is too easy to twist the clubface. It is therefore best to establish your grip and make sure that it is comfortable before you place the clubhead behind the ball. Only then should you aim at your imtermediate target. Always bear in mind this simple rule: first grip the club, then take aim, and then fire.

1 TAKING AIM

One of the most effective ways to aim correctly is to identify an intermediate target just in front of you, on a line directly between the ball and the target. Then aim the clubface at that mark. This process is called "spot marking", and the likes of Jack Nicklaus and Greg Norman swear by its effectiveness. Once you have identified your mark that is on the ball-to-target line – an old divot-mark or a slight discolouration on the ground is perfectly acceptable – make this the focus of your attention. Aim the clubface directly at the spot. As you can imagine, using this technique produces far more accurate shots than if you were aiming at a target that might well be more than 200 m (220 yd) away.

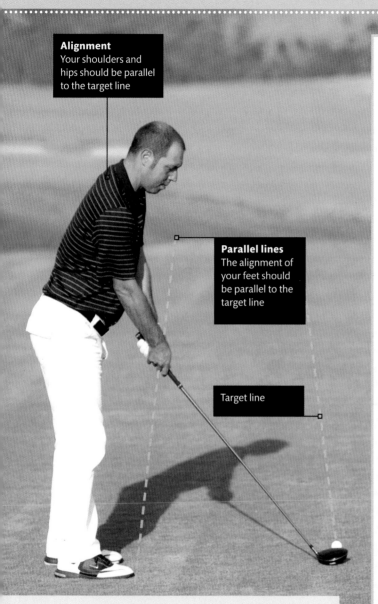

Alignment
Your shoulders and hips should be parallel to the target line

Parallel lines
The alignment of your feet should be parallel to the target line

Target line

2 Once you are satisfied that the clubface is "spot marked", build the remaining elements of your stance around that clubface position. If you want to hit a straight shot, your feet, hips, and shoulders should run parallel to the line along which the clubface is aiming. This position, known as perfect parallel alignment, has a positive influence on the shape and quality of your swing. When you are comfortable over the ball, switch your attentions to your intended target, look back at the ball, and then "pull the trigger" safe in the knowledge that you have aimed the "gun" correctly.

Practise with clubs on the ground

The practice ground is where you develop the "muscle memory" to make a good address position seem like second nature. Equally, if you are careless, you can easily practise the wrong things and damage your swing. This is why you should precisely monitor what you are practising. With aim, this is extremely simple. Lay two clubs on the ground: one just outside the ball, and the other along the line of your toes. The outer club should point directly at the target – it serves as a useful reference that will help you aim the clubface. The inner club should run parallel to the other club – it helps you align your feet correctly. Together the two clubs form a "railway track". Check that your hips and shoulders are also parallel to the clubs on the ground (parallel alignment). If you use two clubs on the ground when you practise, you will become accustomed to aiming correctly for every shot.

AIM AND ALIGNMENT *Two clubs on the ground helps you set up correctly for every shot you hit on the practice ground. This helps instil good habits.*

CHECKING THE FUNDAMENTALS: STANCE

THE STANCE is the aspect of your set-up that relates specifically to the width your feet are apart at address and to the position of the ball relative to your feet.

A good stance is crucial because it enables you to strike the perfect balance between stability and mobility. If your feet are too far apart, this will restrict your mobility, which means that you cannot make the required body-turn (which is essential to a good swing). If this happens, you will lose power and you may find your direction suffers, too. If your feet are too close together, which means that your swing-base is too narrow, you will struggle to retain your balance as you swing and will find it difficult to strike the ball with authority. However, if you spread your feet the correct distance at address, you will benefit from a stable base, which enhances your balance and offers the mobility to make a powerful body-turn in your backswing. Ball position is equally important. If the ball is placed correctly in your stance, this helps ensure that the clubhead meets the ball on the ideal path and angle of attack. You cannot afford to ignore these potential benefits: make sure that you follow the simple but effective guidelines to establishing the ideal stance outlined here.

Alignment
Remember, always practise with clubs on the ground so that you can keep an eye on your alignment

Stance
Start with you feet together and with the ball opposite your left heel

KEY CHECKPOINT

Hang two clubs to monitor the width of your stance

Your stance-width is a vital part of your set-up but it is extremely simple to check. Hold the butt-end of two clubs in each hand, and position one against your left shoulder and the other against your right. Let gravity take its course and note where each clubhead points. If your stance is the ideal width for the driver and long irons, the clubs will point at the inside of each of your heels.

1 **FORMING THE PERFECT STANCE**
Although your stance will change as you move through all the clubs in your bag (see the Key Checkpoint, right), it is a good idea first to establish the correct stance when using a driver. Stand with your feet close together and the ball opposite your left heel. If you stand with your feet side by side as you place the clubhead behind the ball, it is much easier to see where the ball is in relation to your left foot.

Shoulders
Your left shoulder should be higher than your right

Width check
Your shoulder width and the distance between you heels should be the same

Ball position
For a driver, the ball should be opposite your left heel

2 Draw your right foot back, but do not move your left foot (the insides of your heels should be equal to the width of your shoulders – see the Key Checkpoint, left). Flare out each foot very slightly, rather than keeping them square. This will allow your hips and body to wind and unwind as you swing the club back and forth. It is important to ensure that the ball has remained opposite your left instep – the perfect position from which to deliver the clubhead to the ball with a shallow, sweeping blow. This is the ideal width of stance for the driver and all the fairway woods.

KEY CHECKPOINT

The 3-cm (1¼-in) rule dictates the width of your stance

Hitting a driver requires the fullest, most dynamic swing of all the clubs in your bag – it is not surprising that your stance should be at its widest to offer maximum balance to support such a powerful movement. For the 3-iron through to the wedges, however, your stance should become progressively more narrow, and the ball should gradually edge closer to the centre of your stance. Below are three "benchmark" positions from which you can work out the ideal stance for all your irons.

3-IRON: Your feet should be 3 cm (1¼ in) closer together than for the driver, and the ball should be 3 cm (1¼ in) further away from your left instep. This change is necessary to ensure that the ball is positioned at the point where the clubhead reaches the bottom of its swing arc.

6-IRON: Your feet should be another 3 cm (1¼ in) closer together, and the ball should be also 3 cm (1¼ in) further away from your left instep.

9-IRON: With a 9-iron, your stance should narrow another 3 cm (1¼ in), and the ball should again shift 3 cm (1¼ in) back from your left instep. Therefore, there should now be a 9 cm (3½ in) difference in foot and ball position between this club and the driver.

This "3-cm" (1–1¼ in) rule should simplify the confusing questions of where to position the ball in your stance and how far apart to space your feet. The correct stance will give your swing a solid foundation, while helping to ensure that the clubhead meets the ball cleanly and on the correct angle of attack.

CHECKING THE FUNDAMENTALS: POSTURE

POSTURE DESCRIBES the angles in your legs and upper body at address and how you distribute your weight in your set-up. The key elements are: the amount your upper body bends over from the waist; the amount of flex in your knees; and the distribution of your weight on each foot. Together, these factors have a massive influence on the shape of your swing: poor angles and weight distribution invite a bad swing; good angles and weight distribution promote an efficient swing. Since a surprisingly large number of swing faults can be traced back to poor posture, this is undoubtedly one of the most crucial parts of your set-up.

Spine angle
To form the correct spine angle, bend from your hips unitl the clubhead rests on the ground

Legs
There should be a comfortable amount of flex in your knees at address

1 **ASSUMING THE CORRECT POSTURE**
Grip a 5-iron as you would normally (see pp.18–19), and spread your feet as if you were about to hit a proper shot (see pp.22–3). Then stand up straight, and, with your hands just above belt-height, extend the club out in front of you. Make sure that you relax: if you are tense now, you will be tense when you prepare to hit the ball, which will be bad for your swing.

2 Bend over from your waist. Maintain the angle between your body and your arms. Keep bending until the clubhead rests gently on the ground.

3 Finally, flex your knees, and push your buttocks out ever-so-slightly (as a result of this your stomach will be pulled in a little). Distribute your weight evenly over both feet. Your legs should feel quite springy. This posture might feel strange at first because you may well have become accustomed to addressing the ball in a completely different way. However, if you rehearse this three-step technique often enough, good posture will soon start to feel more natural. You will also benefit from a better body-turn, the overall quality of the shape of your swing will improve, and you will enjoy better balance.

WEIGHT DISTRIBUTION

In an efficient golf swing, your body- weight shifts from your back foot in the backswing and to your front foot in the downswing to add power and to provide balance. But you will not enjoy these benefits if your weight is incorrectly distributed at address. What most golfers fail to realize is that the ideal weight distribution is not the same for every club – it varies depending on the type of strike you are attempting to produce. The driver, for example, works best when you strike the ball with a sweeping blow.

Placing your weight so that it slightly favours your right side at address encourages this angle of attack. The principle is the same for lofted woods and long irons.

With the middle and short irons, however, it is a different story. A full swing with these clubs requires evenly spread weight, as this helps promote the necessary (descending) angle of attack.

Unless you are manufacturing a stroke (see pp.304–7), your weight should not favour your front foot at address.

WOODS AND LONG IRONS
If about 60 per cent of your weight favours your back foot at address, this encourages you to shift your weight behind the ball at the top of your backswing. This is essential if you are going to strike the ball with the necessary sweeping blow.

MIDDLE AND SHORT IRONS
For these shorter clubs, you should distribute your weight equally: 50 per cent on each foot. This balanced position promotes the correct angle of attack, which – unlike for the woods and long irons – is slightly descending.

KEY CHECKPOINT

One hand-span separates hands from thighs

If you stand too far or too near to the ball you will struggle to hit it solidly. Only by finding a happy medium will you be in a position to swing the club freely, without having to make compensations. The three-step guide to assuming the correct posture (see p.24) provides a useful guide to how far you should stand from the ball. However, as an additional measure, check how far your hands and the butt-end of the club are from the tops of your thighs – you should see about one hand-span of daylight. This suggests that you have enough room to swing your hands and arms freely, but not so much that you are reaching for the ball – a happy medium.

Although this hand-span rule provides a useful guideline, there is a bit of room to manoeuvre in this area. However, a gap of more than 5 cm (2 in) either side of one hand-span will cause problems in your swing.

SPACE TO SWING *If there is about one hand-span between the top of the grip and your thighs, you are standing the correct distance from the ball.*

GOLF'S SWING ZONES

ALTHOUGH A GOOD GOLF SWING IS ESSENTIALLY a continuous, flowing movement, it is possible to break it down into key areas. In fact, when it comes to learning about your swing and improving your technique it is desirable to look at the swing in sections. This will help you understand how the golf swing works and why it is, in some respects, a chain reaction in which one good move often leads to another. Equally, one poor move is usually followed by another. Aside from that, throughout this book you will constantly come across terminology relating to various stages of the swing. It is therefore worthwhile familiarizing yourself with the key "swing zones".

Going back
In the takeaway, progressive rotation of your hands and forearms ensures that the clubface remains square to the path of your swing

1 | ADDRESS POSITION
The set-up, as the address position is also known, is considered mundane for all the wrong reasons and is consequently neglected by most amateur golfers. However, what you do before your swing begins determines both the shape and quality of your swing. The all-important principles of a good address position will crop up again and again throughout this book.

2 | TAKEAWAY & BACKSWING
The first link in the swing-chain is known as the takeaway. This term encapsulates everything that happens from when the clubhead first moves away from the ball to the time when your hands are just beyond your right thigh.

Technically, the backswing includes the takeaway, but in most golfing circles the backswing relates to the area of the swing where the clubhead is going from halfway back to the point just before the club starts down again (hence the expression "top of the backswing").

3 | TRANSITION
This term describes the moment when you change direction from backswing to downswing. This is a critical moment in the swing, and although the club does not travel far relative to the swing as a whole, it is often make-or-break time in terms of the quality of the shot you hit.

Swing paths

There are three basic swing paths through the hitting zone: inside-to-outside, outside-to-inside, and inside-to-square-to-inside. To hit a straight shot, inside-to-square-to-inside is the correct path. This is the route where the clubhead approaches the ball from inside the target line, then travels square to the target line at the moment of impact, before swinging through inside the line again after impact.

Inside-to-outside	Outside-to-inside	Inside-to-square-to-inside

KEY CHECKPOINT

Weight transfer

In all athletic sports, good weight transfer is an essential ingredient of an effective technique. Golf is no exception. For full shots, your body weight should move in harmony with the direction of the swinging clubhead – that is, on to your back foot in the backswing and then progressively on to the front foot during the downswing and followthrough. This adds power to your shots.

Releasing the club
After this point, your right hand will cross over your left, which means that the clubface effectively rotates anti-clockwise and the toe overtakes the heel

4 **DOWNSWING**
Just as the takeaway is part of the backswing, so the transition is part of the movement known as the downswing. Broadly speaking, the downswing covers the area of the swing from when you start down to just before impact.

5 **HITTING ZONE**
The moment of truth, as it is often described. The hitting zone is the 30 cm (12 in) or so either side of impact, including the point where the clubhead meets the ball. Everything you do in your swing is designed to maximize the quality of the body and club positions you reach in this zone. The optimum swing path through the hitting zone is referred to as: "inside-to-square-to-inside" (see "Swing Paths", above).

6 **FOLLOWTHROUGH**
Just because the ball has gone, does not mean that this area of the swing is irrelevant. A classic, balanced follow through is the hallmark of a good player. You can use followthrough imagery to influence the shape of your swing and therefore control the flight and trajectory of your shots.

OFF THE TEE

THE DRIVER, THE MOST COMMONLY used club off the tee, is also the most powerful club in the bag. Many golfers therefore feel that they should try to hit their drive shots as hard as they can. However, position rather than power is the most important factor off the tee. Professional golfers, who have a far greater awareness of this fact than the average player, hit most of their drives at only 70–80 per cent of full power. This is the kind of attitude you should apply to your tee-shot strategy: accuracy, not length, is paramount. In fact, to help you remember this vital truth, whenever you step on to the tee, you should not simply aim at the fairway in general but should instead identify a more specific target, such as a small mound or discoloured area of grass.

This section of the book will help you hit consistently better tee shots. The merits of teeing off with a lofted wood – which is easier to hit straight yet does not sacrifice much distance – are also discussed. At the end of this section, you should be hitting the ball more solidly, straighter, and – ultimately – further.

TEST YOUR SKILLS

THE OFF-THE-TEE TEST

The first step to better tee shots is to assess your current level of ability. This test will do just that. As you perform the test, bear in mind that the key to good tee shots is position, not hitting the ball a huge distance. The test will assess your consistency and accuracy over 15 shots, the average number of drives in a round.

1 Either: find a fairway that is about 30 m (33 yd) across (the width of an average fairway). Or: go to a driving range and identify two distance boards, or two flags, that are about 30 m (33 yd) apart.

2 Hit 15 balls using your driver, and see how many come to rest in the fairway. For a true reflection of your ability, run through this step three times, and calculate an average score out of 15.

REMEMBER, ACCURACY NOT POWER should be your priority. As your technique improves, and you strike the ball more solidly, you will find that you hit the ball further with no extra effort.

3 Use the performance chart (right) to match your average score to one of the three levels. You are now ready to start working through the drills appropriate to your level of ability.

PERFORMANCE CHART

1
1–5 =
LEVEL ONE
(pp.30–41)

2
6–10 =
LEVEL TWO
(pp.42–54)

3
11–15 =
LEVEL THREE
(pp.55–63)

LEVEL DRILL
1·01   USE YOUR PRACTICE TIME EFFECTIVELY

It is a common sight: every bay at a driving range occupied by keen golfers determined to bash the ball as hard as possible, giving little thought to technique. Although there is nothing wrong with hitting drivers at the range, there has to be a structure and discipline to the procedure, otherwise you might do your swing more harm than good. This drill will give real purpose to your driving practice.

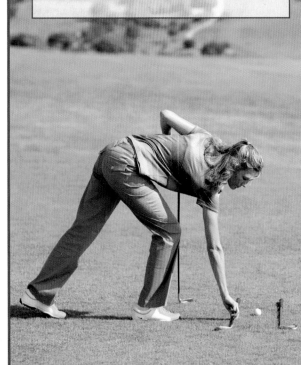

Quality not quantity is what good practice is all about. Most golfers would benefit from hitting half as many balls with twice the application to each one. The old saying "practice makes perfect" is only partly true; "perfect practice makes perfect" is more like it.

1 Identify a specific target. If you are focused on where you want the ball to go, you will make a more focused swing. Lay one club to the right of a ball, pointing directly at the target. Then lay another club parallel to the first, along the line of your toes. This will ensure that every time you address a ball you are in perfect parallel alignment (see pp.20–1).

2 Treat each practice shot as if it is a shot on the course.

LEVEL ONE

LEVEL 1 · DRILL 02

STEP INTO A GOOD YOUR STANCE

In your stance, the ideal distance between your feet is usually the same as the width of your shoulders (see pp.22–3). However, if you are especially tall and slim or have short legs, this rule might not apply. If either of these situations are applicable to you, then this fail-safe exercise, which is as easy as walking down the street, will help you establish the perfect base for your swing.

> *★* Now that you have a sturdy foundation for your swing, do not forget that the ball should be opposite your left heel when using the driver (see the Key Checkpoint on p.35). This helps establish a good upper-body posture and enables you to sweep the ball away, which is essential for solid strikes. Good ball contact contributes to extra distance.

1 | Take the longest club in your bag, your driver, and start walking as you would normally.

2 | After a few paces, stop walking. It is important that you do not move your feet. This is your normal stride length, which provides optimum balance as you walk. Chances are that this distance between your feet will also provide good balance when you swing a golf club.

3 | All you need to do now is turn and face the ball, making sure that your feet stay exactly the same distance apart.

LEVEL ONE

KEEP AN EYE ON YOUR STANCE

Tee height: the 50 per cent rule

Each driving club operates best when the ball is teed up at the correct height. However, as the size of driver heads varies greatly (and many people prefer to tee off with a lofted wood – see the Key Checkpoint on p.39), the ideal tee height is not something you can automatically take for granted.

To guarantee that the ball is always teed at the correct height, no matter what club you are using, make sure that 50 per cent of the ball is visible above the top edge of the clubface. In other words, the top of the clubface should be level with the ball's equator. This, of course, means that the ball must be teed at different heights, depending on the size of clubhead you are using.

Why is this so important? Well, to strike driving shots solidly you need to swing the clubhead into the ball on a shallow angle of attack, sweeping the ball away with a level blow. You cannot do this if the ball is teed at the incorrect height. Teeing the ball too low means you may hit down steeply into impact; too high and you run the risk of hitting the ball on the upswing.

CENTRAL LINE *Whatever the size of clubhead, establish a tee height where the top edge of the clubface sits level with the middle of the ball.*

Hitting the ball consistently well with your driver depends on many factors. One of the most significant of these is making sure that your set-up does not change from one game to the next. It is during practice time that you have the ideal opportunity to instil the right habits. Next time you are at a practice range, try this simple exercise.

✱ At first, this procedure may seem pedantic, but attention to detail is one of the keys to consistent golf – tour professionals are forever monitoring their set-up. With most amateurs it is even more vital: when there may be several days between games it is easy to develop bad habits. With a club as unforgiving as the driver, even the smallest errors can be costly. (Note: this drill can be applied to every club. The longer the club, the further you stand from the ball, so make sure that you repeat this drill with every club change.)

Stance width
Using coins to mark the ideal foot positions ensures your stance is consistent and correct

Ball position
Opposite your left instep is the ideal ball position when using a driver

1 Before you hit your first practice shot with your driver, it is important to perform a few quick checks to ensure that your stance and posture are good (see pp.22–5).

2 Once you have found the perfect set-up, mark the position of your toes with a couple of small coins, and keep them there for as long as you continue to practise with your driver. This ensures that you always stand the correct distance from the ball. Also, if the tee-peg is fixed to the practice mat, you are guaranteed the ideal ball position every time.

LEVEL　DRILL
1·04 REGAIN THE "SWOOSH" TO HELP YOUR RHYTHM

It is extremely frustrating to start suddenly hitting the ball badly for no apparent reason. This annoying occurrence is usually caused by a slight loss of rhythm or timing and is sometimes triggered by one bad shot. Try this exercise to recapture the best rhythm and timing for your swing.

✳ The freedom in your swing often deserts you when you are feeling nervous or uptight. Anxiety can very easily prevent you from swinging the club freely and, instead, you start trying to "steer" the ball. This can be disastrous, especially if it happens during an important round. Next time this problem occurs, try this practice exercise, which should help you not only swing your hands and arms more freely but also release the tension in your swing. This will promote a more powerful swing of the clubhead through the ball, and before long you will find that your game is back on the right track.

1 Hold the clubhead end of the shaft of your driver and make long, rhythmical practice swings back and forth. At the lowest point of your swing, the end of the grip should be about 30 cm (12 in) above the ground. Obviously the club will feel very light, but what you need to focus on is making a loud "swoosh" through the air as the grip end of the club travels into the hitting zone of your swing (where the ball would normally be). You will only produce this sound if your timing is right.

2 Now grip the club as normal, but make the same smooth, rhythmical practice swings. Immediately you will feel the weight of the clubhead at the end of the shaft. Try to recreate the loud swooshing sound at the same point in your swing as in step 1.

LEVEL DRILL
1·05 SWING THROUGH A CORRIDOR OF TEE-PEGS

The purpose of this drill is to establish whether you swing the clubhead on the right path into and through impact. The correct swing path is vital to your chances of producing an accurate shot, as it helps eliminate sidespin, which causes the ball to curve in the air.

* If you consistently avoid contact with the corridor of tee-pegs, you are swinging on the correct path through the hitting area. This will help you hit straighter, and you should notice an immediate improvement in your driving.

1 Line up a corridor of tee-pegs roughly the width of two driver clubheads apart. Place one tee-peg in the middle of the corridor.

2 Swing the club freely through this corridor. The clubhead should clip the lone tee-peg as it swings through. If the clubhead touches either line of tee-pegs, you are swinging on the wrong lines. If this happens, taking note of where you ruin the tee-peg formation will help you correct your swing path.

3 When you are consistently swinging the clubhead cleanly through the corridor, place a ball on the middle tee-peg. Try to recreate the swing you have been rehearsing. Do not swing harder – you will generate all the necessary power if you swing the club freely on the correct path.

LEVEL 1 · DRILL 06
SWING YOUR DRIVER LIKE YOU WOULD A WEDGE

Although few golfers have trouble hitting a solid wedge shot, using the driver is a different story. Most players want to hit their drives hard, which makes them swing more quickly and lose control. Many golfers also have a fear of the driver, which causes them to change their swing in the false belief that something special is needed to hit this club. All of these thoughts are destructive. An excellent way to overcome these problems and improve the rhythm and tempo of your driver swing is to hit alternate shots with your driver and wedge.

✱ The feeling of swinging these two clubs in the same way helps introduce smoothness into your swing, whereas previously there might have been a flurry of uncoordinated moving parts. The most important point to remember is that you do not have to try to hit the driver harder than you do your wedge: a smooth swing produces all the power you need.

Smooth swing
If you swing your driver just as you did your wedge, your rhythm and accuracy will improve

1 Take a bucket of balls and just two clubs, your driver and your wedge. Hit 12 or so smooth wedge shots. Do not worry too much about your aim: focus on striking the ball solidly and with control.

2 Now hit two or three shots with your driver. The key to this drill is to try to swing at the same speed and rhythm as you did for the wedge. Hit another six wedge shots, followed by two or three shots using your driver. Repeat this step as many times as possible.

KEY CHECKPOINT

Ball position affects swing path

Ball position is the forgotten principle of good driving. It is ignored by most golfers, who assume it is too dull to be important. However, where you position the ball in your stance has a huge influence on the direction of your tee shots. There are three basic ball positions: too far forward in your stance, too far back in your stance, and the perfect point.

Only when the ball is ideally positioned, opposite the inside of your left heel, does the clubhead hit the ball on an on-line path – the ball will start its flight on line, too. It is the simplest of things to keep an eye on, yet ball position has massive benefits to your drives. It would be a shame if you ignored this fundamental part of the game.

If the ball is too far forward in your stance (which for a driver is anywhere to the left of your front foot), the clubhead will almost certainly be travelling left of target when it meets the ball, on what is known as an out-to-in path (see pp.26–7). The ball will therefore fly left and then either maintain this flightpath or slice. Neither outcome is desirable.

If the ball is too far back (for the driver this is anywhere near the middle of your stance), the clubhead will travel to the right of target when it collides with the ball, in other words on an in-to-out path (see pp.26–7). The ball will fly right and then either maintain this flightpath or hook.

LEVEL DRILL
1·07

GET YOUR HEAD AND TORSO BEHIND THE BALL AT ADDRESS

Just as a boxer plants his or her weight on his back foot before delivering a knockout punch, so a golfer also needs to shift his or her weight in the same way to deliver maximum power to the ball. It is vital to transfer your weight on to your back foot at the top of your backswing. This is much easier if you start your swing with your weight already favouring your right side. Rehearse the following exercise to help familiarize yourself with the mechanics of good weight distribution.

Check that your head and torso are behind the ball. This should happen naturally as a result of the changes made in step 2.

This exercise makes it easy to load your weight on to your right side and to position your head and torso behind the ball at the top of your backswing. From this position you will find that you can really "punch your weight" and generate much more power. All of golf's big hitters – including the likes of Tiger Woods, Ernie Els, and John Daly – start their swing from behind the ball at address. This helps them produce the massive distances they are capable of generating time and time again.

50%

60%

Stance
This is the correct set-up for a driver, with virtually all your upper body behind the ball

1 Take a driver and stand upright, with your weight spread evenly over both feet. Assume your address position over the ball.

2 Tilt your spine angle away from the target. As you do so, you should feel your balance shift, so that 60 per cent of your weight is on your back foot.

LEVEL   DRILL
1·08 HIT THE BACK OF THE NET

When you are hitting a few balls into the practice net prior to a game, you do not think about mishitting the shot or guiding the ball. You just swing freely and thump the ball into the back of the net. So why not think exactly the same thoughts when you are actually on the first tee? This visualization drill will undoubtedly help you hit better shots under pressure.

* Rather than becoming anxious about the outcome of a shot, or worrying about potential hazards on a hole, simply focusing on "hitting the back of the net" will help you produce much better tee shots. This exercise is a good way to make all your fears disappear and to create a more positive swing.

1 Before you start a round, hit a few shots in a practice net, concentrating only on making a free swing and creating a solid strike. Watch the ball fizz off into the middle of the net.

2 Without hesitation, walk straight to the first tee, and, as you play your first shot, think only of the mental image of the ball flying at great speed into the middle of the practice net.

LEVEL 1·09 DRILL

CHOKE DOWN ON YOUR DRIVER

Too many golfers are obsessed with hitting the ball as far as possible. Yet most players would drive the ball a lot straighter and, strangely enough, further too if they thought of the driver as a positional club. This quick practice drill will teach you how to hit your drives straighter, with no great sacrifice in terms of distance.

1 | Take your driver from your bag, and adopt your normal grip and address position.

2 | Alter your grip so that your hands are 3–4 cm (1¼–1½ in) nearer the clubhead and you can see the end of the club's grip clearly protruding above your left hand. This is described as "choking down" on the club.

Grip
Choke down so that 3–4 cm (1¼–1½ in) of the club's grip protrudes above your left hand

Chin
Move your left shoulder under your chin to promote a full turn in the backswing

* Choking down on your driver is a great trick to have up your sleeve on a really tight fairway. Although you may lose a little distance, the extra control you will enjoy promotes straighter drives, and keeping your tee shots in play on the toughest holes will seem that much easier.

3 | Swing as you would normally: you should experience a feeling of greater control. Although you have effectively shortened the length of the club's shaft – which slightly reduces both the arc and the length of your swing – you do not need to feel like you are making changes to your swing. These things happen automatically.

KEY CHECKPOINT

A 3-wood may offer more than a driver

Many golfers often assume that the driver will give them the most distance off the tee. However, for a number of players this is not the case.

The driver is a straight-faced club, and because of this it sends the ball on a low trajectory. If you do not generate sufficient clubhead speed through impact, the ball will not spend enough time in the air to achieve a decent length. If this is the case, it is perhaps better to use a more lofted club, such as a 3-wood, which will send the ball on a higher trajectory, therefore creating more air-time and a longer drive.

Another good reason to use a 3-wood is if you have a fault in your swing that means that you do not consistently deliver a square blow to the back of the ball. In this situation, the driver's straight face will create lots of sidespin on the ball, which means losing distance as the shot curves through the air. The extra loft on a 3-wood's clubface helps to nullify this sidespin.

However, if either of these situations apply but you feel that teeing off with a 3-wood is too much of a sacrifice, you might wish to explore the possibility of buying a more lofted driver – something with about 13–15 degrees of loft on the face (see pp.326–7).

DRIVER VERSUS 3-WOOD *The clubface of a 3-wood (left) has more loft than the clubface of a driver (right). This makes a 3-wood more forgiving and easier to hit straight.*

Why you should waggle

Virtually all professional golfers "waggle" the club before starting their swing. This move varies from one golfer to the next, but all waggles ensure that the golfer's hands and arms are soft and relaxed at address, which promotes a free-flowing swing.

The waggle can also give you a sneak preview of the path of your takeaway, which allows you to get used to that all-important first move away from the ball. If, for example, you want to make sure you do not take the club back too much on the inside, you can waggle, watching to ensure that the club moves back on the correct path.

Furthermore, the waggle can serve as a preview to the type of rhythm you will achieve in your swing. If, for example, you are feeling nervous (and will therefore tend to swing too quickly), rehearsing a couple of very slow waggles will help settle you down a little and will lead to a smoother start to your backswing. This smoothness should continue through your entire swing.

Develop your own kind of waggle, and use it to get your swing off to a good start. One of the best things you can do for your swing is introduce a waggle.

Pose for a photo to improve balance

A good way to curb any tendency to hit the driver too hard is to think of one simple word: balance. If, while you swing, you concentrate solely on finishing in a perfectly balanced position (as if you are posing for a photograph for the clubhouse honours board), the chances are that your swing is under control. If you cannot maintain a balanced followthrough, you are almost certainly swinging beyond your limits of control.

LEVEL 1 · **DRILL** 10

IF YOU SLICE, TRY STRENGTHENING YOUR GRIP

How you grip the club largely determines how the clubface strikes the ball. If your grip is weak – where the Vs formed by the thumb and forefinger of each hand (see p.19) point towards your chin – it is unlikely that the clubface will be square with the ball at the point of impact. In most cases the face will instead be open, which leads to a glancing blow and a weak (often sliced) drive. If these problems sound familiar, this exercise will help you strengthen your grip.

1 Form your grip on your driver in the normal way. Take your right hand off the club so that you have an unobstructed view of your left hand. If your grip is weak, you will only be able to see one knuckle on the back of your left hand.

2 To steady the club, hold the bottom of the club's grip with your right hand. Loosen your left-hand grip just enough to enable you to rotate your grip to the right until you can see three knuckles on the back of your left hand. Your left thumb should also sit slightly to the right of centre on the grip (but should still be pointing straight down). The V formed by your left thumb and forefinger should now be pointing at your right shoulder.

3 Apply your right hand to the club's grip so that the V of your thumb and forefinger also point at your right shoulder. You should now be able to see just one knuckle on your right hand and three knuckles on your left hand (never more than that).

✳ Strengthening your grip is an excellent way to help ensure that the clubface is square at impact (to produce more solid strikes). This should eliminate sliced drives. Your new grip will also feel so much more powerful than your old, weak grip. A stronger grip can be of particular benefit to women, as well as seniors and juniors, all of whom might be struggling to generate sufficient distance off the tee.

LEVEL DRILL
1·11

IF YOU HOOK, TRY BRINGING YOUR GRIP BACK TO NEUTRAL

The way you place your hands on the club's grip controls the behaviour of the clubface during your swing. If you are plagued by a persistent hook, chances are that your grip is too strong, which means the clubface will be closed at impact. Basically this is the opposite problem to that of a golfer who slices the ball. One of the best ways to cure a hook is to weaken an overly strong grip so that it becomes neutral. This will help you deliver the clubface square to the back of the ball.

✳ Weakening your grip so that your hands assume a more orthodox position on the club will feel strange at first (like any change to your swing). Initially it is wise to restrict yourself to practice swings, so that you can become accustomed to your new grip. As you become familiar with the hand positions, the clubface will stay more neutral – perhaps even a fraction open – during your swing. This reduces the likelihood of hooking and makes it easier to hit straight tee shots.

1 Take your driver from your bag and form your grip as if you were about to hit a tee shot.

Now remove your right hand from the club. If your grip is too strong, when you look down you will be able to see perhaps four of the knuckles on your left hand.

Hold the bottom of the club's grip firmly with your right hand. Carefully rotate your left-hand grip to the left so that you can only see two or two-and-a-half knuckles on the back of your left hand.

2 Now introduce your right hand so that it sits more on top of the grip. While previously you probably could not see any of the knuckles on your right hand, you should now be able to see two knuckles. Also, your right thumb should sit more on top of the grip, rather than to the right (as is the situation if you have an excessively strong grip).

✳
Re-test yourself

Before moving to Level Two, take the test on pp.28–9 again. If you have not improved, it is worth revisiting the Level One drills. However, if the performance chart shows that your tee shots have progressed sufficiently, then you are ready to tackle the more advanced drills in Level Two.

KEY CHECKPOINT

Use existing divot-marks to improve your aim

When searching for a spot to place their tee-peg, most golfers try to find an unmarked patch of turf on the tee. However, to do this is to sacrifice a valuable opportunity to aim correctly. Next time you are teeing up, look for an old divot-mark that is aiming straight at the target. If you place the ball on a tee-peg just behind the divot-mark, you will have a ready-made guide when it comes to lining up the clubface with the target. You can then build your stance around that.

Divot-marks can help your swing path, too. Try to find a divot-mark that points straight at the target, but this time place the ball on a tee-peg just in front of the divot-mark. In your downswing, imagine that you will swing the clubhead into the back of the ball along the line of the divot. This imagery will help promote the correct swing path into impact, which is one of the keys to a good tee shot. This teeing-up method has the added advantage of guaranteeing no interference between the clubface and the ball, which means you can achieve the purest of strikes.

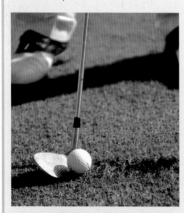

HELPFUL DIVOT-MARKS *Positioning your ball behind a divot-mark pointing at the target (above) will help you aim, while a divot-mark behind the ball will help you swing on the correct path.*

LEVEL DRILL
2·12 PRACTISE A PAUSE AT THE TOP OF YOUR BACKSWING

When using the driver, it is common for golfers to be a little over-aggressive when moving from the backswing to the downswing. This very swiftly wrecks any chance of striking the ball solidly. If you find yourself doing this, but cannot shake the habit, this exercise will be of enormous benefit to you.

Top of the backswing
Practising a brief pause at this point means all body parts can work together in the downswing

"Lazy" downswing
The first movement down must not be rushed

✳ This short pause at the top of your backswing is over in a split-second, but it is an extremely valuable time. It allows you to gather together your moving parts – your hands, arms, body, and club – all ready to surge down towards the ball in one combined movement, culminating in a powerful impact. See Drill 15 (p.45) for a different way to achieve the same result.

1 Start by making a normal backswing, all the way to the top. Pause at this point for no more than a fraction of a second.

2 As you begin your downswing, try to cultivate a "lazy" feeling, as if this all-important first movement down with your hands and arms is little more than a result of gravity taking its course.

LEVEL DRILL 2·13 HIT 4 O'CLOCK ON THE BALL

One of the most common faults club golfers experience is the slice, which is brought about by swinging the clubhead across the ball-to-target line and through impact on an out-to-in swing path (see pp.26–7). The following drill is a practice exercise that, while requiring you to use a little imagination, is an extremely effective way to ensure that you are swinging along the correct path.

Target line

Direction of clubhead

11 12 1
10   2
9   3
8   4
7   6   5

✳ If you swing the club on an out-to-in path through impact, causing a slice, then you are striking the ball somewhere around 2 o'clock. The mental imagery this drill provides will instinctively encourage you to swing the club down on the correct path, attacking the ball from inside the ball-to-target line. After practising this exercise, you should notice that your shots are flying much straighter – your slice may well become a thing of the past.

1 Assume your normal address position and look down at the ball. Imagine the ball's spherical shape as a clock face, with the target line running from 3 o'clock to 9 o'clock.

2 Keep your eyes fixed on a point on the ball correlating to 4 o'clock. As you are swinging, try to move the club down in such a way that the clubhead strikes the ball somewhere around 4 o'clock.

LEVEL 2 · DRILL 14

LOOK FOR A STRAIGHT LINE DOWN TO THE BALL

Anything you can do at address to promote a better swing is worth considering. The following practice drill ensures that when you set up to hit your driver, the club shaft appears to be an extension of your left arm. Bear in mind that when you come to hitting shots, it is acceptable (when using the driver) for the hands to be over the ball rather than ahead of it. This exercise will help give your swing the best possible start.

* The reason this is such a good starting point is because it makes it easier to keep the club and your left arm working together in the takeaway. Lots of swing problems arise from losing that connection early on, so that the club is not synchronized with your arms and body. This exercise should enable you to regain that link.

1 | Make sure the ball is positioned opposite your left heel. Assume your normal posture, but let your left arm hang limp from your shoulder, while holding a driver with your right hand.

2 | Feed the club into your naturally hanging left hand. You will see that it forms an almost straight line with the shaft all the way down to the ball. This is a good position to start from.

SYNCHRONIZE YOUR ARM-SWING WITH YOUR BODY-TURN

Losing coordination between your arm-swing and body-turn is a common fault. It can cause a loss of rhythm and make your swing feel ungainly. When this happens, even well-struck shots lack zip. With most golfers, the body moves too early and races ahead of the hand-and-arm action (the opposite problem is unusual). This is one of the main causes of a sliced drive: the shoulders and upper body unwind too fast in the downswing, throwing the hands and arms outside the ideal swing plane, causing the clubhead to cut across the ball from out to in. If you are slicing your drives, try this drill, which is based on a piece of advice by Harry Vardon, record six-time winner of the Open Championship.

Backswing
Swing the club to the top as normal

Body position
Think of your hands and arms swinging down to hip height before your body starts to unwind

* This drill eliminates the tendency for your shoulders to spin out too early in the downswing, which throws the club outside the correct path and causes a sliced drive. Improved synchronization will lead to better timing and more powerful ball striking.

1 Take your driver and make a normal backswing. From the top of your backswing, concentrate on getting your hands and arms swinging the club down to hip height before your shoulders and upper body even start to unwind.

2 As you continue swinging downwards, your body should start to unwind in harmony with your hands and arms.

LEVEL DRILL
2·16 FEEL A "TURN AND A SWISH" FOR A NATURAL SWING

There are two elements that combine to produce the perfect swing: body-turn and arm-swing. Too much of one and not enough of the other is disastrous – the plane of your swing will be all wrong, and you will struggle to deliver the clubhead to the back of the ball on anything like the correct path or angle of attack. Too much arm-swing, which makes your swing too straight, is a common problem. It is a result of one simple fault: the shoulders not turning enough. If you have had this problem for some time, it can be difficult to put right. This drill, however, should provide a constructive remedy.

Rotary motion
A free swing of the club, a good turn, and a purposeful weight transfer are most important here

Swing height
As the clubhead travels through the hitting zone it should be about 60 cm (2 ft) above the ground

1 "BASEBALL" SWING
Take your driver and stand totally upright, with your arms stretched out in front of you, your hands just below shoulder height. Swing the club around yourself, focusing on the rotary motion of your upper body, and letting your hands and arms swish the clubhead back and forth very freely. Make sure that you also feel your weight transferring to the right in your backswing, as your left shoulder turns under your chin. As you make the return swing from right to left, your weight shifts towards the target and on to your left side as you move into the followthrough position. This movement is not unlike a baseball swing and enables you to familiarize yourself with a powerful upper-body turn – something that may well have been lacking in your swing previously.

2 INTERMEDIATE SWING
Now stand over a ball and bend from the hips ever-so-slightly, until the clubhead reaches a point about 60 cm (2 ft) above the ground. Make the same swing, again focusing on the key elements: a proper weight transfer and a free swish of the clubhead through the hitting area. You should feel your arms straightening as the centrifugal force of the swinging club pulls you into the followthrough.

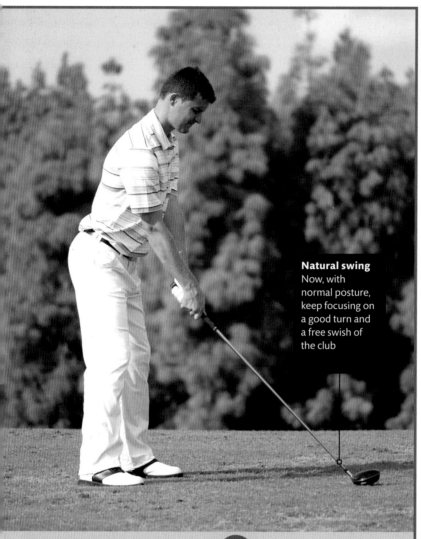

Natural swing
Now, with normal posture, keep focusing on a good turn and a free swish of the club

KEY CHECKPOINT

The right knee maintains its flex

The positioning of the right knee is an important ingredient in a successful swing with a driver. Keeping the right knee flexed during the backswing and well into the downswing provides two benefits. Firstly, it creates resistance in the legs and hips as you make your backswing: this gives a major source of power and is an effective way of stopping your backswing becoming too long and uncontrolled. Secondly, maintaining the right knee flex well into the downswing helps keep your right heel on the ground for longer, which stops your angle of attack becoming too steep. It is a shallow swing that is needed with the driver.

BACKSWING *Keep your right knee flexed to create resistance in your swing. This will stop your backswing becoming too long, which causes a loss of power and control.*

3 **NORMAL SWING**
Bend further still from the waist, until the clubhead rests on the ground, and flex your knees a little. You should now be in the ideal address posture for the driver. As you swing, think only of repeating the sensations experienced in steps 1 and 2 – a full turn of the body, good weight transfer, and a wonderfully free swish of the clubhead as you smoothly accelerate down and through the hitting area.

* If you can recreate the feelings associated with this drill and let the ball get in the way of the swing, rather than becoming too "hit orientated", you will strike the ball sweetly and release the club properly (see p.27). You will have achieved a better balance between body-turn and arm-swing. Drill 15 (see p.45) shows how to correct a loss of synchronization between these two elements.

DOWNSWING *Maintaining the flex in your right knee as you swing the club down promotes a wide downswing arc and a sweeping angle of attack, which is ideal for the driver.*

LEVEL 2·17 DRILL

KEEP YOUR LEFT HEEL GROUNDED TO ADD RESISTANCE

Whether you should lift your heel off the ground in the backswing – one of the most commonly asked questions about the swing – depends on what type of golfer you are. If you are flexible and do not have a problem making a full backswing turn (or even have a tendency to overswing), then you should probably keep your left heel grounded. This stops your hips turning too far in your backswing and keeps your overall swing compact. You will be able to wind-up your body with more resistance from the lower half, resulting in a faster unwinding of the body spring in the downswing. To help you keep your left heel grounded, try this drill.

Standing on a ball
It is almost impossible to retain any sense of balance during your swing if your left heel rises while there is a ball under the toes of your left foot

* Although the guidelines for lifting or not lifting your left heel are not set in stone, if you are very flexible (often young and/or slim golfers) or tend to overswing, then it is probably worth considering keeping your left heel grounded. However, watch out for the reverse pivot – where your weight moves towards the target in the backswing. Make sure that your weight still transfers on to your right side during the backswing (especially if you have been lifting your heel for some time). If you do decide to keep your left heel grounded, you will be in good company – Tiger Woods, Ernie Els, Fred Couples, and many others do exactly the same.

LEVEL TWO

1 Take up your normal address position, and squeeze a golf ball under the toes of your left shoe. You will feel your weight distribution being tipped towards your left heel, which is good.

2 As you move into your backswing, try to keep your weight on your heel. With the ball under your toes, if you do lift your left heel, your balance will become very rocky indeed.

3 Hit a few shots with the ball under your toes (start with practice swings before moving on to practice drives), then remove the ball, and see if you still keep your left heel grounded.

LEVEL 2 · DRILL 18

TURN YOUR BACK ON THE TARGET

Go low and slow: that is a great way to start your backswing with a driver. But where do you go from here? This exercise is very useful for anyone who lacks direction in the backswing, or is simply struggling with driving. It involves two key ideas, which together can have a great influence on the quality of your driving.

* Turning your back on the target ensures a good body rotation, which is essential for generating power, while pointing the club at the target means that the club will be on line. These two key elements combine to put you in a much better position to swing the club down freely and on the correct path through impact, resulting in more clubhead speed and a more solid contact.

1 As you make your backswing, try to turn your back on the target. This will encourage you to make a full turn of your shoulders, will promote a much better weight transfer on to your right side, and will also help you set the club on the correct line at the top of your backswing.

2 When you reach the top of your backswing, try to point the club at the target. This idea is particularly beneficial for golfers who slice the majority of their drives. This is because these players tend to point the club to the left of the target, which results in an outside the line downswing (see pp.26–7), causing them to cut across the ball through impact and produce a sliced drive.

LEVEL 2·DRILL 19

LIFT YOUR LEFT HEEL FOR A FULLER TURN

While keeping the left heel grounded (see Drill 17, p.48) during the backswing has several benefits for some golfers, others may not find this technique so helpful. Indeed, for anyone who lacks flexibility in the swing and, therefore, struggles to make a full turn – most likely senior golfers or those with a heavy physique – lifting the left heel is probably going to be advantageous. It will enable you to make a more complete turn in your backswing, adding length to your swing and power to your shots. Also, if your swing tends to be too short and quick, letting your left heel come off the ground will give you more time to make a fuller, slower – and therefore more effective – swing. And if you have a tendency to reverse pivot (where your weight moves towards the target in the backswing instead of on to your right side), lifting your left heel will force your weight on to the right side, which is essential in a well-executed backswing. If you think lifting your left heel might help your game, the following practice drill will ensure that you develop the correct technique.

Heel up
Lift your left heel in your backswing

1 | Address the ball and start your backswing as normal. When you reach the position in your backswing where you feel that your hips and shoulders will not "give" any more, this is the point when the left heel is effectively pulled off the ground to release the right side and to allow for a bigger turn. This is bound to feel unusual if you have never lifted your left heel off the ground in your swing before, but it will work if you let it happen as a consequence of your turning motion, rather than concentrating on lifting it independently.

✳ It is important to remember that lifting the left heel is not an independent movement – the heel should instead lift in response to the twisting motion of your hips and upper body. Lifting your heel should give you a fuller, more powerful swing. And there is the added benefit that planting your heel back down again is a great way to start your weight transferring towards the target, one of the key ingredients of a powerful swing. Jack Nicklaus and Tom Watson are just two of the many famous players who prefer to lift their left heel.

2 To initiate your downswing, plant your heel back on the ground. This starts your weight moving in the right direction – flowing towards the target. The great Henry Cotton, a three-times Open Championship winner, used to stamp his left heel down so firmly to start his downswing that you could actually hear it thump on to the ground as he changed direction.

Heel down
Stamp your left heel down to start your downswing

LEVEL DRILL 2·20 TILT YOUR SPINE TO PACK A POWER PUNCH

Many golfers with mid to high handicaps have a fundamental problem with their spine angle at address: not so much in the degree of tilt towards the ball, but in the amount of lean to the golfer's left or right. The most common fault is for the spine to lean towards the target slightly, which places the head and upper body too far ahead of the ball at address (and therefore also at impact). Tee shots hit from this position usually have very little power and do not travel as far as they should. This drill will introduce the ideal spine tilt into your address position, which will undoubtedly help you hit your drives more solidly.

Incorrect position
With a driver, your spine angle should not be vertical

* If your spine is tilted away from the target at address, chances are that the same will apply at impact. This also means that your head will be behind the ball at impact, which not only provides maximum leverage in your swing but also allows you to deliver a sweeping blow, with the clubhead perhaps travelling slightly upwards as it meets the back of the ball. These factors will significantly improve the quality of your drives.

1 Stand up straight and bend from the waist to address the ball. Although your spine angle is tilted towards the ball, it should be perpendicular to the ground if you were to see yourself from behind.

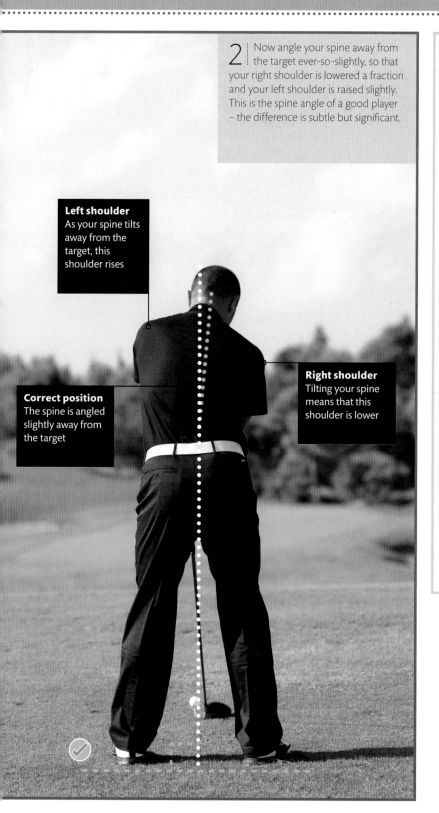

2 | Now angle your spine away from the target ever-so-slightly, so that your right shoulder is lowered a fraction and your left shoulder is raised slightly. This is the spine angle of a good player – the difference is subtle but significant.

Left shoulder
As your spine tilts away from the target, this shoulder rises

Right shoulder
Tilting your spine means that this shoulder is lower

Correct position
The spine is angled slightly away from the target

KEY CHECKPOINT

Think of your forearms touching for a better release

Not releasing the clubhead (see p.27) through the hitting area is one of the worst faults in a swing. This means there will be very little clubhead speed, just when you need it most. To overcome this problem, simply try to think of your right forearm touching your left forearm as you swing the club through impact. This swing thought will help you release the club on every tee shot you hit, which will mean more clubhead speed delivered to the back of the ball and a marked increase in distance.

FOREARMS MEET *Think of the forearms almost touching in the followthrough, and the clubhead will release correctly.*

✳ Re-test yourself

Before moving to Level Three, take the test on pp.28–9 again. If you have not improved, it is worth revisiting the Level Two drills. However, if the performance chart shows that your tee shots have progressed sufficiently, then you are ready to tackle the more advanced drills in Level Three.

LEVEL 3 · DRILL 21

MISS THE HEEL BY ADDRESSING OFF THE HEEL

Many golfers hit a number of their drives out of the heel of the club, which is a tell-tale sign of an out-to-in swing path (see pp.26–7). This causes drives to fly left-to-right through the air. An effective way to cure this fault is, bizarrely, to address the ball out of the heel of your driver – the very spot on which your problem manifests itself. Try this drill and you will soon see the benefits of this technique.

This drill is so effective because once you have addressed the ball out of the heel of the club, your hand-eye coordination will "force" you to re-route the club on the way down so that you strike the ball out of the middle of the clubface. American tour professional Fuzzy Zoeller, a former Masters and US Open champion, has addressed the ball out of the heel of the club throughout his career to help him swing down on the correct (inside) line. Even if you do not introduce this technique into your game "full time", it can at least serve as a very fast and effective way to correct a fault that may have crept into your swing.

Address position
For this drill, address the ball out of the heel of the club

1 Place a ball on a tee as if you were about to hit a tee shot. Adopt your usual address position.

2 Move the clubhead until the heel of the club is level with the ball, and then make a swing.

LEVEL THREE

LEVEL   DRILL
3·22

KEEP IT ALL TOGETHER
IN YOUR TAKEAWAY

If you lose synchronization between your arm-swing and your body-turn at the start of your swing, it is incredibly difficult to regain in the split-second it takes to reach the hitting stage. Here is a fantastic exercise that was popularized by David Leadbetter and Nick Faldo in their time together and has since been adopted by hundreds of golfers hoping that some of the duo's magic might rub off.

When you come to hit shots again, start your swing by recreating the feelings experienced in this drill. This ensures that your arms and body move away together, and if they are together at the start they stand a much better chance of being together throughout the swing.

Grip
Hold the club by the shaft

Eyes
Watch the clubhead as it moves back

Club position
Ensure that the club continues to rest against your midriff during your backswing

1 Take the driver from your bag, and assume your normal stance. Feed the club up through your fingers so that the butt-end of the club rests in your navel and your hands grip the metal of the shaft.

2 Rehearse a backswing movement, turning your body and moving the club away from where the ball would normally be, but focus entirely on keeping the butt-end of the club resting against your midriff. Go no further back than the point where your hands reach just beyond your right thigh. Repeat this movement over and over.

LEVEL THREE

LEVEL   DRILL

3·23 SHAKE HANDS WITH THE TARGET

A good release of the clubhead through impact (see p.27) is part and parcel of a powerful swing. It indicates that the club has been swung freely and with maximum clubhead speed. However, instead of releasing the clubhead, some amateur golfers attempt to guide the club or prod at the ball. Next time you are practising, try the following exercise to ensure that this key move is performed correctly.

* If, when you hit your next tee shot, you make sure that you "shake hands with the target", you will release the club better than ever. This is bound to add power to your shots.

Without a club
The right hand is shaking hands with the target

1 | Adopt your normal posture but without a club in your hands. Let your right arm hang naturally, but fold your left arm behind your back (alternatively, place your left hand in your back pocket).

2 | Make half-swing movements (to approximately hip height on either side of your swing) with your right arm. The key to this exercise is to feel that you are "shaking hands" with the target as you swing your right arm through the hitting zone.

With a club
The right hand is still shaking hands with the target, indicating a good release of the club

3 When you are comfortable with the hand movement described in step 2, rehearse a few practice swings with your driver. Now swing in slow motion, and freeze when your right arm reaches horizontal with the ground in your followthrough. At this point, your right hand should be in line with the target, ready to shake hands. If your hand is pointing to the left or right of the target, or your palm is angled towards the sky or the ground, you need to make some adjustments: try repeating steps 1–2.

LEVEL DRILL
3·24 CREATE A BOX AT THE TOP OF YOUR SWING

At the top of your backswing, the relationship between your right arm, hands, club shaft and upper body is an important one – never more so than with the driver. This drill will help ensure that you are in the ideal position from which to start your downswing.

Perfect position
If your right upper arm, your right forearm, and the shaft of the club form three sides of a box, then your wrists have hinged correctly at the top of your backswing

LEVEL THREE

1 Swing your driver to the top and freeze right there.

2 Now look over your right shoulder. What do you see? The ideal scenario is that the shaft of the club forms a right angle with your right forearm, which in turn forms a right angle with your right upper arm, so that you have three sides of a box. This position encompasses the correct amount of wrist hinge, which is all important with the driver.

Many golfers tend to be too narrow in this part of the swing because their wrists have buckled at the top. This can lead to a loss of control. If you have this problem, at the top of your backswing you will see an angle of less than 90 degrees between the shaft of the club and your right forearm. If this angle is greater than 90 degrees, your wrists are not hinging enough in the backswing. Check the box at the top of your swing to administer the required changes. Your tee shots will almost certainly benefit from keeping this aspect of your backswing in check.

LEVEL   DRILL

3·25

PICK AND MIX YOUR PRACTICE DRIVES

A good player should always be prepared to hit a variety of clubs off the tee in a normal round of golf. You should certainly not automatically reach for your driver on every par 4 or par 5, as it might not be the club that will leave you the easiest second shot. It could, for example, bring into play hazards that would not be a threat with a shorter club. Here is a great exercise you can do at the range that gives you the knowledge necessary to hit different clubs off the tee successfully and provides the confidence to "call the shots" on the course.

1 Once you have warmed up properly (see pp.310–1), put aside 12 or more balls. Select the three longest clubs from your golf bag.

2 Hit the first ball with your longest club – the driver – applying all the principles and skills you have developed throughout this section.

3 Hit the second ball with your next longest club, which will probably be a 3-wood. The only change you need make is to tee the ball lower than you did with the driver, so that the top edge of the clubface sits level with the ball's equator (see the Key Checkpoint on p.32). Other than this minor change, your swing should remain the same.

4 Hit the third ball with the final club selected – either a more lofted wood or a long iron. You will need to tee the ball lower still, and position it 2.5 cm (1 in) further back in your stance. These alterations accommodate a slightly less sweeping angle of attack into impact. One thing that should remain constant with all three clubs is the rhythm of your swing.

5 Hit each subsequent shot with alternate clubs until you have worked through all 12 balls.

Head position
You should feel that your head stays behind the ball at impact

*After you have practised this drill a few times, you should find that there is no dramatic inconsistency from one ball to the next. You can also use this exercise when practising other departments of the game, such as iron play. The idea is the same: to prepare yourself for the fact that you never hit the same shot twice in a row on the golf course.

Coordination
Sense that your body rotates in harmony with the swinging motion of your hands and arms

Impact
Ideal contact means that the ball will be swept away off the tee-peg

LEVEL THREE

LEVEL THREE

KEY CHECKPOINT

Are you a swinger?

There are two distinct types of player: swingers (below) and hitters (opposite). Both styles are effective; the key lies in recognizing which method best suites you.

Great swingers, such as Ernie Els or Davis Love, have stylish swings and a smooth rhythm. They appear to use little effort yet hit the ball a huge distance. The power in a swinger's action comes from the winding and unwinding of the body: this creates tremendous centrifugal force, which is passed out through the arms to the club and on to the ball. To have a good swinger's action you need to be flexible and have a naturally slow rhythm. When making your backswing, think of images associated with slowness and ease. Your downswing should start smoothly, your weight shifting to the left as you start to increase power through acceleration. By the time you get to the bottom of your swing, you should have a sense of the clubhead free-wheeling into the back of the ball. This will pull you into an elegant, balanced finish.

SMOOTH SWINGER *Davis Love has one of the most elegant swings in the game and is also among the longest drivers.*

LEVEL 3 · DRILL 26

TURN YOUR LEFT SHOULDER BEHIND THE BALL

All kinds of mental imagery can help you produce a better swing. Here is an exercise that should ensure that you make a 90-degree turn in your backswing, which is a minimum requirement for generating plenty of power with your driver.

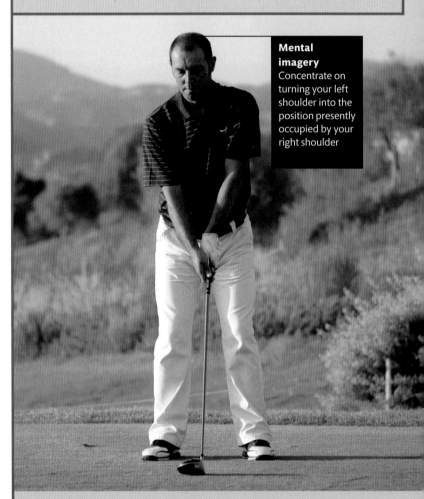

Mental imagery
Concentrate on turning your left shoulder into the position presently occupied by your right shoulder

1 │ Assume your normal address position, but take a brief moment to think about the position of your right shoulder.

2 │ At the top of your backswing, try to turn your left shoulder into the position your right shoulder occupied at address.

Shoulder position
The left shoulder is now situated roughly where the right shoulder was at address

* This exercise encourages two very positive things to happen: firstly, it promotes a better upper-body turn; and secondly, it ensures that you transfer your weight on to your right side. Together, these two factors should help you make a more powerful swing with your driver.

KEY CHECKPOINT

Are you a hitter?

While a swinger (opposite) has a flowing action, a hitter has a less aesthetically pleasing swing, but in the end the results of the swing are all that matter.

A good example of a hitter is big-hitting Spaniard Alvaro Quiros, the longest driver on the European Tour. Although a hitter's drive does not come from strength alone, muscle rather than mechanics generates most of the power. A good hitter needs to be strong and, usually, to have a brisk swing rhythm. If you are adopting this approach, when you start your backswing, take the club back mostly with your hands and arms, but do not forget to turn your upper body as far as you can. Keep your backswing short, so that the club does not become parallel with the ground at the top. Start down slowly, but pummel the ball with your hands and arms through impact. You should sense that there is a definite hit at the bottom of your swing. Your followthrough need not be perfect, but it must be balanced.

POWER HITTER *Alvaro Quiros is a powerful man whose swing may not be classic, but it is very effective.*

LEVEL | DRILL

3·27 CLOSE THE CLUBFACE AT ADDRESS FOR DISTANCE ON THE RUN

There are plenty of situations where it is advantageous to get the ball to run more than normal, such as when you are playing into a strong wind and need to generate maximum distance off the tee. Rehearse this super-effective drill on the practice ground and you will never be found wanting again on a windswept links.

LEVEL THREE

1 Place two clubs on the ground: one parallel with the ball-to-target line, and another pointing slightly right to establish a fractionally closed stance.

2 Rest the clubhead behind the ball, but do not apply your grip.

Normal clubface position

Clubface slightly closed

* This tiny adjustment means that you can make a normal swing, yet will strike the ball with the clubface in a stronger position. This can add approximately 20 m (22 yd) to a drive into a headwind, due to increased run thanks to a lower ball-flight. The exercise can also be used as a quick fix for a slice at times when you do not want to change your swing – in the middle of a round, for example. This is because this technique helps prevent you hitting the ball with a slightly open clubface, which is the cause of many high, sliced drives.

Good aim
This club points at the target

Closed stance
Align your feet slightly right of the target to compensate for the closed clubhead

3 Keeping the clubhead behind the ball, use your right thumb and forefinger to twist the clubface 1 cm (⅜ in) anti-clockwise. Making sure that you do not upset the new position of the clubface, carefully form your grip as you would normally.

KEY CHECKPOINT

Tee up correctly on par-3 holes

Many golfers tee the ball up too high on par 3s in the mistaken belief that this will enable them to hit nice, high iron shots to the green. However, this assumption is wrong. If you tee the ball up too much and make a good swing, you will hit the ball with the top edge of the clubface. The ball will then not fly anywhere near as far as it should. Therefore, teeing the ball up too high encourages you to make a bad swing: you have to hit up on the ball in order to strike it with the centre of the club.

This does not mean that you should not use a tee-peg on par 3s. Although you must hit irons directly off the grass on the fairway, as a tee-peg gives you a perfect lie, this opportunity should not be wasted.

When using an iron off the tee, the ideal teeing height is such that the ball sits just above the level of the ground. Viewed from grass level, you should only see the cup of the tee-peg. If the grass is lush, you may not even see that, and the ball should look as if it is resting on the tips of the blades of grass. This tee-height encourages you to swing the club into the back of the ball, creating ball-then-turf contact – an integral part of a crisp iron shot (see the "Iron Play" section, pp.66–105).

PERFECT HEIGHT *For tee shots with an iron, you should tee the ball up so that only the cup of the tee is visible.*

THE PERFECT TEE SHOT

Probably the most exciting player to emerge since Tiger Woods in the mid-1990s is Rory McIlroy. The Irishman has the temperament and the game to compete with the world's very best, and his driving is spectacular, to say the least. His swing is one we can all admire and learn from. Rory is not a big man, but he produces extraordinary power through good mechanics and superb rhythm and timing. Now that you have completed the drills in the "Off the Tee" sections you're in a good position to pick up pointers from these images of Rory in full flow.

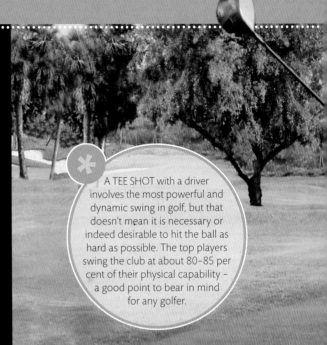

A TEE SHOT with a driver involves the most powerful and dynamic swing in golf, but that doesn't mean it is necessary or indeed desirable to hit the ball as hard as possible. The top players swing the club at about 80–85 per cent of their physical capability – a good point to bear in mind for any golfer.

1 ADDRESS
Rory has the perfect set-up for the driver. His knees are flexed just the right amount, which gives him a balanced stance. His spine angle is such that his arms hang down free from tension and there is a comfortable space between his hands and the tops of his thighs. This means he has room to swing the club on the correct path. His alignment is also spot on: toes, knees, hips, and shoulders all run parallel to the target line, and the clubface looks directly at the target.

2 BACKSWING
You can see here how Rory has perfectly blended his body-turn and arm-swing, with the appropriate wrist action beginning to set the club on the perfect plane. Note also how his left shoulder is turning under his chin.

3 TOP OF THE BACKSWING
Notice Rory's fine upper body rotation, and how his left shoulder is now under his chin. Rory's hands are above his right shoulder: a sure sign that his swing is on the correct plane. Also note the braced leg action.

Keys to consistent tee shots

Off the tee, the most important consideration is position, not power. Here are a handful of final swing thoughts to help you achieve this aim.

To promote solid contact, tee the ball opposite your left heel.

Position your head and torso behind the ball at address to allow a purposeful weight transfer on to your right side during your backswing.

Turn your shoulders fully in your backswing to help set the club on line at the top.

Make a smooth transition from your backswing into your downswing. This will allow your hands, arms, and body to work together in harmony to produce a solid impact.

For a powerful release, feel that your right hand "shakes hands" with the target as you swing the club through impact.

WATCH THE PRO

4 | **DOWNSWING**
Here Rory's hands and arms have swung down almost to hip height, but his upper body has barely started to turn through. This helps slot the club on to an inside track: the perfect pre-hitting position. From this position, Rory can deliver full power to the back of the ball.

5 | **HITTING ZONE**
Rory makes long drives look easy – evidence that power comes from good mechanics, not brute force. By turning his left side, Rory has made room to swing the club into the ball on the correct path. As the clubhead swings through the hitting zone, the club moves back inside the target line, the perfect in-to-in swing path.

IRON PLAY

IRON CLUBS ARE THE PRECISION TOOLS in your bag, each one designed to hit the ball a certain distance. Iron play as a whole encompasses two types of shot: advancement shots, where on a long hole you play for position (in order to make the next stroke easier); and scoring shots, where the flag is the focus of your attention. Whichever shot you look at, trajectory and distance are the primary considerations.

This section of the book will teach you all the skills you need to improve the quality of your ball-striking with each iron. It will also raise your levels of accuracy and consistency.

TEST YOUR SKILLS

THE IRON-PLAY TEST

Hitting the ball a long way with irons is not an issue, then. Hitting the green, however, is an accurate barometer of your ability, and this idea forms the basis of the iron test. Although there are several irons in your bag, a test encompassing every club would be too time-consuming. Therefore, this test should be carried out with a 6-iron, a club that is neither too demanding nor too easy to use.

1 Take 15 balls from your bag, preferably of the same make and construction (to minimize inconsistencies). Ideally you should do this test on a golf course, where you can hit balls at a proper green. But it can also be performed at a driving range, where there are flags and greens to aim at. Perform the test on a calm day if possible, as a strong wind may lower your scores to a level that does not reflect your true ability.

2 Hit some "range finders" to work out your personal 6-iron distance. Position yourself this distance from a medium-sized green, and hit the 15 balls towards the green. See how many come to rest on the green.

ALWAYS REMEMBER THAT
EACH IRON is designed to hit
the ball a certain distance – there
is hardly ever any call to force an
iron shot. All you need to do is
take a lower-numbered club and
swing with the same rhythm.

 Repeat the above step another
two times, and calculate an average
figure based on the number of times you
hit the green. Compare your results with
the performance chart (right).

PERFORMANCE CHART

1
1–5 =
LEVEL ONE
(pp.68–81)

2
6–10 =
LEVEL TWO
(pp.82–94)

3
11–15 =
LEVEL THREE
(pp.95–103)

LEVEL DRILL
1·01 FIND YOUR RANGE WITH EVERY IRON

Each iron in your bag is designed to hit the ball a certain distance. However, every golfer is different, which means that each person will have his or her "personal distance" for each club. The first drill for golfers wanting to improve their iron play therefore involves establishing how far the ball flies with each iron club. This enables you to make more accurate club-selection decisions during a round.

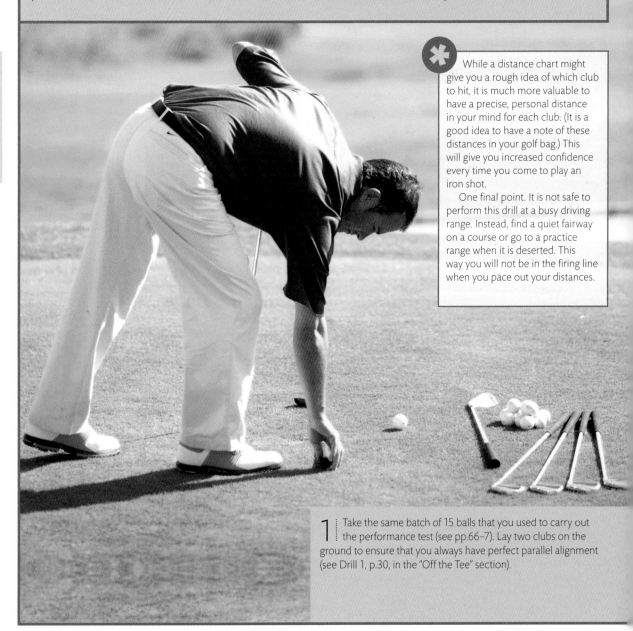

While a distance chart might give you a rough idea of which club to hit, it is much more valuable to have a precise, personal distance in your mind for each club. (It is a good idea to have a note of these distances in your golf bag.) This will give you increased confidence every time you come to play an iron shot.

One final point. It is not safe to perform this drill at a busy driving range. Instead, find a quiet fairway on a course or go to a practice range when it is deserted. This way you will not be in the firing line when you pace out your distances.

1 Take the same batch of 15 balls that you used to carry out the performance test (see pp.66–7). Lay two clubs on the ground to ensure that you always have perfect parallel alignment (see Drill 1, p.30, in the "Off the Tee" section).

Release
Make your right
hand roll over
your left through
the hitting zone

Perfect strike
The ideal contact is
ball-then-turf, which
means that there is a
divot-mark after the
point of impact

2 Work through your irons, hitting all 15 balls with each club.
Once you have hit one "set", pace out the distance to the
main cluster of balls, and take a note of the figure. Ignore the
longest two or three and the shortest two or three, as these
probably do not accurately reflect how far you usually hit the ball.

LEVEL 1 · DRILL 02

ESTABLISH GOOD BALL POSITION FOR ALL YOUR IRONS

In the "off the tee" section, the importance of the correct ball position (opposite your left heel to promote a sweeping blow at impact) was described (see the Key Checkpoint on p.35). Ball position is equally crucial in iron play, as it partly determines whether the clubhead will meet the ball at impact on the correct angle of attack. Obviously there are many different numbered irons, therefore ball position varies as you move through the clubs. This drill will help you appreciate the correct positioning for each iron.

✱ Obviously there are more than three clubs in your set. But this all-in-one stance establishes some benchmark positions from which you can gauge the ideal ball position for the rest of the irons. Using these positions when you swing helps ensure that the clubhead will meet the ball cleanly and on the correct angle of attack (see the Key Checkpoint on p.75).

1 Stand as if you were about to hit a long iron shot, with your feet comfortably spaced so as to provide good balance. Take a 3-iron, a 6-iron, a 9-iron, and three balls from your bag.

Place one ball opposite you, on an imaginary line 3 cm (1¼ in) inside your left heel. Rest the clubhead of your 3-iron behind the ball. Position the second ball 3 cm (1¼ in) further back, and rest the 6-iron behind that. Then, finally, place the third ball 3 cm (1¼ in) further back still, and rest the 9-iron behind that. These three balls indicate the ideal positions for the clubs that you are holding.

LEVEL DRILL
1·03

FROZEN AT ADDRESS? START YOUR SWING WITH A FORWARD MOVEMENT

There are many reasons why you might become tense at address and "freeze" over the ball. Whatever the cause – perhaps an overly tight grip pressure or possibly anxiety about your swing or the upcoming shot – freezing over the ball usually leads to a jerky takeaway, which will ruin your swing when it is barely underway. To become accustomed to the feeling of making a smooth first move away from the ball, try this great drill, which involves starting your swing with a forward movement.

* If you practise starting your swing with a forward movement, you will become accustomed to not freezing over the ball, and your backswing will be much smoother and less rushed than before. This technique also encourages your arm-swing to work more in harmony with your body-turn.

1 | Form your normal address position, but with one subtle difference: position the club so that it is hovering just above the ball rather than behind it.

2 | Now sweep the clubhead about 75 cm (30 in) forwards (in the direction of the target). Without a pause, swing the club all the way to the top, trying to maintain the smooth rhythm of the initial forward movement. Then swing down into and through impact. Take it easy at first: perhaps try a few practice swings before you hit shots using this technique.

LEVEL DRILL
1·04

LET HEEL-TOE-WEIGHTING TEACH YOU GOOD BALANCE

How you balance your weight at address has a much greater influence on the shape of your swing than you might think. This simple exercise will help you appreciate the relationship between weight distribution and how you swing an iron. It involves addressing a ball with the two extremes of poor weight distribution, so that you can then split the difference and find a happy medium.

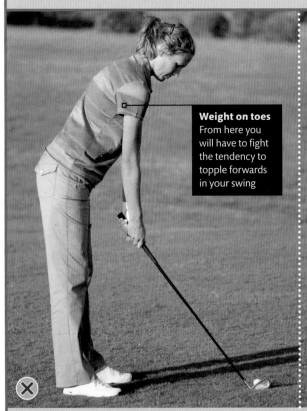

Weight on toes
From here you will have to fight the tendency to topple forwards in your swing

Weight on heels
From this position you will have to guard against falling away from the ball in your swing

1 **WEIGHT TOO FAR FORWARD**
Address a ball as you would normally, but place most of your weight on your toes. Now try to make a swing. You will tend to lift your body and head up and backwards. You will also try to shift your weight back on to your heels, all to stop you falling forwards – just as if you were teetering on the edge of a cliff. You then have to compensate for this sudden extra height by dipping down into impact in an effort to reach the ball. Obviously, this makes your swing very unbalanced, and you cannot achieve any power or consistency.

2 **WEIGHT TOO FAR BACK**
Now for the opposite. Put most of your weight on your heels at address. Although this feels strange, many golfers play this way. With your weight too much over your heels, the tendency is to stand too tall at address. Subconsciously your brain knows this, so the natural compensation is to dip your head and body in the backswing, in an effort to restore the correct height into your swing. With your weight tumbling forwards in the backswing, you lose your balance in the downswing and usually fall back on to your heels – just where you started.

✳ Correct weight distribution encourages good all-round posture, which is reflected in a better-balanced swing. You do not have to dip or lift your body to maintain balance. Without having to make any height adjustments along the way, you can turn your body, swing your arms, and the clubhead will move freely into the back of the ball.

Weight perfect
From an evenly balanced set-up you can make a good swing

3 **CORRECT BALANCE**
Now try to spread your weight evenly between your heels and toes. This is the perfect balance.

LEVEL   DRILL

1·05

FIND BETTER DIRECTION WITH AN INTERMEDIATE TARGET

In order to find the target, the ball must start on the correct line. Although this sounds obvious, many golfers tend to be obsessed with thinking about the last part of a ball's journey to the flag, when instead they might be better off considering the initial portion of the ball's flight. This drill requires only a small bucket (or similar object) to improve the initial direction of your shots.

* Although it is against the rules to place an object in front of you to improve your aim during an actual round, you can continue to imagine the ball flying over a bucket directly in line with the target. This mental imagery will improve the direction of all your iron shots and will help you find more greens.

1 Place a ball-bucket about 5 m (5½ yd) in front of you, along the ball-to-target line. Before you hit a shot, aim the clubface directly at the bucket.

2 As you swing, think of the ball flying directly over the bucket after it leaves the clubface.

KEY CHECKPOINT

When and why you take a divot

Although every iron shot should be struck crisply, with no interference between the clubface and the ball, some iron shots produce a divot and others do not. The reason for this is that to hit a good long iron shot, a sweeping angle of attack – where the clubhead strikes the ball with a shallow blow – is necessary.

Because the ball is swept away, there should never be a divot-mark – perhaps just the merest bruising of the turf. However, with more lofted clubs, good contact demands a progressively more descending angle of attack. Therefore, with a club such as a 6-iron, where the ball is positioned slightly further back in your stance (see Drill 2, p.70), the clubhead will meet the ball on a more downward path. This means that the clubhead should first strike the ball and then the turf, taking a divot after the ball has been struck. The more lofted the club, the further back in your stance the ball is placed, and the more pronounced the descending angle of attack becomes. A divot taken with a club such as a 9-iron will therefore be larger than a divot taken when using a 6-iron.

Ball-then-turf contact is what solid ball-striking is all about: the divot should start after the point where the ball was struck. If you take a divot before impact, lots of turf will be trapped between the clubface and the ball. This is known as "heavy" contact. Taking no divot at all is fine with longer irons, but if there is no divot-mark after impact with any club from a 5-iron upwards, then you are not striking the ball as you should be. Drill 9 (see pp.118–21) in the "Pitching" section describes how you can learn about your swing by examining your divot-mark.

LEVEL 1 · DRILL 06

VIDEO YOURSELF TO LEARN ABOUT YOUR SET-UP AND SWING

If you own or can borrow or hire a video camera, you have an excellent opportunity to examine and improve your swing. This drill focuses on a mid-iron swing, but you can use a video camera to check aspects of your game covered in other parts of this book.

Alignment
Place clubs on the ground and check that your stance and aim are correct

1 Before you begin filming, you must position the camera correctly. When you are checking your alignment, posture, and swing plane the camera must be looking "down the line". If you imagine a railway line extending back from the target, with the inner rail on the line of your toes and the outer rail on the ball-to-target line, then the camera should be midway between these two rails. (It is a good idea to place two clubs on the ground to mark the positions of these "railway lines".)

When checking your ball position, stance, followthrough, and weight transfer the camera must be "face on" (in front of you). It should be exactly opposite the middle of your stance, facing your navel. If the camera position is even a fraction out, it will give you the wrong information about your swing.

2 Begin by examining your address position. This is the easiest part of your technique to monitor and is conveniently also probably the most important. Many players do not believe that the only static element of the swing is the most vital, but this rule applies to every golfer, from the complete beginner to the tour professional.

With the camera positioned directly opposite you ("face on"), and with a mid-iron in your hand, begin filming. When you watch the video, start by checking that the width of your stance is correct: the inside of your heels should be about the same width apart as your shoulders. Now examine the ball position: about two ball-widths inside your left heel is good for a mid-iron. Also ensure that your grip is neutral: ideally you should be able to see two knuckles on your right hand and two, perhaps three, on your left hand. If your stance, ball position, and grip are in good shape, you are off to a good start.

3 While still in the address position, you must also check that your alignment is correct. Move the camera to your right and place it so that it is looking "down the line".

When you watch the video, check that your shoulders, hips, and toes run on a line parallel to the left of the flag, and that the clubface is aiming directly at the flag. Check that there is a comfortable gap between your hands and the tops of your thighs, and that your posture is neither too hunched nor too upright. Look out for the tell-tale signs of good posture, which include that your right shoulder is over your right toe and that your knees are a little bent.

Backswing
Check that you complete a full shoulder turn

Followthrough
Your right shoulder should be over your left foot

4 Now position the camera opposite you and make a few backswings. When you watch the video, check that your weight shifts on to your right foot in your backswing and that your head moves laterally to the right (your left as you watch yourself) – anywhere between 5 cm (2 in) and 10 cm (4 in) is adequate.

5 Switch the camera angle again so that it is looking "down the line". Rehearse your backswing, and freeze when your left arm is horizontal to the ground. If your wrists hinge correctly, the club should set on to the ideal backswing plane, whereby the butt-end of the shaft will point at a spot on the ground midway between the ball and your toes.

6 Now hit some shots. Later, you can use the freeze-frame facility on your video player to confirm that your backswing is on the correct plane (as described above). You can also check your downswing: freeze the video when your left arm is horizontal to the ground. The butt-end of the shaft should point at the ball or perhaps a little outside it. Finally, analyse your followthrough. Position the camera opposite you, and hit some shots. When watching the tape, check that your right shoulder is roughly over your left foot. This shows that your weight has moved fully on to your left side, as it should do.

* Watching your swing on video can be an alarming experience: what you see is often different from what you feel. But do not be disheartened. If you know what to look for, this process is incredibly informative and beneficial to your long-term progress. Even if you do not have a video camera, it is worth borrowing one every couple of months to see how your swing is developing.

LEVEL 1 · DRILL 07
FREEZE-FRAME ALL THE RIGHT MOVES

A few minutes swinging a club and rehearsing key positions in the swing can make all the difference when it comes to keeping your swing on track. Therefore, even if you do not have time to hit balls during the week, this "maintenance" exercise will at least stop you becoming too rusty between games. It will help you develop the muscle memory and sensations of a good technique.

1 Make a "stop-go" swing in slow motion, and freeze-frame the key positions. Try to become accustomed to the feeling of what you see, thereby introducing "muscle recognition" of the most important positions in a swing.

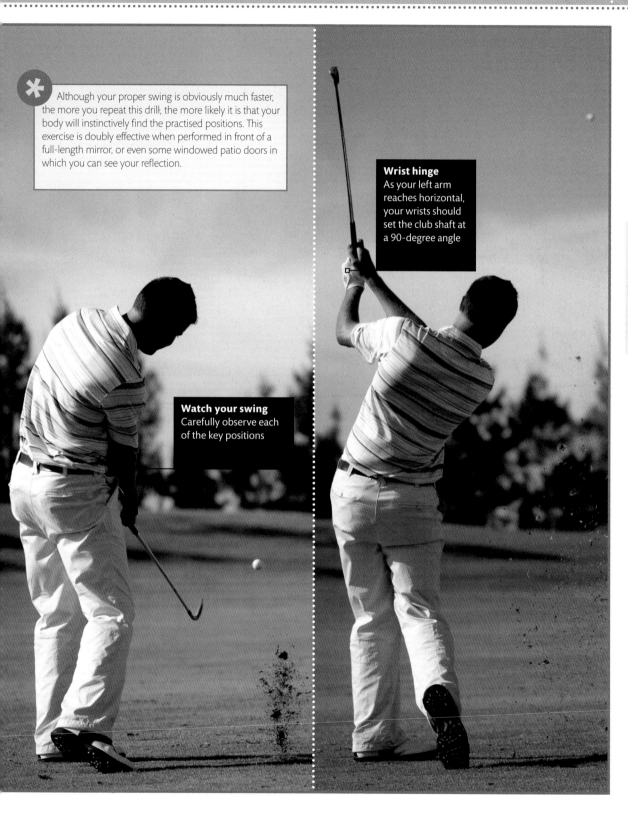

✱ Although your proper swing is obviously much faster, the more you repeat this drill, the more likely it is that your body will instinctively find the practised positions. This exercise is doubly effective when performed in front of a full-length mirror, or even some windowed patio doors in which you can see your reflection.

Wrist hinge
As your left arm reaches horizontal, your wrists should set the club shaft at a 90-degree angle

Watch your swing
Carefully observe each of the key positions

LEVEL 1·08 DRILL

SPLIT THE DIFFERENCE TO FIND THE IDEAL SWING SPEED

Going to extremes in your game can often help you find the happy medium. The following practice drill, which is a good example of this theory, might just help you find the perfect balance between control and speed when you swing an iron.

> * Once you have worked through this drill and found the happy medium – a perfect balance between control and power – it is a good idea to spend the next 10–15 minutes becoming as familiar as possible with the tempo of this swing. You will quickly discover that this is the kind of swing that will work most effectively for all of your iron shots.

1 Take a 6-iron and three golf balls. Hit the first ball with every ounce of strength you can muster.

2 Hit the second ball as if you want it to fly half the distance of the first. Swing as slowly and lazily as you can.

3 With the final ball, split the difference. Make a swing that is halfway between overly hard and ridiculously easy.

LEVEL 1 · DRILL 09

MAKE SURE THAT ALL YOUR PRACTICE SWINGS ARE FOR REAL

There have been few better swingers of the club in the past 30 years than Davis Love. He has a wonderfully smooth rhythm and the sort of effortless power that is magnificent to watch. Much of this must stem from one of his favourite swing thoughts, which he has stuck with throughout his long career: "I feel like when I make a practice swing it should be a rehearsal for what I'm getting ready to do. Then when I get the clubhead behind the ball I'm trying to copy the practice swing I just made". This drill shows you how to incorporate this idea into your game.

 Since most amateur golfers seem to make better practice swings than they do real swings, this drill can be marvellously effective. You might well be surprised how solidly, and how far, you can hit the ball.

1 Next time you are practising your iron shots, before you hit a ball, make a smooth practice swing. Concentrate on your rhythm and on building acceleration through the hitting area.

2 Then address a ball and try to repeat your practice swing. Just let the ball get in the way of the clubhead as you smoothly accelerate down and into impact. There is no hit, as such: it is more of a swinging motion.

KEY CHECKPOINT
Know when to quit

If long irons are causing you trouble, you might be better off swapping your two longest irons, say your 3- and 4-irons, for two lofted woods, maybe a 5- and a 7-wood. There is no shame in it: many top players carry a 7-wood in their bags.

These clubs are easier to hit and more forgiving than long irons. Your good strikes will be rewarded with a high-flying, relatively long ball-flight, and your mishits will not be so bad. And a small-headed, lofted wood is versatile: you can hit it off the tee, from the fairway, and from light rough, where an iron might become snagged. Drill 27 in the "Off the Tee" section (see p.62–3) will help you hit shots with a fairway wood.

FAIRWAY WOODS *As you move from a 7-wood (left), to a 5-wood (middle), to a 3-wood (right), the loft on the clubface gradually decreases.*

Re-test yourself

Before moving to Level Two, take the test on pp.66–7 again. If you have not improved, it is worth revisiting the Level One drills. However, if the performance chart shows that your iron play has progressed sufficiently, then you are ready to tackle the more advanced drills in Level Two.

LEVEL 2·10 DRILL — LET A ROPE TEACH YOU NEW TRICKS

One of Britain's most respected teachers, Jim Christine, is a great advocate of the benefits of swinging a rope in practice. Although you might wonder how this could possibly help your game, after trying this drill you will realize that a humble length of rope can improve the rhythm and efficiency of your swing, enabling you to create more clubhead speed with less effort. A worthwhile exercise, then.

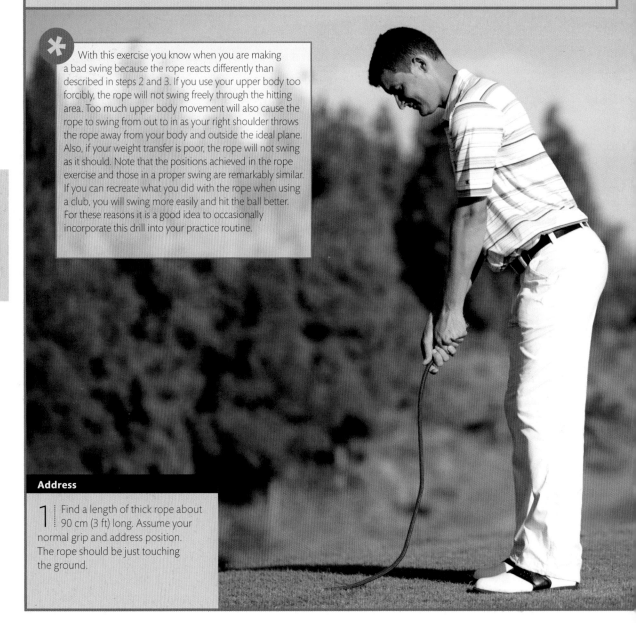

* With this exercise you know when you are making a bad swing because the rope reacts differently than described in steps 2 and 3. If you use your upper body too forcibly, the rope will not swing freely through the hitting area. Too much upper body movement will also cause the rope to swing from out to in as your right shoulder throws the rope away from your body and outside the ideal plane. Also, if your weight transfer is poor, the rope will not swing as it should. Note that the positions achieved in the rope exercise and those in a proper swing are remarkably similar. If you can recreate what you did with the rope when using a club, you will swing more easily and hit the ball better. For these reasons it is a good idea to occasionally incorporate this drill into your practice routine.

Address

1 Find a length of thick rope about 90 cm (3 ft) long. Assume your normal grip and address position. The rope should be just touching the ground.

Top of the backswing

2 Swing your hands and arms upwards in tandem with your upper-body rotation. If your backswing is on the ideal plane, the rope will curl gently around your left shoulder. If your backswing is too flat – if your body is doing too much turning, and your arms not enough swinging – you will find that the rope will not make it that high. Conversely, if your backswing is too upright – if your arms are swinging too high, and your body is tilting rather than turning – then the rope will hit you on the head or neck.

The hitting zone

3 The change in direction from backswing to downswing is one of the most important split seconds in the swing (see Drill 15, p.88), and the rope will teach you a valuable lesson in not rushing this first move down. So, take your time at the top of your backswing: you should feel a slight lag as your weight starts to shift to the left. When your hands and arms start to swing down, the rope will respond to this movement. As you continue to move down, smoothly building up speed, the rope will rapidly catch up with your hands and arms and "snap" straight at the bottom of your swing, like the cracking of a whip. This is centrifugal force taking effect, which means the rope reaches maximum speed at the perfect time: when it is in the hitting zone.

KEY CHECKPOINT

Identify your go-for-the-flag range

Many pin positions are designed to catch you out. If the flag is close to either side of the green, or is situated just over a front bunker, you have to be very careful about aiming for the flag because if you miss you will probably be left with a delicate shot and very little green to work with. You should therefore determine which clubs are "go for it" clubs and which are "middle of the green" clubs. If, for example, you feel very confident about your accuracy with every club from a wedge to an 8-iron, then when using a 7-iron or lower, you should switch to a "middle of the green" approach. Do not ever be tempted to step out of this comfort zone.

In fact, if club golfers ignored the flag during a round and aimed for the centre of each green, there is a good chance that their scores would fall over a period of time.

IRON ATTACK *Be clear in your own mind which clubs you can go for the flag with. Any clubs longer than these are "middle of the green" clubs.*

LEVEL **2·11** DRILL

MONITOR YOUR STRIKE WHEN YOU PRACTISE

If you are practising your iron play from grass, rather than on the mats at a driving range, this routine will help you monitor the quality of your strikes. The exercise produces the clearest results when the grass is closely mown.

* The moment of impact happens so quickly that even with the best eyesight in the world you cannot possibly keep track of everything that is going on. However, the kind of feedback provided by this practice exercise gives you valuable information that you can use to improve your technique.

1 After placing the ball you are going to hit on the grass, put a second ball about two ball-widths outside the ball-to-target line, but in line with the original ball. With an 8-iron, hit the first ball. Swing as you do normally.

2 Check where the divot-mark starts by comparing it to the position of the second ball. With a crisply struck mid-iron shot, the divot-mark should start fractionally after the point of impact.

LEVEL DRILL 2·12

USE YOUR SHADOW TO LEARN ABOUT YOUR SWING

This exercise can tell you a lot about your swing. But it does require one vital ingredient: sunshine. You will be amazed what you can learn from your shadow.

However, this is a drill for practice swings rather than hitting shots, as it requires you to take your eye off the ball.

* This practice drill is invaluable because weightshift and head-position are very difficult to keep tabs on as you swing. Seeing your swing via your shadow can shed a whole new light on your game. The next drill (see p.86) reveals another way to monitor head movement.

1 With the sun directly at your back, take up an address position so that the ball is right in the middle of your shadow. Using a long iron, swing to the top of your backswing. Ideally, your shadow should move to your right, so that the ball is in direct sunlight. If this happens, it indicates that your weight has moved on to your right side, an essential ingredient in any successful backswing. If this is not happening, your shadow will tell you as much.

2 With the sun still at your back, address the ball again. Have a helper place a club on the ground so that it sits on the top of your shadow's head. As you swing back, watch your shadow and see how your head behaves. It should not move up or down: in any good swing the head always stays almost level from address until impact.

LEVEL TWO

KEY CHECKPOINT
Downswing speed should match backswing speed

Bobby Jones was a magnificent golfer who, despite retaining amateur status, dominated the game in the 1920s and 30s, winning seven major championships before he turned 30. He was also a guru of golf instruction, shaping the way the game was played at that time. One of his favourite pieces of advice is still relevant and indeed is adopted by many of today's great players. His tip was that you should start your downswing at the same speed as you began your backswing. This avoids the tendency to rush the first move down, which will ruin any golf shot, and gives the hands, arms, club, and body plenty of time to work together. It is such a simple thought, yet is so very effective. That was part of Jones's genius as an instructor.

LEVEL 2·DRILL 13

MOVE YOUR HEAD TO THE RIGHT AS YOUR WEIGHT SHIFTS BACKWARDS

This drill, which requires a helper, enables you to determine exactly how much your head moves during your backswing. It is an especially revealing exercise for any golfers who believe the false assumption that the head should remain completely still throughout the swing.

* Head position is something you should definitely be conscious of, not so much when you are playing, but certainly when you are working on your game.

1 | Address the ball as normal, and position a helper opposite you. Instruct the helper to dangle a club vertically in front of him- or herself so that as the helper looks at you, your head is bisected by the shaft. The helper can now monitor the movement of your head as you swing.

2 | If you are swinging correctly, all of your head should move to the helper's left of the dangling club during your backswing, as you load your weight on to your right side. If your head stays where it was in step 1, or worse still, drifts to the helper's right, then your weight is not moving correctly in your backswing.

3 | If necessary, repeat steps 1–2 until your helper confirms that your head has moved sufficiently to the left of the shaft during your backswing.

LEVEL **2** DRILL **14**

TRAIN YOUR HEAD NOT TO MOVE UP OR DOWN

Unlike the previous two drills, which examined the importance of lateral head movement, this exercise concentrates solely on becoming accustomed to not moving your head too far up or down as you swing into impact. This is important because if you lose or gain height during your downswing you will struggle to hit the ball cleanly.

1 Position yourself so that you are right next to a wall, and assume your normal posture. Rest your head on a pillow up against the wall. Your head will hold the pillow in place.

2 Rehearse your backswing. Your head should not move up or down.

3 Now swing down. Your head should maintain its original height until the point where impact would be. This means that your spine angle will have remained the same as well. If these things occur in your proper swing you will swing the club freely into the back of the ball and not have to make adjustments for head movements up or down.

* In your backswing, your head must move 5–10 cm (2–4 in) to the right to facilitate a good weight transfer. As you swing into impact, your head may even move a fraction towards the target. So while this drill, which ensures that you keep your head still, may seem to advocate something incorrect, it is designed to eliminate excessive up or down head movement.

LEVEL DRILL
2·15 WAIT, THEN APPLY THE HIT

The transition from backswing to downswing is a critical phase in your swing. In the split second when you change direction, you have two choices: you can make a great first move down and successfully store the power in your swing, or you can rush it and forget about producing a good shot. This simple drill will ensure that your swing falls into the former category every time.

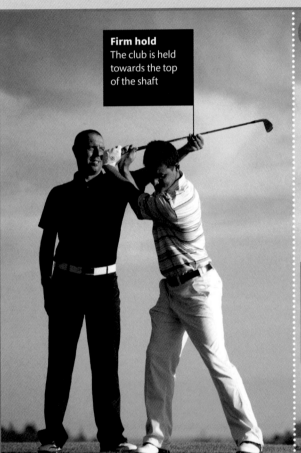

Firm hold
The club is held towards the top of the shaft

✱ This vital move from backswing to downswing is the one that stores the energy in your swing, enabling you to unleash power into the back of the ball as your wrists uncock. It is like the motion of cracking a whip (see Drill 20, p.95): if you time it correctly, the clubhead speed at the bottom of your swing will be phenomenal.

Wrist pressure
With the club held in position, there will be some resistance in your wrists

Top of the backswing

1 Make a normal backswing, but have a helper hold the clubhead in position at the top. Initiate your downswing by moving your weight on to your left side, unwinding your hips a little. With the helper holding the clubhead firmly in position, you should feel some pressure in your wrists, as the angle between your forearms and the club shaft becomes more acute.

Beginning of the downswing

2 Now make some practice swings and try to recreate the feelings experienced in step 1. Remember, as you change direction you should feel that the clubhead lags behind for a fraction of a second.

FOCUS WITH YOUR LEFT EYE FOR SOLID STRIKES

If your upper body slides towards the target prematurely in your downswing, this is called "getting ahead of the ball". If this happens, you will lose leverage and therefore power because there is no point of resistance at impact. You will probably hit weak shots to the right of the target, and will struggle to hit the ball from the middle of the clubface. This drill might help cure the tendency to get ahead of the ball.

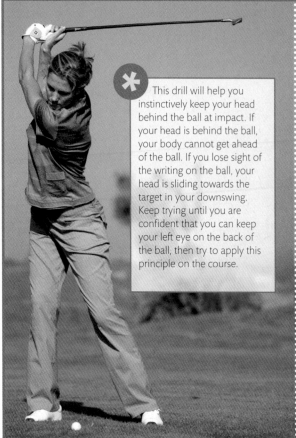

* This drill will help you instinctively keep your head behind the ball at impact. If your head is behind the ball, your body cannot get ahead of the ball. If you lose sight of the writing on the ball, your head is sliding towards the target in your downswing. Keep trying until you are confident that you can keep your left eye on the back of the ball, then try to apply this principle on the course.

LEVEL TWO

1 Place a ball on the ground in such a way that the manufacturer's logo is horizontal to the ground. Turn the ball until the logo sits along the ball's equator. From your address position you should just be able to see the edge of the writing on the ball. Swing to the top of your backswing and focus on the writing on the back of the ball with your left eye only (closing your right eye might help).

2 Maintain this focus until the clubhead makes contact with the ball.

LEVEL 2·DRILL 17

STAY SQUARE IN THE TAKEAWAY

As you make your backswing, the clubface should stay square to the path of your swing. If this is not the case, you will be forced to make compensations mid-swing in order to present the clubface square to the ball at the point of impact (which is vital for a straight shot). It is therefore prudent to check the position of the clubface in your swing, using this simple drill.

* Try to perform this exercise on a regular basis so that you can keep track of the clubface position as you start your swing. Remember, square to your swing path is correct; open and closed are incorrect. The great thing about this move is that you can use it any time you like as a "dry run" to help capture the correct sensations prior to starting your actual swing. This way your first move away from the ball is more likely to be a good one.

Square face
In a good takeaway, the clubface is square to the path of your swing

1 Make your normal takeaway, but stop when your hands are just above your right thigh. Compare the position of your clubface with the three images (see right).

CORRECT POSITION
The clubface is looking just a little to the right of the ball as a result of the correct rotation of the hands and forearms in the takeaway. This is the position you should try to emulate in your swing.

CLOSED CLUBFACE
As a result of a lack of hand and forearm rotation, the clubface is still looking at the ball, which means it is closed to the path of the swing. Because it is difficult to achieve a more neutral clubface position later in the swing, this kind of takeaway will probably lead to a pull or hook.

OPEN CLUBFACE
The hands have fanned the clubface too much in the takeaway. The clubface is looking too far right, which means it is open in relation to the swing path. It will be difficult to bring this back to a square position later in the swing: the result will probably be a push or slice.

LEVEL 2·18 DRILL

SQUEEZE YOUR ELBOWS TO STAY CONNECTED

This drill is based on the concept of developing better synchronization in your swing to ensure that your moving parts operate as a team, rather than independent of one another. The exercise specifically examines the relationship between your arm-swing and body-turn in your backswing, which often becomes a little disjointed.

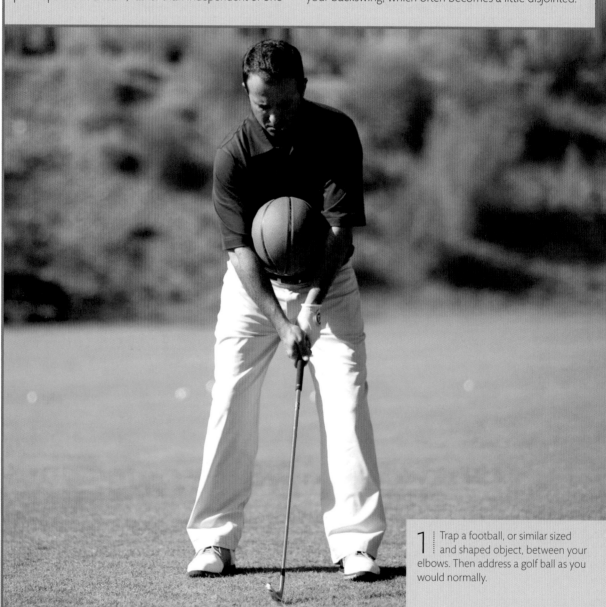

1 Trap a football, or similar sized and shaped object, between your elbows. Then address a golf ball as you would normally.

* This simple one-two procedure keeps the start of your backswing more "connected", which means that your arm-swing and body-turn are taking place simultaneously. This retains the width in your swing (which means the clubhead travels in a wide arc that extends away from you), and forces your left side to wind-up behind the ball, all the way to the top of your backswing. Rehearse this drill occasionally between shots when you are hitting balls at the range. If you can recreate the feelings experienced in this exercise in your normal swing, you will be a better ball-striker.

LEVEL TWO

2 Now make a backswing, squeezing your elbows together to prevent the ball from falling. Stop when the club is horizontal with the ground.

KEY CHECKPOINT

Learn to move on

Everyone hits bad iron shots. However, a good player can forget a poor stroke and get on with making up for the mistake, while a bad player might dwell on the error and compound it with another bad shot. In this situation, every mishit becomes a potential disaster. It is therefore important to remember that the only shot that matters is the next one. By all means curse yourself when you hit a bad shot, but let that be the end of it. Walk on and make sure that one error does not become the first of many.

SHORT MEMORY *A good player should be able to forget about a poor performance on one hole and instead concentrate on playing the next hole well.*

✳ Re-test yourself

Before moving to Level Three, take the test on pp.66-7 again. If you have not improved, it is worth revisiting the Level Two drills. However, if the performance chart shows that your iron play has progressed sufficiently, then you are ready to tackle the more advanced drills in Level Three.

LEVEL DRILL
2·19 THROW A FOOTBALL TO IMPROVE YOUR RELEASE

This drill provides an interesting way to recreate the hand movements required to release the clubhead (see p.27) powerfully through the hitting area. The exercise, which is best performed outside, requires only a football and a little imagination.

✳ You do not necessarily need to take a football with you every time you go to the range, but if you keep the image of throwing a ball in mind as you practise, you might find it easier to release the clubhead freely. It is amazing how a strong mental picture can sometimes trigger the appropriate physical reaction and therefore improve your ball-striking.

1 | Hold a football with both hands, and try to assume something resembling your normal posture for a mid-iron shot.

2 | Move your hands and arms back to hip height. Then swing the football down and through the hitting zone. Try to spin the football 30 degrees to the left of the ball-to-target line. To achieve this your right hand must cross over your left in the area where impact would normally be made. If the ball goes straight ahead of you, your hands are moving in such a way that you will not release the clubhead properly when you make a real swing.

3·20 HIT AT THE RIGHT TIME

The so-called "late hit" – a feature of every good player's swing – is not a conscious move or technique. It is merely the product of a well-timed downswing whereby the angle between the wrists and the club shaft is maintained from the top of the backswing to late in the downswing, until the wrists gradually unhinge to release the clubhead into the back of the ball at maximum speed. However, as this is something that you swing through very quickly (you cannot "freeze" this position), it is very dangerous to try to copy. This drill will teach you how you can correctly integrate the late hit into your swing to help you release the club with more speed through impact.

Do not be in a hurry to hit shots: it takes a while to become familiar with this technique. Instead, rehearse this drill frequently, then make practice swings with a conventional grip, and finally move on to hitting balls. If you can carry the same feelings evoked during this drill into your actual swing, your ball will think a different golfer is hitting it.

1 Take a 6-iron and hold the club so that there is at least a 7.5-cm (3-in) gap between your hands.

2 Now make some smooth practice swings, and feel that your right arm straightens through the hitting area. Your wrists should unhinge progressively as you accelerate down and through the hitting zone, so that there is a definite "swish" at the bottom of your swing.

KEY CHECKPOINT

A straight left arm?

Over the last few decades of golf instruction, a few nuggets of advice have echoed around the clubhouses of the world. However, not all of them are correct. One saying that often does more harm than good is to "keep your left arm straight in the backswing". This is often neither practical nor conducive to making a good swing. Probably only a handful of the world's top 50 golfers keep their left arm perfectly straight. This is because to make a full backswing – with a proper pivot and weight transfer – while keeping the left arm ram-rod straight, you have to be incredibly flexible. Most tour players allow a little softness in the left arm – with a degree of bend at the elbow – so as to make a full and tension-free backswing. You should, too – unless you are flexible enough to comfortably keep your left arm straight all the way to the top of your backswing. A slightly bent left arm will do your swing no harm, as long as you make sure that the club does not travel way beyond horizontal at the top of your swing.

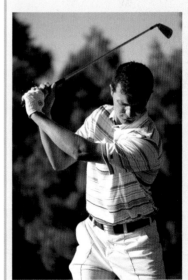

THE LEFT ARM *For most club golfers, contrary to popular belief, it is perfectly acceptable to bend the left arm slightly at the top of the backswing.*

LEVEL 3·21 DRILL
PLAY SHOTS WITH YOUR FEET TOGETHER

The golf swing is a complex action consisting of many separate moving parts working together. Nevertheless, it is possible to identify two core elements: arm-swing and body-turn. Arm-swing is often neglected, mainly because many golfers tend to rely too much on the bigger muscles found in the shoulders and torso. Rehearse this drill to ensure that your arms play an appropriately active role in your swing.

1 Take a 6-iron and address a ball with your feet no more than 15 cm (6 in) apart. Grip the club lightly.

2 Swish the ball away with a free-flowing swing of the club. Try to swing so that you feel that your arms are doing much more work than your body.

* It is a good idea to punctuate your practice sessions with spells of hitting 12 or so shots with your feet together. This will remind you of the role of your arms in your swing. It will also promote a free swing of the club through the hitting area, which adds speed to your swing just where it is needed most. If too much upper-body motion is a persistent problem, you might like to emulate former US Open champion Hale Irwin, who would occasionally spend days hitting nothing but feet-together iron shots.

LEVEL THREE

3 If you lose your balance, your body is doing too much and your arms too little. Keep trying until you do not lose balance.

LEVEL   DRILL

3·22   HITCH A RIDE ON BOTH SIDES OF THE BALL

The correct rotation of the hands and arms is an essential ingredient in a golf swing: without it you can never deliver the clubface square to the back of the ball with enough speed. Anyone struggling to achieve this rotation need think only of "thumbs up" in the backswing and through swing. Rehearse this drill to understand exactly what this means and how to integrate it into your iron play.

(see p.27)

Backswing
Your thumb points upwards when your arm is horizontal

* The two "thumbs-up" positions – as if you are hitching a ride on both sides of the ball – is what happens when good players release the club properly (see p.27). For these golfers, this is almost an instinctive move, but you might have to work at it before it becomes second nature. After practising this drill a few times, try to introduce this feeling into your swing. You should notice an immediate improvement in the crispness of your ball-striking.

After impact
When your arm is horizontal, your thumb once again points to the sky

1 Adopt your address position, but without a club in your hand. Now place your left hand in your pocket or behind your back.

2 Raise your right arm as if making a backswing, and let your body start to turn. Pause when your forearm is horizontal to the ground. In this position your thumb should be pointing at the sky, and the back of your hand facing behind you. This indicates the correct forearm rotation and wrist hinge has taken place.

3 Swing down and through the hitting zone. Freeze when your forearm is horizontal to the ground. Again, your right thumb should point at the sky, but the back of your hand should face directly in front of you.

HIT SHOTS WITH THE BALL ABOVE YOUR FEET

Swinging the club into the ball on an inside path (see pp.26–7) is one of sport's greatest challenges: perhaps on a par with serving an ace in tennis. If you find most of your shots curve from left-to-right through the air, you are not swinging the clubhead into impact on the correct (inside) path. Rehearse this practice drill to help correct this problem and to give your swing a better shape.

* With a more rounded backswing you can deliver the club to the ball from the inside, promoting a free release of the club (see p.27) through impact. You may be pleasantly surprised to discover that a straight ball-flight, or even a draw, is not an impossible dream, after all.

1 Find a sloping lie on your home course that allows you to set up with the ball noticeably above the level of your feet, as much as 30 cm (12 in) if possible. Use a 6-iron to hit shots from this position. Instinctively, this immediately establishes a more rounded backswing and encourages a better body-turn.

2 When you have hit about 12 shots from this sloping lie, find a flat area of ground, and see if you can replicate the swing sensations experienced in step 1.

KEY CHECKPOINT

Maintain a straight line at the start of your takeaway

Losing coordination in your swing often stems from a bad first move away from the ball. The ideal address position is such that your left arm and the shaft of the club form a straight line down to the ball (see Drill 14 in the "Off the Tee" section, p.44). As you start your backswing, that line should remain intact for the first 60 cm (24 in) of the clubhead's journey away from the ball. This promotes a one-piece takeaway, which helps synchronize your arm-swing with your body-turn.

ONE-PIECE TAKEAWAY *If your left arm and the shaft of the club form a straight line for the first 60 cm (24 in) or so of the takeaway, there is a better chance of making a synchronized swing*

LEVEL **3** DRILL **·24**

SQUEEZE YOUR SHOTS WITH YOUR PALM FACING DOWN

When hitting iron shots, all good players decrease loft at impact, which means that the club's shaft is angled towards the target. This produces a powerful ball-flight. Poor players, on the other hand, increase loft at impact, which means that the club's shaft is leaning away from the target. This can produce a weak, high ball-flight. If the clubhead reaches its lowest point before impact, heavy contact is possible, as is a "thin" (where the ball shoots along the ground). One fundamental difference between these two situations is in the position of the right palm as the club enters the hitting zone. This is because what the right palm does influences what the clubface does. This exercise simulates what the right palm should not and should do in your swing. You can compare the two and become accustomed to positioning your right palm correctly.

✱ In an actual swing, this all happens very quickly. But by rehearsing this drill, your brain can become familiar with the correct movements. If you can recreate this right-palm position in your swing, you will compress the ball more strongly – literally squeezing it against the clubface – producing a powerful ball-flight for all of your iron shots. This is how the tour professionals do it.

1 INCORRECT HAND POSITION
Stand as you would normally to hit a ball. Swing your right arm back, then down towards the hitting zone. At the moment where you would be striking the ball, position your right palm so that it is starting to flip upwards. This is how many amateur golfers deliver the clubface to the ball.

2 CORRECT HAND POSITION
Repeat step 1, except as you swing your right arm into the hitting area, make sure that your palm is angled down towards the ball. This means there will be a slight angle in the back of your wrist, which was not there in step 1.

FLEX YOUR KNEE TO ADD RESISTANCE TO YOUR SWING

For most golfers, keeping the right knee flexed throughout the backswing stops the hips turning more than 45 degrees. This provides a point of resistance against which the upper body can "wind up". The following simple practice exercise will help you focus on maintaining your right-knee flex.

* By keeping your right knee flexed throughout your backswing, your hips can only turn so far, which enables you to wind your upper body tight, like a spring. The tighter you wind up in the backswing, the faster your upper body will unwind in the downswing, and the more power you will generate. (Note: older or less supple golfers will probably not be flexible enough to coil their upper body sufficiently and therefore need to allow their hips to turn more than 45 degrees. This will help provide the necessary twisting motion.)

1 | Take any iron, and assume your normal address position. Make sure that you introduce the appropriate amount of flex in your knees (see p.24). Take your left hand off the club.

2 | Rehearse a backswing. As you do so, shift your weight on to your right leg, keeping the knee braced. At the top, your head should be over your flexed right knee. Repeat several times, always focusing on turning your upper body and shifting your weight on to your right knee.

3 | Now put both hands on the club and try to replicate the same feelings in your proper backswing. If your knee straightens in your backswing, you are probably reverse pivoting, where your weight moves on to the left side instead of the right. If your knee slides to the right you are probably swaying off the ball too much. These situations are to be avoided.

LEVEL 3 · DRILL 26

LEARN ABOUT TRAJECTORY BY EXAMINING THE LAUNCH ANGLE

By now you probably have a good idea how high or low the ball flies with each iron you hit, but are you aware of the ball's launch angle? This is the trajectory of the shot in the first 18 m (20 yd) or so of its flight – a distance that is traversed so quickly that your head usually does not come up in time for you to see where the ball is going. However, establishing the launch angle for each iron is far more important than you might think, as it enables you to make informed club selections when, for example, overhanging branches are partly blocking your way to the target. It is also useful when you need to control the trajectory of your iron shots on a breezy day. The following exercise will prepare you for such eventualities.

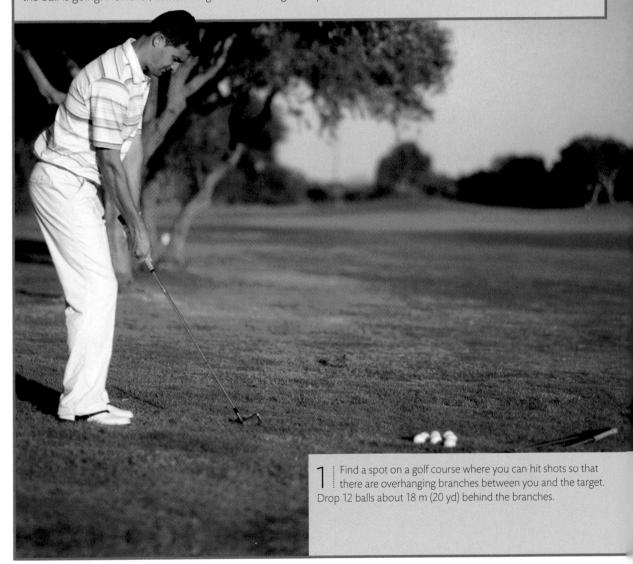

1 Find a spot on a golf course where you can hit shots so that there are overhanging branches between you and the target. Drop 12 balls about 18 m (20 yd) behind the branches.

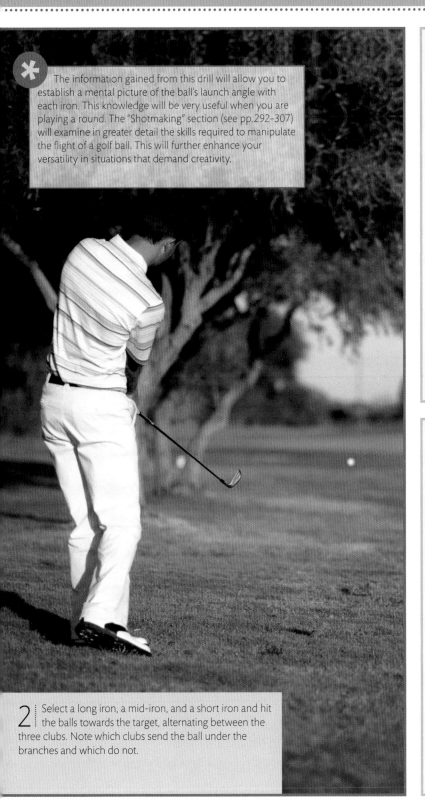

The information gained from this drill will allow you to establish a mental picture of the ball's launch angle with each iron. This knowledge will be very useful when you are playing a round. The "Shotmaking" section (see pp.292–307) will examine in greater detail the skills required to manipulate the flight of a golf ball. This will further enhance your versatility in situations that demand creativity.

2 Select a long iron, a mid-iron, and a short iron and hit the balls towards the target, alternating between the three clubs. Note which clubs send the ball under the branches and which do not.

KEY CHECKPOINT

Find a rhythm that suits your personality

Golfers with good rhythm swing at a pace that allows them to generate power while maintaining control of the club. This rhythm also helps them achieve perfect balance from start to finish. But rhythm varies. Some golfers swing fast; others swing slow. Which is best for you?

While there are no strict rules, a useful guideline is to think about what type of person you are. If you are a naturally lively person who tends to do everything quickly, then the chances are that your ideal swing rhythm is relatively brisk. Golfers such as Alvaro Quiros and Anthony Kim fit into this category. If, on the other hand, you tend to go through life at a fairly sedate pace, then a slower swing speed will probably suit your game. Think of golfers like Ernie Els and Fred Couples.

KEY CHECKPOINT

Keep checking your personal distances

If you have worked through all the drills in this section, you will undoubtedly be a much better iron player than you were when you performed Drill 1 (see pp.68–9). This means that, because of the improved quality of your ball-striking, your personal distances for each club will have increased. It is therefore a good idea to repeat Drill 1 periodically, especially if your handicap and scores are lowering. This helps ensure that you are not inadvertently selecting the wrong clubs, which could easily result in costly errors. Always remember to ignore the longest and shortest few balls hit with each club, as these do not accurately represent your normal average length. Instead, pace out your distances to the centre of the main cluster of balls.

LEVEL THREE

THE PERFECT IRON SHOT

One could take almost any aspect of Tiger Woods' game and hold it up as a beacon of excellence – such is the man's greatness – but for the purposes of this book, we focus on his iron play. The positions in Tiger's swing are perfection within motion; that much is evident from this swing sequence. However, it is the rhythm of Tiger's swing that warrants extra mention here; like all great players he has the ability to swing every club at the same tempo. He swings within himself, maintaining superb balance, which yields the perfect blend of power and control. That encapsulates one of Tiger's greatest skills.

* TIGER WINDS and unwinds his body over a very stable leg action, which is an object lesson in how to create lots of power in your golf swing. He combines this with a lovely, free swing of the hands, arms, and club, down and through the hitting zone.

1 GREAT POSTURE

Tiger's posture is perfect at address, which goes a long way to promoting his very correct action. This is because the angles established at address to a large degree determine the shape of the swing. Tiger's alignment is also perfect; the feet, hips, and shoulders being parallel to one another. This in turn promotes an on-line swing path. So, together, posture and alignment have significant benefits.

2 PERFECT PLANE

Here, a perfect body pivot combined with the appropriate hand-and-arm swing produces a backswing that is on the ideal plane. The club does not quite reach horizontal at the top of the backswing, but it does not need to. Tiger has completed all the body turn he needs and the wrists have hinged fully and correctly.

3 CONSTANT SPINE ANGLE

As Tiger approaches impact, his spine angle has retained its original angle as it was at address. Maintaining this angle means that he does not need to make any significant height adjustments mid-swing to return the clubface to the ball. It is then a free and uninhibited swish through the hitting area.

Keys to accurate iron play

Pinpoint accuracy should be your objective with every iron in the bag. These four keys will remind you of some of the primary moves essential to achieving this goal.

To give you extra confidence on the golf course, use your practice sessions to establish exactly how far you hit each of your irons.

Make sure that the clubface remains square to the path of your swing in your takeaway. This way you will not have to make adjustments later in your swing in order to hit a straight shot.

If you retain the flex in your right knee as you make your backswing, your hips will turn no more than 45 degrees, allowing you to effectively coil your upper body.

Swing each iron with the same rhythm and trust the loft on the clubface to produce the exact shape of shot and yardage you require. Swinging longer irons harder does not help you hit further; in fact it results in poor striking and loss of accuracy.

WATCH
THE PRO

4 **LEFT SIDE CLEARS**
Tiger gives himself plenty of room to swing the club freely into and through impact on the correct path. This is facilitated by the action of his left side clearing out of the way quite early in his downswing. If the left side fails to clear, the arms and the club become trapped too far on the inside. Tiger has no such problems in this instance.

5 **TOTAL CONTROL**
As we referred to in the introduction to this swing sequence, Tiger swings the club well within his own physical limitations, which are admittedly quite exceptional. The point is worth making again: whether you are using a 3-iron or a 9-iron, the rhythm of the swing must stay the same. Tiger's perfectly balanced followthrough is the ideal sign-off for a controlled golf swing. The sense of balance should be a key feature of your golf swing, too.

PITCHING

THE PITCHING WEDGE comes into operation anywhere from approximately 35 m (38 yd) to 110 m (120 yd) away from the green. From this position, a tour professional will more often than not land the ball close enough to the flag so that only one putt is required. Most amateurs, however, are just happy to hit the green. Even allowing for the remarkable skills of top tour players, this difference is too big. For one thing, distance is not an issue: you do not need to worry about generating lots of power. Also, because a shorter swing is required, accuracy and control should be much more attainable.

THE ART OF PITCHING

Theory is all well and good, but you need to turn your pitching aspirations into reality. Although there are similarities between pitch shots and other iron shots, there are nuances in technique and touch that are unique to pitching. This section of the book will provide you with all the necessary knowledge to master these skills. But first you must perform the all-important test, which will accurately establish your current level of ability with a pitching wedge.

TEST YOUR SKILLS

THE PITCHING TEST

You are likely to be using your pitching wedge when you are 35 m (38 yd) to 110 m (120 yd) from the green (although this upper limit is higher for the likes of Tiger Woods). However, forgetting the two extremes of pitching, somewhere midway between these two parameters is a good distance from which to gauge your ability. Therefore, shots of about 75 m (82 yd) form the basis of the

1 Locate an average-sized green, ideally with the flag positioned centrally. Pace out approximately 75 m (82 yd) from the flag into the fairway.

2 Hit 15 balls from a good lie with your pitching wedge. Walk up to the green and note how many balls finish within seven paces of the hole. (Note: if you are performing this test at a driving range, you will not be able to actually walk on to the green and check your results. However, it is better to make your best guess from a distance [as to how many balls are within seven paces of the hole] than not do the test at all.)

* ACCURATE PITCH SHOTS CAN SAVE you several strokes during a round. They will not only set you up for a greater number of birdie opportunities on par 4s and par 5s but also help you salvage valuable pars when your long game goes awry.

3 Hit two more batches of 15 balls, and calculate your average score. Then use the performance chart (right) to establish your current level of ability.

PERFORMANCE CHART

1
1–5 =
LEVEL ONE
(pp.108–121)

2
6–10 =
LEVEL TWO
(pp.122–135)

3
11–15 =
LEVEL THREE
(pp.136–145)

LEVEL 1 · DRILL 01

THINK OF DISTANCE NOT DIRECTION

One of the biggest problems golfers have with their approach play is not knowing precisely how hard to hit shots of different distances. Drill 1 (see pp.68–9) in the "Iron Play" section discusses the importance of knowing your personal distances for each club. It is critical that you practise with this information in mind.

1 | Next time you are at the range and you want to work on your pitching, identify a specific target, whereby you know exactly how far it is from you. Do not aim at something beyond the distance you can comfortably hit with a wedge.

2 | Hit pitch shots to this target, and judge every one in terms of distance. Whether the ball comes up short, long, or perfect will provide you with feedback you can use to make adjustments to the feel of your swing.

* The essence of a good pitch shot is being able to see a target and make an appropriate length swing to produce the required amount of carry through the air. If your wedge shots are flying in all directions, then your technique needs work. But, assuming direction is not a problem, which it should not be with such a short shot, getting the right distance is your priority. Distance technique is further refined in Drill 13 (see pp.126–7).

LEVEL DRILL
1·02 OPEN YOUR STANCE

When playing most shots, perfect parallel alignment – where your toes, hips, and shoulders all run along the same line – is required. However, as explained in the introduction to this section (see pp.106–7), pitch shots are not like any other iron shot. To be a good pitcher your stance needs to be slightly open, and this drill will help you make the appropriate change.

1 Address the ball as you would to hit a normal iron shot, with your stance parallel to the target line. Place two irons on the ground to help you find perfect parallel alignment.

2 Now draw your left foot back about 5 cm (2 in), to open your stance. Make sure you keep your shoulders square, though. This element of your set-up must remain the same.

✱ This small adjustment has two key benefits to your pitching. Firstly, it creates more resistance in your legs and hips, curtailing your backswing so that the club does not reach a point where it is horizontal with the ground. This is preferable when pitching, as a shorter swing equals more control. Secondly, because you are making a shorter swing, you need assistance to clear your left side out of the way in your downswing. An open stance provides this help and produces a better impact position.

Open stance
Draw your left foot back approximately 5 cm (2 in)

LEVEL. DRILL

1·03 FIND THE BOTTOM OF YOUR SWING FOR CRISP STRIKES

Controlling the distance you hit your pitch shots is impossible unless you learn to strike the ball consistently out of the clubhead's sweet spot. To do this, the ball must be positioned at the bottom of your swing arc – the point where the clubhead first comes into contact with the turf. Anywhere else in your stance and you have to make unnatural compensations to avoid hitting the shot heavy or thin. This straightforward drill will help you locate the bottom of your swing arc and will confirm the ideal place to put the ball in your stance.

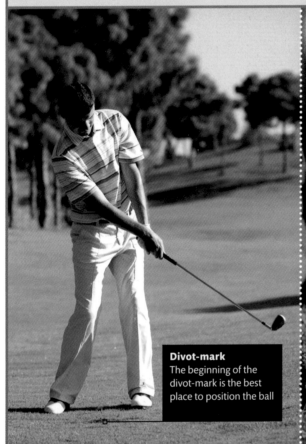

It is a very good idea to make regular checks on this aspect of your swing. You can also use this drill to find the bottom of your swing for every iron club in the bag. This will help you identify the correct ball position for all your irons.

Check ball position
Hit balls placed along a line that indicates the bottom of your swing. The divot-mark should start slightly in front of the line.

Divot-mark
The beginning of the divot-mark is the best place to position the ball

1 | Stand in a closely mown area of grass and make a well-disciplined practice swing – not a half-hearted swish, but a dynamic movement that closely resembles your actual swing.

2 | Take note of where the clubhead first comes into contact with the ground. This is the perfect place to position the ball in your stance.

LEVEL DRILL
1·04

KEEP YOUR HANDS SOFT FOR A FREE-FLOWING SWING

If one thing is guaranteed to hamper your chances of making a good swing, it is tension. It only takes a little extra tightness in your grip for tension to spread into your arms and shoulders. This tends to lead to a poor first move away from the ball (see Drill 3, p.71), and your whole swing will lack fluidity and rhythm. This is disastrous for a pitch shot. Lee Trevino, who won six majors in his career, used to say that just before he took the club away he consciously eased his left-hand grip to free up the muscles in his hands, arms, and upper body. If he did not do this he felt his swing was in danger of becoming a little tight and too short. Many golfers are guilty of doing the opposite to Trevino, actually tightening their grip just before they start to swing.

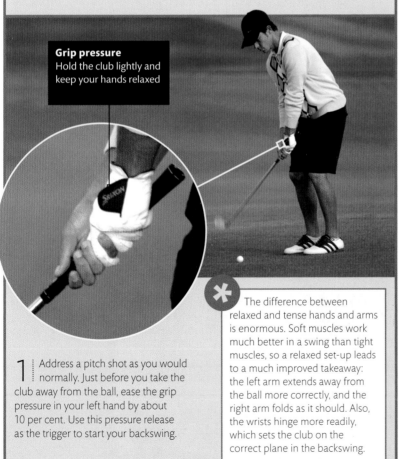

Grip pressure
Hold the club lightly and keep your hands relaxed

1 Address a pitch shot as you would normally. Just before you take the club away from the ball, ease the grip pressure in your left hand by about 10 per cent. Use this pressure release as the trigger to start your backswing.

* The difference between relaxed and tense hands and arms is enormous. Soft muscles work much better in a swing than tight muscles, so a relaxed set-up leads to a much improved takeaway: the left arm extends away from the ball more correctly, and the right arm folds as it should. Also, the wrists hinge more readily, which sets the club on the correct plane in the backswing.

KEY CHECKPOINT
Grip as you hold a child's hand

Short shots tend to create greater anxiety than almost any other shot. This usually leads to tension, especially in the grip. But what is the ideal grip pressure? Well, Sam Snead – who holds the record for the most tournaments won by any professional golfer in history – said you should grip a golf club using the same pressure you would to hold a live bird.

Another analogy is that you should hold the club as if you were holding a child's hand while crossing a road: you hold the hand tight enough not to let the toddler break free, but soft enough so as not to cause discomfort. This is the ideal grip pressure for holding a golf club: firm enough to provide a secure hold on the club, but soft enough to promote flexibility in the wrists, which allows you to make a free-flowing swing. Holding your wedge at the correct pressure will undoubtedly improve your pitching. The Key Checkpoint on p.19 describes another way to attain the correct grip pressure.

SOFT HOLD *Imagine the grip pressure you would use to hold a toddler's hand. This is very close to the grip pressure you should use when pitching.*

LEVEL 1·05 DRILL

FIND YOUR PERSONAL SPEED LIMIT

How hard should you hit a full wedge shot? As with most things in golf, this varies, depending on the individual. This drill shows you how to find the correct amount of force you should use – a speed limit, so to speak. You can then apply this to every pitch you hit, using the length of swing and changes of club as necessary to regulate the distance you will hit your shots.

1 Hit pitch shots in three-ball batches. Start with a very easy swing, using barely 50 per cent of full power.

2 Swing the club using progressively more force with each batch of balls. Build up gradually.

3 Eventually you will start to lose control, not just in terms of balance but also in the consistency of your ball-striking and the accuracy of your shots. If all three balls are coming off the clubface differently or are flying erratically, you have exceeded your speed limit. When this happens, drop down a level. The amount of force used on the batch of balls hit just before you lost control is how hard you should hit a full wedge shot.

* No one can tell you your personal swing speed limit: you have to find out yourself. This practice exercise allows you to do just that. Once you have this information, it is a simple matter to determine how far you hit a full wedge shot. Knowledge of your personal speed limit and distance with a wedge will help you manage your game more efficiently and should lead to lower scores. The more you know about your swing, the better your pitching will be.

LEVEL ONE

LEVEL 1·06   DRILL

SWING DOWN ON THE PATH OF YOUR BACKSWING

Sometimes the simplest of thoughts can clear your mind and clarify your swing objectives. With pitching, for example, it is easy to become so obsessed with hitting the target that you actually forget what you have to do in your swing. This simple drill will provide a clear swing thought that will improve your pitching.

* Swing path is one of the most important ingredients of a well-struck pitch shot. If you can combine the proper swing path with the correct angle of attack (see the Key Checkpoint on p.143), you will soon find that your pitch shots become much more precise.

Downswing
Try to swing the club down on the same path it went back on

1 | As you start your swing, be conscious of your takeaway path. Ideally, the clubhead should move straight back for the first 30–45 cm (12–18 in) and then gradually arc inside in response to your body-turn (see p.26–7).

2 | Perform a couple of "dummy run" backswings to help establish a strong visual reference.
Make it the sole objective in your downswing to swing the club into impact on exactly the same path that it went back on. Do not think about anything else.

Have a trigger to start your swing

Most golfers find that the closer they are to the flag, the more anxious they become. And anxiety usually leads to tension and a poor swing. That is when you need a trigger to start your swing smoothly. A lot of the greatest players in history have relied on a "swing trigger". Gary Player, for example, kicked in his right knee just before taking the club away; Jack Nicklaus turned his head to the right – different move, same principle. Next time you are practising your pitching, take time to try out a few swing triggers of your own – trial and error is the key. Maybe either of the two moves mentioned above will suit you. Perhaps a final waggle of the club or a little nudge forwards of your hands at address will do the trick. And do not forget the possibility of easing the pressure in your left hand, as discussed in Drill 4 (see p.111). Keep experimenting until you find a trigger that feels comfortable. Having a swing trigger means that you will never freeze over the ball.

HEAD TURN *Simply moving your head slightly to your right just before beginning your backswing is an effective way to trigger the start of your swing. It will also facilitate a fuller body-turn.*

LEVEL 1 · DRILL 07

MAKE A RIGHT ANGLE IN YOUR BACKSWING

Poor pitching is often the result of either too much wrist hinge in the backswing, where the hands pick the club up too abruptly; or too little wrist hinge, where the wrists remain stiff as the club swings back. Either situation damages your ball-striking because if you cannot set the club correctly in the backswing, you will never produce the ideal angle of attack into impact. This drill will ensure that the appropriate wrist hinge takes place in your backswing – and at exactly the right time.

Right angle
The wrists have hinged correctly and at the right time. The shaft of the club and the left forearm form a right angle.

Obtuse angle
The angle between the left forearm and the club is too wide: the wrists have not hinged sufficiently (a common problem). Set your wrists a little earlier in your takeaway.

Acute angle
The wrists have done too much too soon, and there is a poor body-turn. Try to keep your wrists passive for longer and to get the club a little wider as you turn your upper body.

1 Take your pitching wedge and address the ball as normal. Begin your backswing, but freeze at the point where your left arm is horizontal. Compare your position with the three images shown here.

✱ Working on this aspect of your swing is time well spent. Correctly hinging your wrists in your backswing helps promote the ideal angle of attack in your downswing, enabling you to strike your pitch shots with authority.

LEVEL   DRILL

1·08   CHECK YOUR SWING PLANE
HALFWAY BACK

This drill uses the same "frozen" position employed in Drill 7 (see p.115). It will show you a very simple way to check if your swing is on the correct plane in the backswing, which is vital to your chances of making a good swing.

1   Position either a mirror or a helper to your right. Assume an address position whereby you would be hitting away from the mirror/helper.

2   Begin your takeaway, but freeze when your left arm is horizontal.

3   Use either the mirror or your helper to check your position. If your wrists have hinged correctly (see Drill 7, p.115), the butt-end of the club's grip will point at a spot on the ground between the ball and your toes (slightly closer to the ball than your toes). This is the perfect swing plane. If the grip is pointing too far – say more than 10 cm (4 in) – either side of this spot, your swing requires corrective action.

*This drill, coupled with Drill 7 (see p.115), is terribly important to the future success of your pitching. If you can be correct in this early stage of your swing, it is so much easier to develop a repeatable action. Certainly, if you take the time to perfect this part of your swing, the targets set by the drills in Levels Two and Three will be much more achievable.

LEVEL ONE

Wrists
The correct wrist hinge is vital to a good swing

Swing plane
If you are swinging on the correct path, the butt-end of the club will point between your toes and the ball

KEY CHECKPOINT

Choke down to increase control

Any opportunity to enhance the control in your pitch shots has to be seized. One good way to do this is to hold the club about 5 cm (2 in) further down than you would normally. This might not seem much, but choking down on the grip (see Drill 9 in the "Off the Tee" section, pp.38–9) brings your hands slightly closer to the clubhead, which gives you greater control over the it. And if you control what is happening to the clubhead, you can control the ball better, too. Try choking down on your wedge, and you should notice an improvement in your pitching.

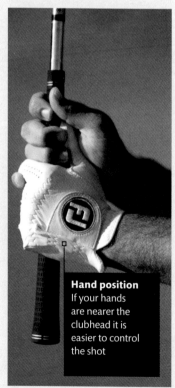

Hand position
If your hands are nearer the clubhead it is easier to control the shot

CHOKE DOWN *When choking down on a pitching wedge, the right hand is almost in contact with the metal of the shaft. This aids control.*

LEVEL DRILL
1·09

CHECK YOUR DIVOT-MARKS FOR SWING INFORMATION

The divot-mark (or lack of one) you leave in the ground after playing a pitch shot can tell you a great deal about the shape and quality of your swing. Each divot-mark is like a fingerprint that reveals one or more of the individual traits of your game. Knowing how to interpret what your divot-mark is telling you can lead to some dramatic discoveries and, more importantly, clues as to how you can hit better pitch shots. Use the information in this drill to decode the information your divot-marks are giving you.

DEEP DIVOT-MARK AND HEAVY CONTACT

Taking a divot is part and parcel of good short-iron play. However, if your divot-marks become too deep and your ball-striking is very erratic, it is obvious that you are doing something wrong. These symptoms suggest that your swing is too narrow, causing you to swing the clubhead into impact on an excessively steep angle of attack. This means you will be chopping down into the ground behind the ball. If these problems sound familiar, this short exercise will improve the quality of your ball-striking immensely.

1 Make sure the ball is not too far forward in your stance – in other words, close to or directly opposite your left heel – as this might cause you to hit behind the ball.

2 To shallow your angle of attack and start striking the ball more cleanly, try to delay hinging your wrists in your backswing.

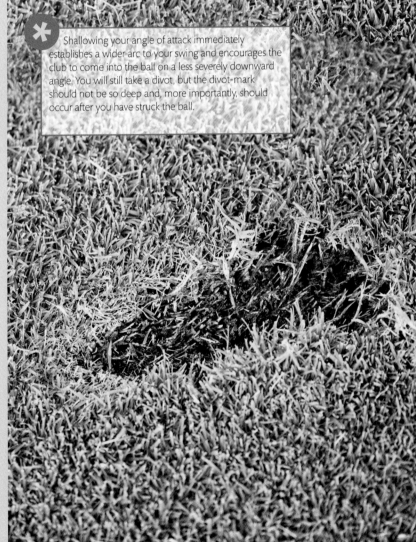

★ Shallowing your angle of attack immediately establishes a wider arc to your swing and encourages the club to come into the ball on a less severely downward angle. You will still take a divot, but the divot-mark should not be so deep and, more importantly, should occur after you have struck the ball.

NO DIVOT-MARK AT ALL

Chances are that you are trying to help the ball into the air with a scooping motion if many of your shots leave no divot-mark at all in the ground, and you are also occasionally hitting very heavy shots, where the ball flies barely half its proper distance. These problems indicate that the clubhead has travelled beyond the lowest point in its swing arc (see Drill 3, p.110) and is on the way up at the moment of impact. This is the worst possible angle of attack for pitching. Try this quick and easy drill to correct this destructive fault.

1 Check that the ball is positioned correctly – in the middle of your stance. This alone will help promote the required descending blow.

2 Examine the weight transfer in your swing. If you are hitting up on the ball, you are probably hanging back on your right side in your downswing. Eliminate this problem by ensuring that your weight flows on to your left side as the club swings down towards impact. With your weight travelling in the same direction as the club, you can hit down on the ball.

* You should notice straight away that you start taking a divot after you have struck the ball. This is an immediate signal that you are back on the right track.

DIVOT-MARK POINTS LEFT OF THE TARGET

When a pitch shot finishes left of the target, there is every chance that the divot-mark will be pointing that way, too. This problem is caused by the clubhead approaching the ball from outside the correct line (see pp.26–7) and travelling to the left of the target through impact.

1   Narrow your stance by about 5 cm (2 in). This encourages your arms to play a more active role than your body (see Drill 21 in the "Iron Play" section, pp.96–7), which in turn encourages a more correct swing path.

2   When you are at the top of your backswing, start down with your hands and arms. Try to feel that your downswing consists of more hand and arm swing and less body movement. This will enable you to swing the club into impact from slightly inside (see pp.26–7), which is ideal.

* Once you have effected the suggested changes in this drill, you should find that instead of the ball (and your divots) flying left, everything is now back on line.

Target line

These adjustments create more room in front of you, which promotes a more correct line of attack in your downswing.

Target line

DIVOT-MARK POINTS RIGHT OF THE TARGET

A divot-mark pointing right of the target is much less common than the mark pointing to the left, especially at amateur level. This problem is caused by your hips not clearing out of the way as they should in your downswing. This means that the clubhead becomes trapped on the inside, which leads to a severe in-to-out swing path (see pp.26–7). Therefore, when the clubhead approaches impact it will travel to the right as it makes contact with the ball. This means that the ball will fly to the right of the target. The following drill will eliminate such tendencies.

1 Firstly, check that the ball is not too far back in your stance (nearer your right foot than your left foot) because this ball position can create an excessive inside-the-line attack, and cause your shots to fly to the right of the target. Remember, the centre of your stance is the perfect ball position for pitch shots.

2 Open your stance so that your toe-to-toe line runs slightly left of the target (see Drill 2, p.109).

3 At the top of your backswing, initiate your downswing by turning your hips so that there is plenty of space for your hands and arms to swing on the correct path.

Re-test yourself

Before moving to Level Two, take the test on pp.106–7 again. If you have not improved, it is worth revisiting the Level One drills. However, if the performance chart shows that your pitching has progressed sufficiently, then you are ready to tackle the more advanced drills in Level Two.

LEVEL ONE

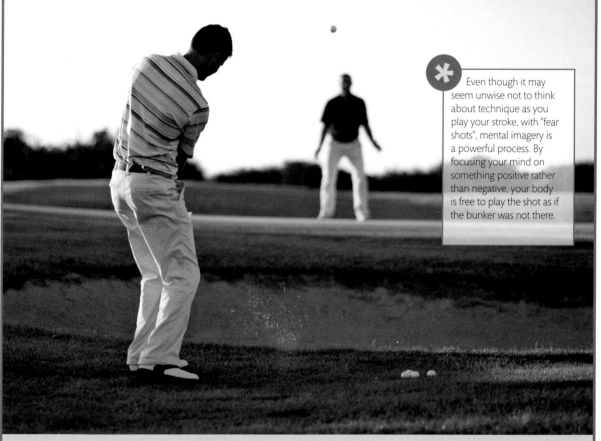

LEVEL 2 · DRILL 10   PITCH TO A CATCHER

Just about the scariest shot in golf, certainly for most amateurs, is the pitch shot over a bunker. Strictly speaking, it is no different from a pitch with nothing in the way, but of course it never feels like that: psychologically, this is an intimidating shot. Often, the fear of landing the ball in the bunker becomes a self-fulfilling prophecy, and you end up hitting the exact shot you most wanted to avoid. However, the positive mental imagery this drill provides will help eliminate the fear of such shots and will allow you to function normally. This means that pitching over a bunker will soon become much less problematic.

* Even though it may seem unwise not to think about technique as you play your stroke, with "fear shots", mental imagery is a powerful process. By focusing your mind on something positive rather than negative, your body is free to play the shot as if the bunker was not there.

1 Find a position on the course where you have a pitch shot of approximately 40 m (44 yd) to the flag, with a bunker between you and the green.

2 Instead of fretting about hitting the ball into the sand, as perhaps you might have formerly, imagine someone standing on your landing area on the green, waiting to receive the ball.

3 As you hit the shot, concentrate 100 per cent of your mental capacity on lobbing the ball to the person on the green. Try to give him or her an easy catch.

HIT THE BUCKET TO IMPROVE YOUR ACCURACY

It is easy to hit pitch shots on the practice ground and be satisfied with a loose grouping in the distance. In reality, this is not good enough: pitch shots should be incredibly accurate. You should be looking to knock pitch shots close to the flag every time: merely hitting the green is not good enough. Try this exercise to completely transform your attitude to pitching.

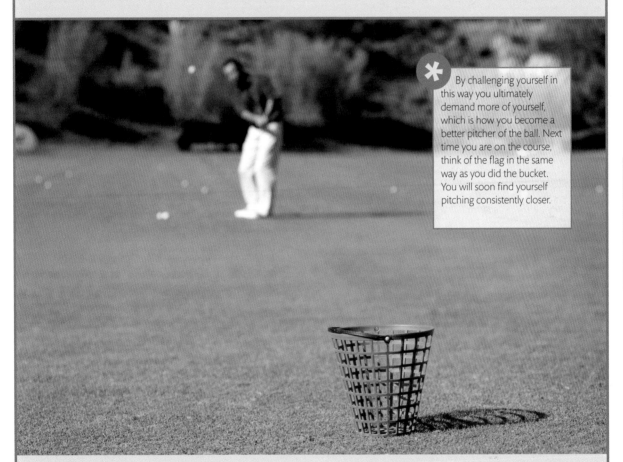

✱ By challenging yourself in this way you ultimately demand more of yourself, which is how you become a better pitcher of the ball. Next time you are on the course, think of the flag in the same way as you did the bucket. You will soon find yourself pitching consistently closer.

1 Place a large bucket on the range, about 30 m (33 yd) away, and think of this as your target. From such a short distance you will almost certainly find it beneficial to pitch with your most lofted wedge (see the Key Checkpoint on p.125), because greater loft allows you to be more positive while not having to worry about hitting the ball too far.

2 Now hit a few pitch shots, and try to get the ball into the bucket (without the ball bouncing on the turf first). This forces you to be very specific about your target and subconsciously raises your expectations.

LEVEL 2·12 DRILL

FEEL CONTROLLED AGGRESSION
THROUGH THE BALL

Pitch shots are predominantly "touch" shots played from a distance, which means many golfers become a little tentative with the strike. You cannot afford to do this. Yes, pitch shots are control shots, but they still need to be struck with authority. Watch the likes of Tiger Woods or Phil Mickelson, both great pitchers of the ball, if you need confirmation of this fact. Here is a simple exercise that will help you make a more authoritative strike.

1 Take your pitching wedge and find a thick area of rough.

2 Make some smooth practice swings. Build up speed gradually in your downswing, and feel as if you are swishing the clubhead through the long grass. Be very positive and get used to the feeling of the clubhead zipping through the hitting area. If you become too tentative, the clubhead will become snagged in the grass. However, do it properly and the clubhead will rip through the grass and enable you to swing through to a full finish.

KEY CHECKPOINT

Smart golfers carry three wedges

If you were to take a peek into any tour professional's golf bag you would find at least three different wedges, perhaps even four. If professionals feel it necessary to have this many wedges all to hit from 35 m (38 yd) to 110 m (120 yd) from the green, then so should you. Wedges will be discussed again in the reference section (see p.330), but now is a good time to stress the importance of carrying several types. This is because during a round you will have to play many different wedge shots. Lofts on wedges start from around 46 degrees for a standard pitching wedge and move up through the gap wedge and sand wedge to the lob wedge, which has a loft of around 62 degrees. Having this array of wedges is smart thinking because it means you will have a club to suit every situation. Drill 25 (see pp.144–5) shows you how to determine your personal distances for these clubs.

CLUB SELECTION *There is probably not a single tour professional in the world who does not carry at least three different wedges, and you should do the same. Make sure you carry clubs with an even spread of lofts, such as a lob, sand, and gap wedge (above).*

＊ The next time you hit a pitch shot you should try to recreate the feeling of the clubhead swinging positively through the hitting zone, except that this time there will be a ball in the way rather than a thick patch of grass. This controlled form of aggression will help your ball-striking enormously.

LEVEL DRILL
2·13 MATCH YOUR SWING LENGTH TO EVERY PITCH

If golf was an exact science you would be able to leave yourself with your ideal-distance pitch shot every time – and you would never hit a bad shot. But golf is not like that, and inevitably you have to play pitch shots from a variety of distances during a normal round. This is part of the game's charm and challenge. The following drill will improve your ability to match the correct swing to shots of different lengths. Drill 24 (see pp.142–3) shows another way to do this. It will also help you establish your favourite pitching distance, which will make you better at seeing a certain length shot and matching the correct swing to it.

1 Arm yourself with a bag of balls and however many pitching clubs you have in your bag (you should have at least three: your pitching wedge, another slightly more lofted wedge, and your sand wedge).

2 Find a quiet green. Starting from about 35 m (38 yd) from the flag, drop a ball, move 5 m (5½ yd) back, drop another ball and so on. Stop when you are about 110 m (120 yd) from the green.

3 Starting with the shortest shot, simply work your way back from the target, pitching each ball towards the flag. As there are 5-m (5½-yd) gaps between each ball, you will have to alter your swing very slightly for every shot. You may also want to swap clubs at the appropriate time, going with progressively less loft as the shots become longer.

* Since you only have one chance at each shot on the course, this practice drill accurately recreates the challenge of a proper round (this idea is elaborated on in Drill 23, p.141). It also reveals the exact distance from which you feel most comfortable pitching. Somewhere along the line of balls you should have hit upon a distance where you felt most confident.

This distance represents a strength in your game that you can deliberately play to. For example, if you are on a hole where the green is out of range in two shots – say on a long par five or if you have hit a poor drive into trouble on a par 4 – your first consideration should be to leave your second shot in a position whereby you can pitch from your favourite distance. This is one area of the game that tour professionals are very good at exploiting, which is one reason you see them hit so many of their pitch shots close to pin-high. Once you have practised this drill, there is no reason why you cannot do the same.

LEVEL DRILL
2·14 HIT THREE SHOTS WITH ONE SWING

The key checkpoint on p.125 discusses the merits of carrying at least three, or even four, wedges in your bag. The following drill, which teaches you how to hit three different-length pitch shots with the same technique, will help you appreciate why this is such a sensible plan. It is an easy exercise to carry out and can only be of benefit to you when you are on the course playing a proper round.

1 Hit 10 balls with your most lofted wedge.

2 Use exactly the same swing to hit another 10 balls, but this time use your gap wedge, which probably has a loft of around 56 degrees.

3 Hit 10 more balls, again using the same swing, with your regular pitching wedge.

4 Walk up to the three clusters of balls, and make a note of the different distances. Your regular pitching wedge shots might fly about 90 m (100 yd), gap wedge shots around 70 m (75 yd), and the most lofted wedge shots will reach no more than 45 m (50 yd).

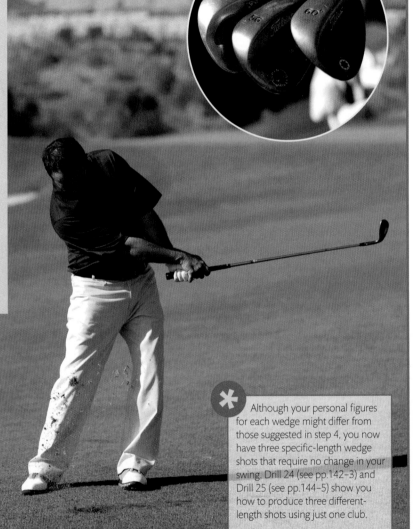

✳ Although your personal figures for each wedge might differ from those suggested in step 4, you now have three specific-length wedge shots that require no change in your swing. Drill 24 (see pp.142–3) and Drill 25 (see pp.144–5) show you how to produce three different-length shots using just one club.

LEVEL · DRILL 2·15

FORCE THE CLUB UPWARDS IN YOUR BACKSWING

Drill 16 (see pp.130–1) discusses how easy it is to let the club swing too flat from an open stance, which destroys your chances of swinging the club on the correct plane. While Drill 16 is for the practice ground only, this exercise can be rehearsed just about anywhere. This drill trains you to swing the club on the correct plane going back, which increases the likelihood of a good swing path coming down.

1 Stand with your buttocks resting lightly against a wall or similar object (such as a tall fence or hedge). Pretend that you are about to hit a proper pitch shot.

Small gap
The clubhead should not touch the wall during your backswing

Upper body
There should be a full upper body turn

2 Now rehearse your backswing, making sure that as you swing back and upwards the clubhead does not come into contact with the wall. If you can get to the top of your backswing without the club hitting the wall, while keeping the clubhead no more than 8–10 cm (3–4 in) from the wall, you are swinging on the correct plane. If you have been swinging the club too far on the inside, this will probably feel quite strange. But rest assured that this swing path represents the correct movement, providing you continue to make a good shoulder turn.

3 Step away from the wall and hit a few pitch shots. Try to imagine that you are still up against the wall.

✱ Periodically rehearse this practice exercise to ensure that you are not swinging the club too flat in your backswing. This will encourage the ideal blend of arm-swing and body-turn, which is one of the most significant balancing acts in the game. It will help your pitching considerably.

Address position
Align your feet parallel to the wall

Knees
Your knees remain flexed during your swing

LEVEL   DRILL
2·16   FOLLOW THE PROFESSIONALS' SWING PATH

A good pitching action relies on a slightly open stance (see Drill 2, p.109), but you have to be careful that this does not allow faults to creep into your swing. Some golfers have a tendency to take the club back too much on the inside, which leaves them trapped at the top in a very flat, behind-the-body position. From this situation it is inevitable that the club will be thrown outside the correct line (see pp.26–7) resulting in a pull or even a shank. This practice drill involves a slight exaggeration of a perfect pitching swing, but as an exercise it helps eliminate that damaging inside-to-outside loop.

1 Stick the shaft of an old club, or a rolled-up umbrella, in the ground about 60 cm (2 ft) to the right of the toes on your back foot. Position it so that it leans at the same angle as the club at address (have a helper check this for you).

2 Practise mini-swings in which the clubhead travels above the umbrella during your backswing and under the umbrella on your downswing. Do not be in a hurry to hit shots too soon: become familiar with the feeling of the clubhead travelling on this path. It might feel strange at first, but every swing change will seem unusual at first.

* After practising this drill, you should notice a difference in the quality of your ball-striking and also in the accuracy of your pitch shots. Drill 15 (see p.129) addresses the problem of a flat swing in a different way.

3 Continue rehearsing this swing, slowly building up to full speed. Then remove the umbrella, and hit some shots, recreating the feelings experienced in step 2.

KEY CHECKPOINT
Which ball should you use?

There are three main ball categories, and it is important that you are aware of the differences to ensure that perfectly decent pitch shots do not go unrewarded simply because they are inappropriate for the type of ball you are using. Ball types are also discussed in the reference section (see p.331).

Control ball: Most golfers would gain more than they would lose by switching to a control ball. Any distance lost off the tee will be more than made up for by the enhanced control you will enjoy around the greens. You will find that a well-struck wedge shot spins back more, which gives you the confidence to attack the flag when you are playing well. The downside is that a badly struck shot, and even normal bunker shots, will scuff and cut the soft cover, which is made of balata (an artificial rubber compound). However, providing expense is not an issue, these balls are well worth the money.

Distance ball: What you gain in length with a distance ball you lose in control. This means that around the greens you have to work a little harder to compensate. In summer months you should pitch the ball well short of the pin and allow for some run. Whenever possible, load your shots with plenty of height and maximize the backspin you generate to give yourself some degree of control. Only in the winter months, when the greens are soft and receptive, can you start pitching the ball well up to the pin.

Compromise ball: This type of ball occupies the middle ground between control balls and distance balls. You cannot expect a compromise ball to spin back as much as a control ball, but on all except the hardest putting surfaces you can expect reasonable spin and control. However, even with your most lofted club, you will not be able to stop the ball dead unless the greens are very spongy. On the plus side, you will not be losing much yardage off the tee, as these balls will fly almost as far as a distance ball. This balance between distance and control suits golfers who are unwilling to make too great a sacrifice in either area.

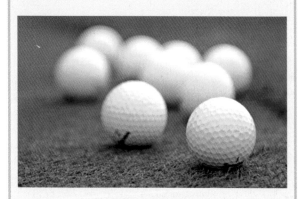

LEVEL DRILL
2·17
PRACTISE YOUR BODY-TURN, THE HUB OF YOUR SWING

When playing short shots it is easy for your hand-and-arm action to become independent of your body-turn, which can upset the timing of your swing. Whenever you play a pitch shot, whether it is from 110 m (120 yd) or 35 m (38 yd), you must ensure that your hands and

arms swing the club up and down in harmony with the appropriate body action. Here is a good drill that you can rehearse between hitting pitch shots at the range. All you need is one of the clubs from your bag.

Backswing
Your left shoulder turns under your chin

Posture
Your set-up should be as for a normal pitch

1 Trap a club across your chest and fold your arms to hold it in place.

2 Assume good posture for a wedge shot, making sure your knees are flexed and your spine angle is correct (see pp.24–5).

3 Turn your body to simulate a backswing movement, your left shoulder moving under your chin. Keep turning until you see the end of the shaft move behind the ball.

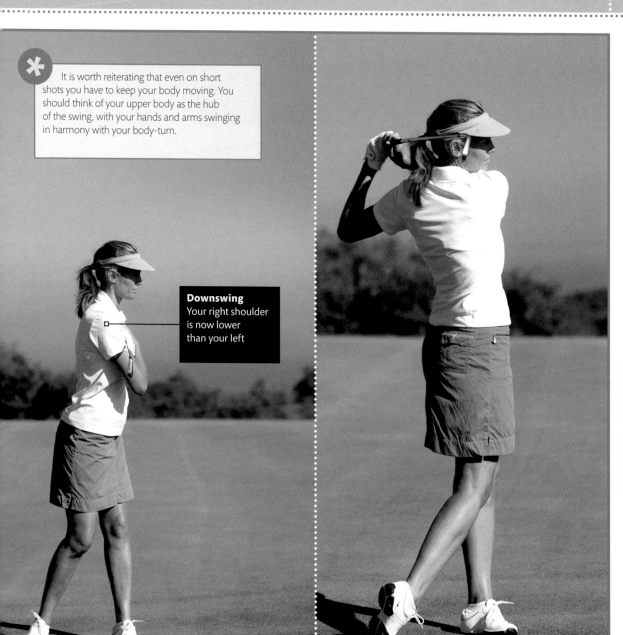

✱ It is worth reiterating that even on short shots you have to keep your body moving. You should think of your upper body as the hub of the swing, with your hands and arms swinging in harmony with your body-turn.

Downswing
Your right shoulder is now lower than your left

4 Turn your body back again as you would in a downswing, until your chest faces the target. Because your spine is tilted forwards at address, during your backswing your left shoulder will be lower than the right shoulder; during your downswing, your right shoulder will be lower than the left.

5 Now hit some shots, and try to feel the same body motion you created in steps 3 and 4 in your proper swing.

PRE-SET IMPACT TO TRAIN A CRISP STRIKE

LEVEL **2**·18 DRILL

A slightly descending angle of attack is essential for accurate short-iron play (see the Key Checkpoint on p.143). This produces the right kind of strike – ball then turf – which in turn creates lots of backspin, and with backspin comes that much sought-after ingredient: control. Try this exercise to help promote the correct angle of attack.

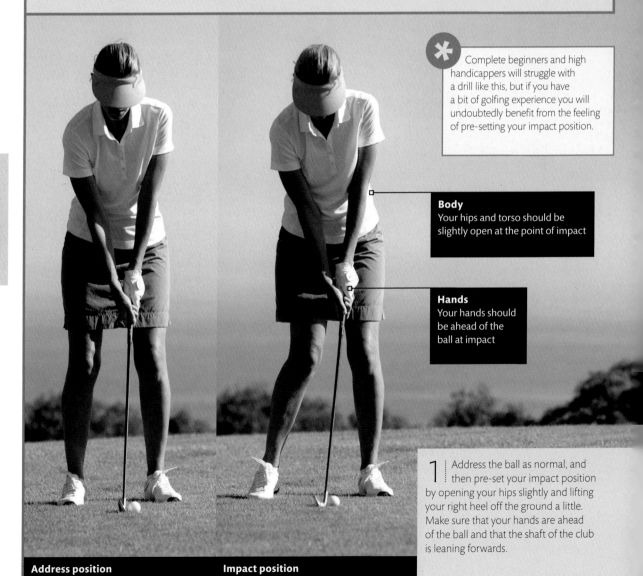

* Complete beginners and high handicappers will struggle with a drill like this, but if you have a bit of golfing experience you will undoubtedly benefit from the feeling of pre-setting your impact position.

Body
Your hips and torso should be slightly open at the point of impact

Hands
Your hands should be ahead of the ball at impact

1 Address the ball as normal, and then pre-set your impact position by opening your hips slightly and lifting your right heel off the ground a little. Make sure that your hands are ahead of the ball and that the shaft of the club is leaning forwards.

Address position   **Impact position**

Re-test yourself

Before moving to Level Three, take the test on pp.106–7 again. If you have not improved, it is worth revisiting the Level Two drills. However, if the performance chart shows that your pitching has progressed sufficiently, then you are ready to tackle the more advanced drills in Level Three.

2 Make your swing and try to return to the position created in step 1. It should be easier to replicate a good impact position because you started from a good impact position.

3 Once you have repeated step 2 a number of times, try hitting a few shots using this pre-setting technique.

KEY CHECKPOINT

Softer metals provide more feel

All types of equipment will be discussed in depth later in the book (see pp.326–31), but now is an apt time to consider the possibility of using a wedge with a clubface made of a metal compound other than steel, to give you more feel around the green. (Wedges with different lofts are discussed in the Key Checkpoint on p.125.) The most popular alternative to steel is beryllium-copper because it is softer than steel (and pleasing to the eye). This softness allows you to gain more backspin on the ball. This means that, especially if you are using a soft-covered ball (see the Key Checkpoint on p.131), you can make your pitch shots "sit down" incredibly quickly on almost any green. For this reason it is well worth having at least one alternative-metal wedge in your bag – probably the most lofted of your wedges, as this is best suited to the most delicate shots.

Soft metal
Wedges with beryllium-copper heads are popular because they provide extra feel

FEEL THE CONTROL *Since the essence of a great short game is touch, you can only benefit from having a wedge featuring a soft-metal clubhead, as the ball comes off the face with more spin.*

LEVEL 3 · DRILL 19

FREE UP YOUR SWING

If you struggle to get your swing off to a smooth start, this exercise might just release the tension in your swing and help you wield the club more freely. It also removes the tendency to hit at the ball too aggressively, which can cause problems in your swing.

* At first you might struggle to hit every ball out of the middle of the clubface. However, providing you maintain a flowing, easy rhythm, after a couple of tries you will notice certain things happening to your swing. Your rhythm will indeed be smoother and more natural. Your swing will not be restricted by tension, and as a result you will start to feel what it is like to release the club more freely through the ball. Once you are confident that these feelings are ingrained in your swing, try to replicate them when you hit pitch shots during a round.

1 | Tee up five or six balls in a row, approximately 10 cm (4 in) apart.

2 | Address the first ball in the line. For the purposes of this drill, use either a pitching wedge or a 9-iron.

3 | Hit each ball without stopping between balls. Start with a half swing and build up gradually. From the time you address the first ball, the clubhead should not stop moving until the last ball is dispatched.

HOVER THE CLUB FOR A FREE AND EASY TAKEAWAY

If you are pitching from rough, it is easy for the clubhead to become snagged in the grass during your takeaway. You can prevent this happening if you hover the clubhead behind the ball at address. This technique, advocated by two-times US Masters champion Bernhard Langer, guarantees a smooth, uninterrupted start to your swing, which can only enhance the rhythm of your entire swing. However, it takes a bit of practice.

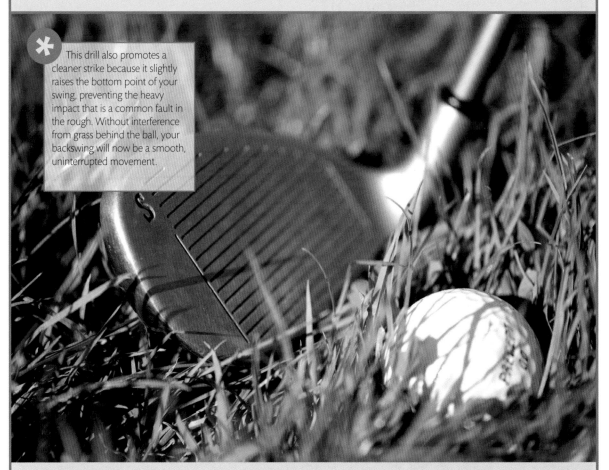

* This drill also promotes a cleaner strike because it slightly raises the bottom point of your swing, preventing the heavy impact that is a common fault in the rough. Without interference from grass behind the ball, your backswing will now be a smooth, uninterrupted movement.

1 Place a ball in light rough and address it with your pitching wedge just as you would normally, with the clubhead resting on the ground.

2 Raise the clubhead so that it is hovering in a position approximately level with the ball's equator. Do this by standing a little taller from your spine, rather than lifting the clubhead up with your hands alone.

3 You are now in a good position to sweep the clubhead back freely.

LEVEL 3·21 DRILL
THINK OF GRADUAL ACCELERATION IN THE DOWNSWING

Mickey Wright, probably the greatest female golfer of all time, once said: "You cannot start a car from a dead start and put it immediately up to 70 miles an hour. No matter how powerful your engine, you must have a gradual acceleration of speed. So it is in the golf swing". Mickey was referring to the need to build up clubhead speed gradually in the downswing. Another way to look at this is to think of a rollercoaster as it begins its plunge downwards. At first it descends quite slowly, but gradually it picks up speed until, when the rollercoaster reaches the bottom of the dip, it is travelling at full speed. Although pitch shots are control shots, gradual acceleration is still required in the downswing to produce a proper strike. A rollercoaster analogy forms the basis of a useful way to work on your swing.

Beginning of the downswing
Your hands and arms should start down smoothly

Halfway down
The club should be gradually accelerating

1 Forget targets and distance for the time being. Simply set up a shot at the practice range, and make what feels like a comfortable-length backswing with a pitching wedge.

2 Imagine that your hands, arms, and the club are the cars of a rollercoaster, that the top of your backswing is the highest point on the rollercoaster ride, and that the ball is at the bottom of the ride's dip. Make sure the "rollercoaster cars" start their descent slowly and then pick up speed gradually but purposefully. At the bottom of the ride the clubhead should reach top speed. After that your hands, arms, and the club (the rollercoaster cars) are simply freewheeling to the finish of your swing.

* For the purposes of this drill, it is not important to concern yourself with hitting towards a target. The idea is to develop smooth acceleration in your swing (see Drill 12, pp.124–5), rather than to work on your accuracy.

Hitting zone
The club should be moving at optimum speed

Followthrough
Your hands, arms, and club freewheel through to the finish of your swing

LEVEL 3·22 DRILL

TRY RIGHT-ARMED SWINGS TO TRAIN A BETTER RELEASE

With golf's shorter shots there can be a tendency to want to guide the ball towards the target. But this usually ends in misery because you cannot possibly strike the ball with any conviction or confidence if you are trying to guide the ball. Ironically, your preoccupation with greater accuracy usually results in a missed green. To produce a good pitch shot, you have to release the club properly (see p.27) and trust your swing. This practice drill will help you attain a free release of the clubhead through the hitting area.

1 Hold the club halfway down the grip with your right hand. Tuck your left hand away from the action, either in your pocket or behind your back. To begin with, do not use a ball.

2 Make a three-quarter-length backswing. Allow your right elbow to fold as it does in a proper golf swing.

3 Swish the clubhead in your downswing so that the club is freewheeling through the hitting zone.

4 When you are confident with this one-handed swing, try hitting a shot. Tee up the ball (to give you the best chance of a clean strike) and reproduce the movements described in steps 2 and 3. You will be surprised at the quality of shot you can hit.

* When you attain the correct freedom of movement in your one-armed swing, you will find that your right arm straightens through the impact area, due to the centrifugal forces built up in the swinging motion of the club. It is this feeling that you need to cultivate in your actual pitching swing.

AIM AT MULTIPLE TARGETS WHEN YOU PRACTISE

When you play a round of golf, you only ever get one attempt at each shot. Once you have hit that shot, the chances are you will not get another like it in the same round. The pressure on your pitching is perhaps the greatest of all the shots, because you are aiming at the most well-protected area of the course where all manner of hazards, such as sand or water, guard the green. Work on this "multiple-target" drill in your practice sessions so that on the golf course you will be up to the challenge of hitting the right shot first time.

1 Identify as many separate targets as possible within your pitching range: five or six is just about the right number, but as few as three will still be sufficient. The targets should be at a variety of distances and in various directions.

2 With a bucket of balls by your side, hit the first ball at the first target, the second ball at the second target, and so on. Try not to rush. Make sure you treat each shot just as you would if you were playing a round. The key is not to hit the same shot twice in a row.

* By not hitting more than one shot at a time at a particular target, your swing never has the luxury of getting into a groove as it can do if you beat dozens of balls in the same direction. In that sense, this drill is much like playing a proper round. If you can hit good pitch shots in this practice routine, you will know you can do it on the course, too.

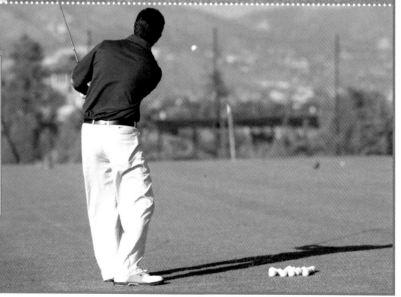

LEVEL DRILL
3·24 SWING AROUND THE CLOCK TO VARY YOUR DISTANCE

To produce a pitch shot of a certain distance requires a length of backswing that enables you to swing down and through the hitting zone with smooth acceleration (see Drill 21, p.138–9). A good way to determine which backswing-length matches which distance is to work through the following drill. It requires you to make three different-length backswings based on the numbers on a clock face.

9 o'clock

10 o'clock

1 Address a ball as normal and imagine that the ball is at 6 o'clock on an imaginary clock face and that your head is at the centre. With your first shot, swing your arms back until your hands reach 9 o'clock. Then smoothly accelerate into your downswing and through impact. Note how far the ball flies. (Use the same wedge throughout this drill.)

2 With your next shot, stop your backswing when your hands reach 10 o'clock. Swing down with the same smooth acceleration and see how far this ball travels.

11 o'clock

* You should use the same amount of acceleration in your downswing for all three shots: it is the length of your backswing that determines how far the ball will travel. Armed with the knowledge gained from this exercise, you can think of every pitch shot you play during a round as merely a function of swing length. Rather than guessing about how hard to hit each shot, you simply have to judge whether it is a 9 o'clock, 10 o'clock, or 11 o'clock swing.

3 Finally, make a swing in which your hands move all the way to 11 o'clock in your backswing and check the distance this ball achieves.

KEY CHECKPOINT

The geometry of a good pitch shot

A properly struck pitch shot requires a fairly steep angle of attack. But it is not necessary to work on this aspect of your swing in isolation, since you need only adhere to the fundamentals dealt with in the Level One drills (see pp.108–21) to ensure your angle of attack is correct. In particular, check that your stance is very slightly open, that the ball is in the middle of your stance, and that your wrists are set correctly in your backswing. If all of these factors are in order, you will produce the necessary downward blow, which gives a clean contact and lots of backspin. As explained in the section on iron play, the divot-mark should start after the point of impact (see the Key Checkpoint on p.75). If the mark occurs before the point of impact, the turf will be interfering with a clean strike. If there is no divot-mark, you are not hitting down on the ball properly. Drill 9 (see pp.118–21) shows that divot-marks can teach you much about your swing.

DIVOT-MARK *A descending angle of attack will automatically create a divot-mark. This mark should start just after the point of impact.*

LEVEL DRILL

3·25 HIT THREE SHOTS WITH ONE CLUB

Drill 14 (see p.128) demonstrated how you can hit three different-length pitch shots with the same swing. This might be the easiest way to play different-length pitch shots, but for more advanced players, there is another way. By manipulating the clubface and adjusting your stance accordingly, it is possible to vary the trajectory and length of your pitch shots using just one club. If you like the sound of that, the following drill outlines the points you should work on next time you are at the practice range.

1 Hit a few standard pitch shots. Note the trajectory of the balls' flight and the distance achieved.

2 Now try to hit a low-flying wedge shot, which can be useful in windy conditions. To do this, place the ball back in your stance with your hands forward so that the club's shaft is angled slightly. This delofts the clubface. To ensure this lack of loft is maintained through the hitting area, keep your hands and wrists firm so that they do not hinge as much as normal. Grip the club a fraction more tightly than usual as well, since this will restrict your hand and wrist movement. It should feel like more of a shoulders-and-arms swing than a hands-and-arms swing. Finally, think of your hands and the club finishing low.

* Hitting three shots with one club is a more advanced technique, requiring skill and practice. The major benefit is that, if you have a favourite wedge – a club that feels great in your hands – you can use it in a variety of situations.

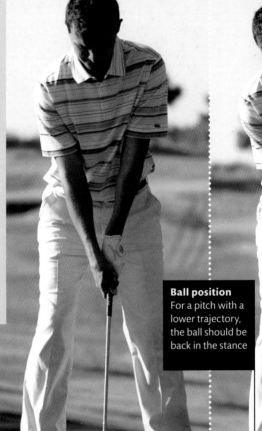

Ball position
For a pitch with a lower trajectory, the ball should be back in the stance

Address position for a regular pitch   **Address position for a low pitch**

3 Now aim for a much higher shot, which could be used to clear an obstruction between you and the target. To achieve this shot, move the ball forward in your stance to a point opposite just inside your left heel. The clubhead will then meet the ball on a relatively shallow angle of attack, delivering lots of loft at impact, so that you end up with a higher ball-flight. Rather than gripping the club quite tightly, as you would with the low-flying wedge shot, hold the club more softly to promote a longer, more flowing swing. As with the low shot, let your followthrough reflect your intentions and aim to finish with your hands high.

Ball position
For a pitch with a higher trajectory, the ball should be forward in the stance

Address position for a high pitch

KEY CHECKPOINT

Be wary of too much backspin

The key checkpoint on p.143 describes how, through a steep angle of attack, clean contact, and a high degree of loft on the clubface, it is possible to generate lots of backspin on pitch shots. On a receptive green this can make the ball "suck back" quickly. However, there are times when lots of backspin will hurt you more than it helps.

Take, for example, a green that slopes upwards from front to back: as soon as the ball lands it will spin back down the slope. If the flag is at the back of the green, lots of backspin will make it difficult for you to hit the ball close to the hole. It is sometimes wiser to play a less lofted club, such as a 9-iron, and hit the shot a little softer and lower to generate less backspin. Of course, backspin will help you place the ball close to the hole if the flag is at the front of the same green. In this scenario you can pitch the ball into the middle of the green and be confident it will spin back down the slope towards the hole.

SOFTER SWING *If you want the ball to run rather than stop quickly on the green, take a less-lofted club and make a softer swing. This generates less backspin.*

THE PERFECT PITCH SHOT

England's Ryder Cup star and multiple tournament winner Paul Casey is known for his Popeye-like forearms and power-hitting, but like all top tour professionals he has a wonderful pitching action. Perfect pitching requires a good sense of touch combined with sound mechanics, in which the body-turn and arm-swing are perfectly synchronized. It is captured nicely in this superb swing sequence.

Keys to sharp pitch shots

While control is vital for pitch shots, you must still remember to make a positive swing. The following reminders will help you combine these two key elements while you are pitching.

Choke down on the grip by about 5 cm (2 in), and make sure that your grip pressure is soft. These factors will enhance your control over the clubhead.

Open your stance to stop you swinging back too far and to help you clear your left side out of the way at impact.

Feel that you create the same amount of acceleration in your downswing on every pitch shot you hit, using the length of your backswing to vary the distance the ball flies through the air.

Since you must hit down in order to create height and spin on your pitch shots, think of generating ball-then-turf contact to promote the ideal impact factors.

1 ADDRESS
Some golfers tend to adopt a very slightly open stance for pitch shots, but Paul's address position is perfectly square – an example well worth emulating. Note how the clubhead is barely touching the ground, as if Paul is resting it on an eggshell. This helps remove tension from the hands and arms. It also facilitates a smooth first move away from the ball.

2 BACKSWING
Note how Paul's hand-and-arm swing works with his body pivot. As he turns his body, his hands and arms follow. While this is happening, the wrists hinge, setting the club on the perfect plane at the top. The lower half of his body is very stable; his knees remain flexed, and his hips have resisted the turning motion of his torso.

3 HALFWAY DOWN
Paul's pitch boasts a nice smooth transition into the downswing. Note the obvious transfer of weight on to his left side, in the direction of the target, and how the right shoulder is tucked in to help deliver the club to the ball from an inside path of attack.

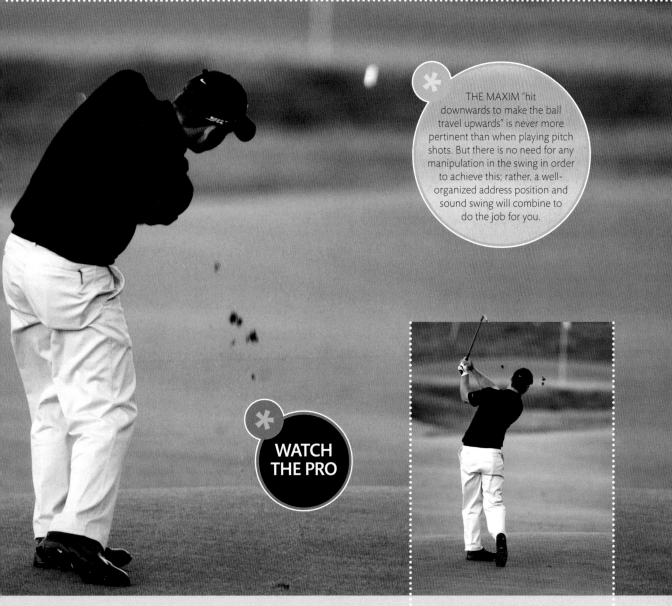

THE MAXIM "hit downwards to make the ball travel upwards" is never more pertinent than when playing pitch shots. But there is no need for any manipulation in the swing in order to achieve this; rather, a well-organized address position and sound swing will combine to do the job for you.

WATCH THE PRO

4 | **IMPACT**
Hitting a golf ball could scarcely ever have looked so easy and controlled as this. Just as Paul's body wound up as his hands and arms swung the club upwards in the backswing, so his downswing is controlled by harmonizing the unwinding of his body with his arms and hands as they swing down and through impact. This smooth, controlled acceleration brings him into the wonderful impact position shown here.

5 | **FOLLOWTHROUGH**
Paul's followthrough is the same length as his backswing, a useful point to bear in mind for pitch shots as it helps produce smooth acceleration through the hitting zone. When professionals such as Paul play this shot, the clean strike is what creates plenty of backspin on the ball. There is no need to hit the ball hard in order to achieve this; instead, simply improve your mechanics.

CHIPPING

IT IS A WIDELY HELD belief that all tour professionals are masters of the short game (they know that this is where the money is). They must be highly skilled around the greens because even the best golfers in the world cannot find the green every time with their approach shots. Indeed, they often miss the target as many as five or six times in a round. On average, you might miss many more greens than that, which shows how vital chip shots are. A nicely played chip gives you an outside chance of a "chip-in" birdie, which will send you off to the next tee with a spring in your step. Even if you do not hole the shot, the ball should finish close to the hole. This takes the pressure off your putting – a significant factor when you are under pressure to produce a good score. Altogether, a sharp chipping technique can save you between five and ten strokes per round.

DELICATE CHIP SHOTS

A proficient chipper must control the four key ingredients that combine to determine where the ball comes to rest on the green: height, carry, spin, and roll. Everything you read and do in the forthcoming section is designed to enhance your understanding of these elements, and to give you the necessary skills to master them. By the end of this chapter you will have a versatile short game, spanning a range of clubs.

TEST YOUR SKILLS

THE CHIPPING TEST

There are dozens of different kinds of shots you can play around the green. However, the following test uses just one shot-type and asks the one simple but incisive question that matters most: how sharp are you around the greens?

1 Find a green to which you can play chip shots of approximately 10–20 m (11–22 yd). Ensure that there is more green than fairway between you and the flag, and do not position yourself so that it is necessary to chip over a bunker.

2 Make a circle of tee-pegs – with a radius of about 1 m (1 yd) – around the hole. Use your wedge as an approximate measuring device. It is best to use only five or six tee-pegs because if you place too many around the hole they can deflect balls from their natural course. This makes it difficult to obtain accurate results from the test.

EVEN AT THE HIGHEST LEVEL, the ability to turn three shots into two is one of the keys to consistent scoring. This is why chipping plays such an important part in your game. No matter how confident you are in your ball-striking ability, you cannot hit every green – so you will need to be able to chip and putt.

3 Take your 9-iron or pitching wedge and chip 15 balls towards the flag. Your objective is to get as many balls as possible inside the tee-peg circle. Repeat this step another two times, average your scores, and use the performance chart (right) to determine your current level of ability.

PERFORMANCE CHART

1
1-5 =
LEVEL ONE

2
6-10 =
LEVEL TWO

3
11-15 =
LEVEL THREE

LEVEL DRILL

1·01 ORGANIZE YOUR SET-UP TO MAKE CHIPS SEEM EASY

If you have a fundamental problem striking your chips cleanly, then the prospect of playing any shot from around the green can be intimidating. If this is the case, it is likely that your set-up is to blame. Many problems, in every department of the game, can be traced back to what you do before you start your swing, and even

those who consider themselves reasonable chippers would be wise to take this opportunity to revisit the basics. This simple exercise – which can be done at home, in the garden, or at the course – will ensure that you have the correct address position.

✳ The correct set-up position for a chip shot can be summed up like this: ball back, hands and weight forward. It is worth pointing out that the chip shot is one of the few strokes in golf where the impact position is virtually identical to the address position. Improving your set-up by working on this drill will, therefore, also improve the quality of your impact position.

Left arm
The shaft of the club and your left arm form a straight line

Weight
Sixty per cent of the weight is on the left foot

Hands
Position your hands slightly further forward than the clubhead

Open stance
Pull your left foot back slightly

Target line
The clubface aims directly at the target

1 Stand with your feet, hips, and shoulders slightly open to the target (if you imagine the target as 12 o'clock, align yourself to 11 o'clock). Your feet should be only 15–20 cm (6–8 in) apart.

2 Place the ball back in your stance: opposite your right instep. Settle your weight to favour your leading foot. A ratio of 40 per cent of your weight on your right foot and 60 per cent on your left is ideal for a standard chip shot.

3 Place the clubhead behind the ball and move your hands forward so that your left arm and the shaft of the club form a straight line down to the ball. The clubface should be positioned so that it is aiming straight at the target.

LEVEL **1** · DRILL **02**

GO BACK LOW, THEN RELEASE AND HOLD

Drill 1 (left) demonstrated the perfect set-up; now for the perfect swing. The technique described in this exercise applies to a medium-length chip of about 12 m (13 yd). However, to play shots of different lengths, you can still apply the same techniques described in this drill – the only thing that changes is the length of your backswing (shorter to send the ball a lesser distance; longer to send it a greater distance).

✳ It is important to remember that your body must move, even in a swing that is as short as this. As your arms swing back and forth, your body rotates backwards and through everything works in harmony. If your body is motionless in your downswing, the clubhead will pass your hands before impact, and the club will meet the ball on an upward path, which is far from desirable. How your body should move during a chip shot is examined in a different way in Drill 3 (see p.152), and in Drill 13 (see pp.168–9).

1 Take a pitching wedge and assume the address position described in Drill 1 (left). Be meticulous about your set-up and, to begin with, perform this exercise without a ball. Sweep the clubhead away, mostly using your hands and arms, and maintain your body's connection to this motion. The clubhead should stay low to the ground for the first 30 cm (12 in), and your wrists should hinge softly to bring the club up. Your backswing should stop when your hands reach 8 o'clock (see Drill 24 in the "Pitching" section, pp.142–3).

2 As you change direction, from backswing to downswing, you should feel a softness in your hands and wrists, which is often referred to as "lag". This puts your hands in a dominant position as you lead the clubhead on a downward path into the ball. Effectively, lag prevents the clubhead overtaking your hands before impact.

3 When you are familiar with these movements, you can then move on to hitting a ball. Simply try to recreate the swinging motion described in steps 1 and 2.

LEVEL   DRILL
1·03

USE AN EXTENDED CLUB TO FEEL THE CORRECT BODY MOTION

This practice exercise, which is slightly unusual in that it requires you to swing holding two clubs, shows you how your body should move when you chip. The feedback you gain from rehearsing this drill highlights with great clarity the difference between good and bad body motion.

* Keep rehearsing this movement back and forth. Focus on what your arms and body are doing when the second shaft does not hit you: this is the motion of a good chipping action. Then try to recreate the same feelings in a proper swing.

1 Take your pitching wedge and hold it end to end with another club, with the grips touching. The shaft of the second club should run up your left side.

2 Now rehearse a chipping swing. If your body does not move properly, and you let the clubhead pass your hands in the downswing, the shaft of the second club will hit you in the ribs as you swing through the hitting area. Only by keeping your hands ahead of the club and moving your body correctly through the downswing will the second shaft not come into contact with your left side.

LEVEL DRILL
1·04 BRUSH THE GRASS TO FIND THE PERFECT BALL POSITION

It is amazing how many golfers put the ball too far forward in their stance for chip shots; even good players are occasionally guilty of this. Although having the ball forward in your stance may feel comfortable, it can also cause problems with ball-striking: either you hit the ball on the up or hit the turf before the ball – both scenarios are disastrous. However, this drill will confirm the ideal spot to place the ball in your stance.

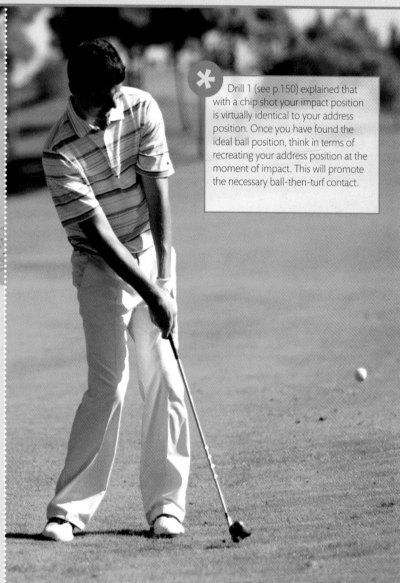

* Drill 1 (see p.150) explained that with a chip shot your impact position is virtually identical to your address position. Once you have found the ideal ball position, think in terms of recreating your address position at the moment of impact. This will promote the necessary ball-then-turf contact.

1 Stand on an area of closely mown grass. For the moment do not have a ball positioned in your stance. Make some practice swings, working on the techniques described in drills 1, 2, and 3 (see pp.150–2). Note where the clubhead first comes into contact with the ground. This is where you need to position the ball in your stance to ensure clean contact.

2 Place a ball on the spot described in step 1. Swing as before, but let the ball get in the way of the swinging club. You should strike the ball first and then the turf, leaving a small divot-mark if the ground is soft or the faintest bruising of the ground if conditions are hard underfoot.

KEY CHECKPOINT

A bare left hand can offer extra touch and feel

As you will learn in the "Putting" section (see pp.232–79), most golfers putt with their bare hands. This gives a more delicate feel for the putter throughout the stroke. Many of the world's top golfers find this also applies to chip shots (the enhanced grip a glove offers for long shots is not required for most short shots). You too might consider the benefits of chipping without a glove. However, you must find an "outer limit" (determined according entirely to personal preference), after which you wear a glove. Stick to this limit so that you are never undecided about whether to play a chip with or without a glove. Chipping with bare hands might be a welcome change.

BARE HANDS *Many golfers take their glove off to chip, as this tends to enhance control of the club, while also offering increased feel in the hands.*

LEVEL 1 · DRILL 05

CREATE A DOWNWARD STRIKE FOR CRISP CHIPS

One of the worst crimes you can commit while chipping is to try to help the ball into the air with a scooping motion through impact. For short shots you need to hit down on the ball in order to make it go up. This drill shows the benefits of this technique.

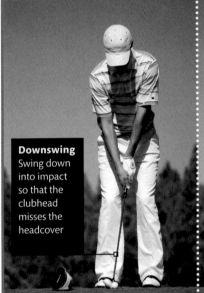

Downswing
Swing down into impact so that the clubhead misses the headcover

Impact
By striking down on the ball, you generate height in your chips

Address position

1 Place a ball on a good lie, and position a headcover about 20 cm (8 in) behind the ball. Take a pitching wedge, and adopt your address position. Make sure that your hands are well ahead of the clubhead and that the ball is back in your stance, opposite your right instep (see Drill 1, p.150).

✱ If ever you find that you are struggling with chip shots, this is a good drill to go back to because you can immediately discover if your angle of attack is incorrect.

2 Hit a chip shot of about 18 m (20 yd). To avoid hitting the headcover you have to strike down on the ball. This produces ball-then-turf contact, a nice ball-flight, and a bit of backspin on landing. If you try to help the ball into the air with a scooping motion, the clubhead will collide with the headcover during your downswing.

3 After repeating step 2 a few times, remove the headcover and continue chipping.

CLIP A TEE-PEG TO PROMOTE A FREE SWING

In a full swing, the clubhead is travelling so fast that there is no danger of the club stopping at impact. But with chipping, where the swing is short and delicacy is often required, it is easy to stub the clubhead into the ground behind the ball. The turf instead of the ball then soaks up the energy. This drill shows you how to be more positive in your approach to chipping, encouraging you to make a freer swing of the clubhead.

1 Tee up a ball about 1 cm (⅜in) off the ground. Address the ball as you would for a normal chip, using your pitching wedge.

2 Make a smooth, free swing of the club: focus on flattening the tee-peg into the ground at impact (below). This encourages you to accelerate the clubhead through the hitting area. Try to ignore the ball. When you succeed in flattening the tee-peg, you will produce nicely flighted chips. Repeat a few times and then dispense with the tee-peg.

* If you can translate the freedom in your swing when the ball was teed up into your actual swing, you will never "quit" on a chip shot (which is so often the cause of heavy contact). Instead, you will find that you can make a positive move through impact, while still retaining control.

LEVEL 1 · DRILL 07

ONE BALL AND ONE CLUB AT A TIME

Visualization is a vital component of an effective short game. However, although it is important to see shots in your mind's eye (visualizing the path of the ball through the air and along the ground), you still have to select the club to match your mental image. This drill will give you a crystal-clear understanding of how the ball reacts relative to the amount of loft on the club.

1 Select an even patch of ground about 5 m (5½ yd) to the side of a green, with about 5–7 m (5½–7½ yd) between the apron of the green and the flag. Count out nine balls of the same make and construction and line up nine clubs, ranging from a 3-iron to a sand wedge.

2 Start with the 3-iron, and hit a chip shot. Note the amount of height (not much) and run (lots) on the shot. Work your way through the clubs until you play the final ball with your sand wedge, which will provide plenty of height but little run.

※ Throughout the exercise, use exactly the same, standard chip shot technique (see drills 1–5, pp.150–4). You do not have to change your swing each time you change club; instead, the different lofts on the clubs will produce shots of a different nature. Always pay close attention to the ball's height, carry, spin, and roll. Then, when you are on the course, you will be able to select the most appropriate club for every chip.

LEVEL ONE

KEY CHECKPOINT

The "Texas Wedge" shot is sometimes better than a regular chip

Putting from off the green (known as the Texas Wedge shot) can be an effective alternative to a chip if it is used in the correct circumstances. It is certainly not a cowardly decision, as some golfers seem to view it.

If your ball is lying on the fairway near to the green, and the grass is closely mown between you and the putting surface, you will be amazed how easy it is to knock the ball inside a 60-cm (2-ft) radius of the hole. This takes all the pressure off your next putt. This is partly because most people find it is easier to judge the distance of a long putt than a chip. Also, you are unlikely to completely mishit a putt. With a lofted club, however, it is easier to make a hesitant swing and send the ball only halfway to the hole. The only adjustment you need to make to your putting technique (see the "Putting" section, pp.232–79) when putting from off the green is to stand a little taller to facilitate a longer, freer swing of your hands and your arms.

However, there are some occasions when you should not attempt this shot: if the ball is lying in rough (you cannot make a decent strike); if there is rough between you and the green (you cannot expect a ball to run through long grass); if the grass is wet from early morning dew or rain (the ball will be quickly slowed down by the surface moisture); or if you are more than about 18m (20 yd) from the putting surface (even if the fairway is closely mown, you will have to hit the ball so hard that you are unlikely to strike it properly).

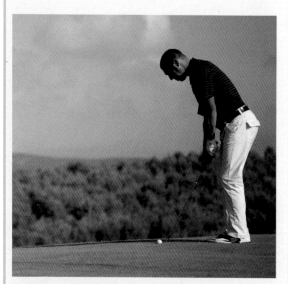

PUTTING OFF THE GREEN *If the conditions are right, the Texas Wedge is a useful alternative to a standard chip shot. You might be surprised how accurate you can be.*

LEVEL 1 DRILL 08

USE UPTURNED UMBRELLAS TO INCREASE ACCURACY

To be a good chipper, you have to control the height, carry, spin, and roll of the ball. The following exercise is based on a popular practice drill, but with an added twist to enhance your judgement of two of the four key elements: height and carry. One of the good things about this exercise is that you do not have to be at the golf course to gain full benefit from it: your garden at home will do just as well.

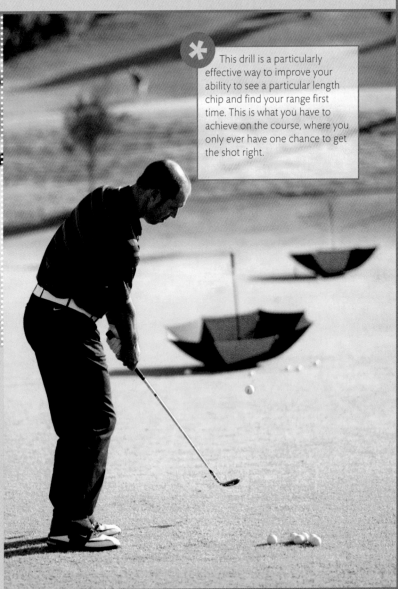

* This drill is a particularly effective way to improve your ability to see a particular length chip and find your range first time. This is what you have to achieve on the course, where you only ever have one chance to get the shot right.

1 Stick two open umbrellas into the ground, approximately 5 m (5½ yd) apart. Place a batch of balls about 5 m (5½ yd) from one of the umbrellas.

2 Using your pitching wedge, alternate hitting one ball to the closer umbrella and the next ball to the further umbrella. See if you can land every ball in an umbrella (the balls do not necessarily have to stay in). Try a less-lofted club for an even stiffer challenge.

REHEARSE, LOOK, AND HIT

Many golfers chip poorly because they fail to make use of their natural "touch" and hand-eye co-ordination. By practising chipping as outlined in the following drill, you will use these attributes to improve your performance around the greens.

1 Set yourself up with a chip shot about 10 m (11 yd) from the flag. Make a couple of practice swings, but keep your eyes firmly fixed on the target, not on the ground. Try to get a feel for the length and force required to send the ball the correct distance.

2 Then address the ball, take one look at the hole, and hit the chip. Do not hesitate any longer than you have to, just recreate the same swing that you practised, only this time with the ball in the way.

✱ By making a practice swing while looking at the target, your eyes pass visual signals to your brain. In turn, your brain sends the appropriate message to your hands and arms. This information needs to be fresh, so one look at the hole before you hit is enough. If you take too long, you will lose the visual and physical feedback gained from the practice swing. This is a great way to chip when you are on the course: rehearse, look, hit – and let your instincts take over.

LEVEL 1 · DRILL 10

THROW SOME BALLS TO READ THE ROLL ON THE GREEN

This is one of many drills in this section designed to train you to visualize shots before playing them. It uses the simple action of throwing a ball to improve your understanding of height and roll. A better grasp of these key concepts will be of great benefit to your chipping.

1 Stand about 27 m (30 yd) from a flag. Have to hand at least 10 balls and a selection of clubs, from a 7-iron to a sand wedge. Lob a ball underarm, and try to finish as close as possible to the flag. Use a low trajectory, which will produce plenty of roll. After a couple of tries you should find your range quite accurately.

2 Now throw a ball underarm high into the air so that it bounces near the flag and does not roll far. You will find it much more difficult to get the balls to finish close to the flag. Not only that, but the general dispersion of the "high" balls will probably be more erratic. Keep throwing balls, always varying the height and roll.

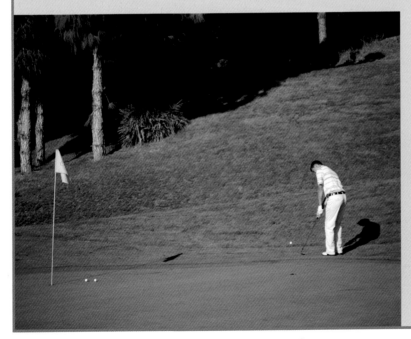

3 Now hit some chip shots. Think of the trajectory and roll you achieved with your throws, and try to recreate these by selecting clubs with different lofts. Again you will find that the low shots nearly always finish closer than those hit high.

✱ On the course, whenever possible, use a low trajectory and get the ball to roll as early as possible in its journey (although the first bounce should ideally be on the green). Only when hazards force you to take a more aerial route should you play a high-flying chip.

LEVEL DRILL
1·11
MONITOR YOUR SWING PATH WHEN YOU CHIP

A chip shot involves a short swing, and the clubhead travels through impact at a much slower speed than with a full iron shot. Even so, it is still very hard to monitor the exact path of the clubhead into and through impact. The following drill can provide you with this crucial information.

1 Place any club from your bag approximately one clubface-length the other side of the ball, lying parallel to the ball-to-target line.

Take your pitching wedge and address the ball, remembering the importance of a slightly open stance. Keep your hands and weight forward, and the ball back in your stance (see Drill 1, p.150).

2 Now play a chip shot. In a correct swing the clubhead will not strike the obstruction in the backswing, downswing, or followthrough. The club should travel on an inside arc during the backswing, then parallel to the obstruction through the hitting zone, before arcing to the inside again in the followthrough. This is an "in-to-in" swing path (see pp.26–7).

✱ This exercise gives you immediate feedback on your errors. If you strike the obstruction in your backswing, the clubhead is travelling too far outside the correct line. To rectify this, take the club back more on the inside. If you hit the obstruction in your followthrough, your swing is excessively in-to-out through the hitting zone – the result of taking the club back too far on the inside in the takeaway. To cure this, take the club back more on a straight line, and swing the clubhead to the left of the target through impact. This practice drill is an excellent way to straighten out your chipping.

The anatomy of a good chip shot

One of the first things you should know about chipping is that the way the ball behaves through the air and on the ground varies enormously from club to club. As a general rule, loft creates height and backspin, which combine to reduce roll. This means that the most lofted clubs in your bag, such as the wedges, produce lots of carry and not much roll, whereas clubs such as the mid-irons produce little carry and lots of roll. Long irons produce nearly all roll and almost no carry.

If you want to be more specific, however, the following simple table might help when you are trying to visualize a shot and attempting to match a club to your requirements. These figures are a useful guide, but bear in mind that extreme ground conditions, such as those encountered after a heavy frost, might alter these percentages.

CLUB	◼ CARRY	ROLL ◼
7-iron		
9-iron		
Pitching wedge		
Sand wedge		

Re-test yourself

Before moving to Level Two, take the test on pp.148–9 again. If you have not improved, it is worth revisiting the Level One drills. However, if the performance chart shows that your chipping has progressed sufficiently, then you are ready to tackle the more advanced drills in Level Two.

LEVEL 2 · DRILL 12

ADD AND SUBTRACT HOURS TO ACCELERATE INTO IMPACT

In his heyday, Tom Watson was probably the best player of the chip shot in the world. He maintains that one of the worst chipping faults is making too long a backswing and then decelerating into impact. This he compares to a boxer pulling his punches. Try this drill, which – like Drill 24 (see pp.142–3) in the "Pitching" section – is based on the principle of determining your swing length using positions on an imaginary clockface. It will also help you learn to accelerate into the ball on every chip shot.

(see pp.142–3)

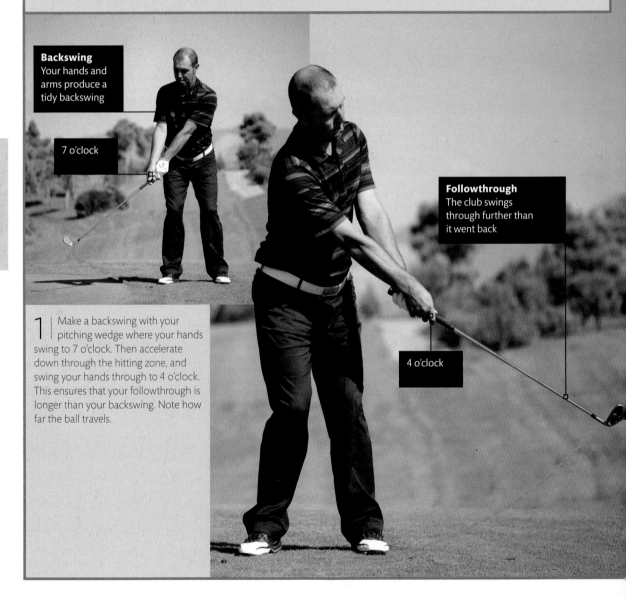

Backswing
Your hands and arms produce a tidy backswing

7 o'clock

Followthrough
The club swings through further than it went back

4 o'clock

1 Make a backswing with your pitching wedge where your hands swing to 7 o'clock. Then accelerate down through the hitting zone, and swing your hands through to 4 o'clock. This ensures that your followthrough is longer than your backswing. Note how far the ball travels.

LEVEL TWO

Backswing
Your body turns as your hands and arms swing back

8 o'clock

2 Now add an hour to the backswing so that your hands swing back to 8 o'clock. To compensate for the extended backswing, take an hour off your followthrough so that your hands reach 3 o'clock. Again, your followthrough is proportionately longer than your backswing. This extended swing will make the ball travel further.

Followthrough
Again accelerate the club through further than you swung it back

3 o'clock

* You should feel as if you are using the same acceleration through the hitting zone for both lengths of backswing (although with the longer swing, the clubhead will in reality be moving slightly faster). If you add an hour in your backswing and subtract one in the followthrough – so that your followthough is always longer than your backswing – you will always accelerate through impact. Keep this formula in mind when you make practice swings, and watch the clubhead as it swings back and through. Try to associate what you see with what you feel in your hands and arms. If you can replicate this when playing shots, you will not "pull your punches".

LEVEL TWO

LEVEL 2 · DRILL 13 ROCK THE SHAFT TO KEEP YOUR BODY AND ARMS TOGETHER

The relationship between your upper body and your arms is critical for any golf shot, even chip shots. These two core elements of your swing must work together to ensure reliable and consistent shots. If you can maintain the harmony in your body's motion during the swing, you will strike the ball the same way every time, which makes it easier to judge the distance of your chip shots. This drill trains your body and arms to work together.

LEVEL TWO

1 | Trap a club under your armpits so that the shaft is horizontal across your chest. Take a 9-iron or pitching wedge and assume your normal address position, while keeping the horizontal shaft in place.

2 | Rock the shaft up and down by turning your body smoothly back and through. Let your arms respond to this turning movement, and you will find that the club tracks a neat path back and forth, with the clubhead just brushing the ground as it travels through the hitting area. The shaft should stay trapped against your chest throughout. If it becomes dislodged, your arms are working independently of your body-turn, and your ball-striking will suffer.

* When you are comfortable with this movement, remove the horizontal shaft and hit 18-m (20-yd) chip shots with no target in mind. If in your proper swing you can recreate the same feelings experienced in this drill, you will hardly ever mishit a chip shot.

KEY CHECKPOINT

Choose shots that reflect the type of ball you use

Your choice of ball, which is discussed further in the reference section (see p.331), has a direct influence on what shots you can and cannot play around the green.

Control ball: Just about every chip shot is available to you if you play a balata-covered ball. These balls spin more and consequently run less than a ball designed for distance, which means you can pull off the very difficult shots when there is little green to work with. But there are pitfalls. For example, if you have a chip to a long green with the pin at the back, a crisp strike with a lofted club will give lots of backspin, which makes it very easy to leave the ball short. In this situation, a smart control-ball club selection would be an 8-iron. Less loft equals less backspin, so you can play a chip-and-run and the ball will roll towards the hole.

Distance ball: There is no problem playing chip-and-runs with this type of ball. Your difficulty is to impart much backspin with a distance ball, because it is designed for length and durability. Do not expect to emulate the professional who gets the ball to bite and slow down, or perhaps even spin back, on the second bounce. A distance ball is most problematic when you have little green to work with. If, for example, you are chipping over a bunker, you may have to accept that you cannot get the ball to stop close to the pin.

Compromise: There are many balls, of differing construction, that bridge the gap between control and distance balls. They offer durability and a degree of control.

USE LESS LOFT ON AN UPSLOPE

When you work on your short game, it is not enough to play all your shots from a perfect lie. After all, that is not what happens in a real round of golf. You have to put yourself in tricky spots if you are going to learn how to play the tough shots. This drill shows you how to chip from an upslope lie.

*The reason for this club change is simple: an upslope effectively adds loft to the clubface. If you were to use a 56-degree wedge, there could be up to 70 degrees of loft on the clubface at impact. This means the ball's trajectory would be too steep, and you might leave the ball short.

1 Place a ball on an upslope by the side of a green.

2 Determine which club you would take from a similar range if the ground was flat, then subtract two. For example, if you would usually use a pitching wedge, then use an 8-iron instead.

3 Use your usual chipping technique to hit the ball on to the green and watch it run towards the hole.

LEVEL TWO

LEVEL 2·15 DRILL
PRACTISE ON A DOWNSLOPE TO HEIGHTEN YOUR SKILLS

Playing from an upslope (see Drill 14, p.165) is an easy proposition compared to chipping on a downslope. Hitting good chips from a downslope demands a very sound chipping technique. Therefore, when you revert to chipping from a flat lie, the shot seems much easier and your confidence soars. If you work on this drill, you will find that all your chip shots – not just those on a downslope – will improve greatly.

*A downslope naturally delofts the clubface, resulting in a flatter trajectory than normal. This makes the shot very difficult. When you are striking the ball cleanly from the downslope, try some chips on even ground – these shots will never have seemed so easy.

1 | Place a ball on a downslope to the side of a green. Put the ball 5 cm (2 in) further back in your stance than usual, and move your hands further forward than normal. These two adjustments allow you to strike the shot cleanly but deprive the club of even more loft. The best solution is to use your most lofted club: the sand wedge. This means that you can still deliver about 45 degrees of loft to the ball, even on a severe slope. This should be enough to create a relatively soft-landing chip shot – one with sufficient height for the ball not to run out of control.

2 | Keep most of your weight on your lower foot, and ensure that your hands are ahead of the clubhead, as you swing down the slope. Do not try to help the ball into the air – focus on hitting down through impact. Trust your technique to create the necessary height.

LEVEL 2 · DRILL 16

PLAY OFF A HARD SURFACE FOR A CLEAN STRIKE

Drills 14 (see p.165) and 15 (left) highlighted the benefits of practising from a tough spot to improve your overall technique. This exercise is based on the same theory. Although it is challenging at first, the drill ultimately improves your chipping action and makes playing normal chip shots seem simple. This will give you lots of confidence around the greens, which is a valuable asset to have.

Do not rehearse this exercise with a sand wedge. The bounce (the rounded sole of the clubhead) raises the leading edge off the ground, which makes it virtually impossible to get the clubface to the bottom of the ball. Instead, the wide flange tends to bounce over the bare lie so that the leading edge of the clubhead strikes somewhere around the ball's equator, sending it shooting low across the ground. For this reason you should never choose a sand wedge to play a shot from a bare lie on the course. Always go with a club that has a straighter leading edge, such as a 9-iron or pitching wedge. Clubs such as these will help you get the clubface under the ball and will promote a better strike. Smart club selection sometimes makes all the difference.

1 Place a ball on a hard, bare surface, such as tarmac, tiling, concrete, or paving stones – anything that has no give in it. Use an old pitching wedge that you do not mind scratching. Put the ball back in your stance and push your hands forward and body-weight on to your left side – refer to the keys to a good set-up outlined in Drill 1 (see p.150).

2 Hit some short chip shots of no more than 18 m (20 yd). For now, a target is irrelevant: the aim of this exercise is to strike the ball cleanly from an unforgiving surface. Keep your hands in front of the clubhead all the way into the hitting area. This will help prevent the clubhead hitting the bare surface before it reaches the ball. After a few tries you should achieve some success. Next time you play a chip shot from grass, it will look far more inviting.

Hands
At impact your hands should be ahead of the ball

Impact
The clubface should strike the ball first, not the bare surface

LEVEL **2** · DRILL **17**   BE A RECORD BREAKER

The principles of trying to visualize a shot in your mind's eye and then matching that to the appropriate club and length of swing were explored in Drill 7 (see pp.156–7) and Drill 10 (see p.160). The following drill is a great way to further enhance those skills, although you do need to be at a course. You will need three or four old vinyl records. (You can use small towels if you do not have any unwanted albums.)

1 Scatter the records around a green, making sure that they are well spread out. Choose a spot to the side of the green and select your preferred chipping club.

2 Hit some chip shots, trying to land each ball on to one of the records. Do not aim at the same record twice in a row. Instead, alternate between shorter and longer chip shots as much as possible. If you can hit a record regularly – say one in five times – from a distance of about 7 m (8 yd), you can be very pleased with yourself. And, if the balls that do miss the target pitch within a 60 cm- (2 ft-) radius of the record, this is a good indication that your chipping is improving.

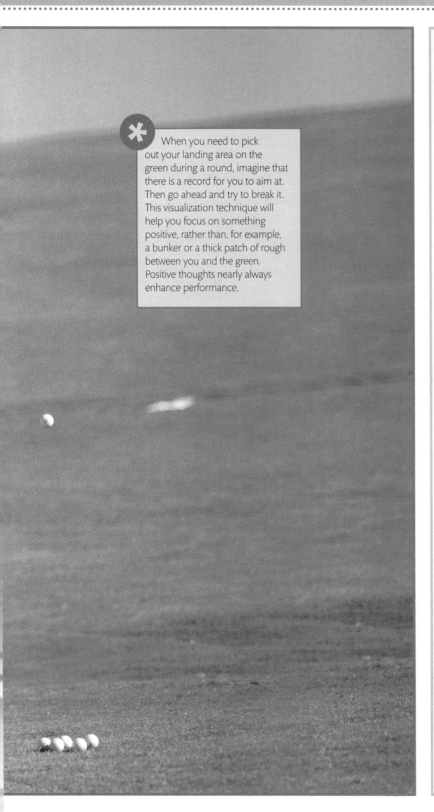

When you need to pick out your landing area on the green during a round, imagine that there is a record for you to aim at. Then go ahead and try to break it. This visualization technique will help you focus on something positive, rather than, for example, a bunker or a thick patch of rough between you and the green. Positive thoughts nearly always enhance performance.

KEY CHECKPOINT

Analyse your landing errors

Drill 17 is an invaluable aid in helping train you to hit your chosen landing area on the green. However, if you consistently struggle to hit the mark, you need to analyse your mistakes and learn from them. Try not to chip away without pausing for thought, hoping you will improve but not knowing how. Here are some clues that will help you learn more from the shots you miss.

Too many shots land short: This is the most common problem among poor chippers. You are probably decelerating into impact and making a tentative swing. Alternatively, you could be reading the shot wrongly – visualizing a landing area too far up the green and taking a club that has not enough loft on it (for short shots, less height means less carry). Try visualizing a landing area nearer to you, or take a more lofted club and pitch the ball further up the green.

Too many shots land long: Look at the length of your swing. You might be taking too long a backswing and accelerating into the ball. You should be making a shorter backswing, but still accelerating in the hitting zone. Also look at your club selection. It might be wise to use a less-lofted club, aim to land the ball nearer to you, and allow for some run on landing.

Too many shots land left or right of the target: This indicates a fundamental problem with your technique. Check that you are aiming accurately. Also look at the path of your swing through impact (see Drill 11, p.161) and revisit Drill 1 (see p.150) to establish the correct address position.

LEVEL TWO

KEY CHECKPOINT

Aim for flat spots on the green

Even with the best planning in the world, once the ball leaves the clubface, the outcome of any shot is to some degree down to chance. The ball might, for example, bounce badly (through no fault of your own) or be affected by a gust of wind. Therefore, if there is anything you can do to eliminate some of the unpredictability that is part of every shot, you have to take the opportunity to do so. One way to do this when chipping is always to aim for a flat part of the green. This way you can more accurately predict the first bounce and how the ball will behave from then on, reducing the margin for error. Your misjudged chips will be less wayward, and your well-judged chips will finish consistently closer to the hole. If the ball does not land on a slope or on top of a hump, it is easier to judge the first bounce and determine where the ball will finish. Whenever possible, try to take this into consideration as you make your club selections.

AVOID SLOPES *One of the many things you should take into account when chipping is to try to land the ball on a flat portion of the green.*

LEVEL DRILL
2·20 HAVE A CHIPPING CONTEST

What makes this drill so beneficial to your chipping is that it introduces the intensity and pressure of a competitive round into your practice sessions. Trying to better an opponent in a point-scoring game such as this is an excellent way to sharpen your skills.

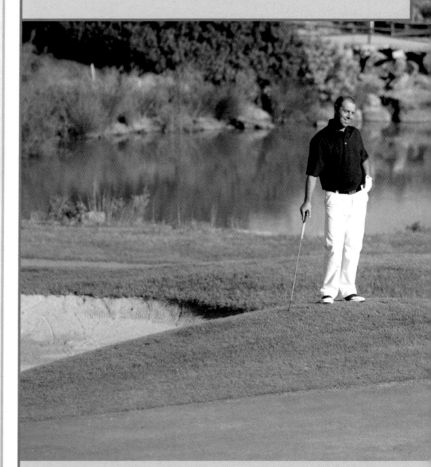

1 | Team up with another golfer, and find a green surrounded by as many interesting features as possible, such as bunkers, slopes, and different levels of rough. Take turns to nominate a place around the green from which you will both chip (using a sand wedge).

2 | Have one attempt at each shot, and the closest to the pin scores a point. Make sure that you constantly move to different locations around the green so that you do not become overly familiar with one situation. Keep score as you go.

Remember, loft equals height and spin

It is amazing how often golfers leave chip shots short of the hole. The most common explanation for this is playing a club with lots of loft while not allowing for the fact that the ball will run only a short distance when it lands. Remember, loft equals height and backspin (see the Key Checkpoint on p.161). If you choose to play your chip shots with a lofted club, you have to carry the ball roughly three-quarters of the way to the pin (even further if the greens are soft). If you want to take this high-trajectory route, be positive and make sure that you pitch the ball well up. On the other hand, if you want the ball to run, take a less-lofted club, such as an 8-iron. Whichever option you choose, make your decision before you take a club out of the bag – do not become caught in two minds.

Also consider the condition of the putting surface. In winter, when greens are often slow and soggy, use less loft than you would in summer. This will encourage the ball to run out towards the flag.

LEVEL TWO

Re-test yourself

Before moving to Level Three, take the test on pp.148–9 again. If you have not improved, it is worth revisiting the Level Two drills. However, if the performance chart shows that your chipping has progressed sufficiently, then you are ready to tackle the more advanced drills in Level Three.

LEVEL 3·DRILL 21

USE A WEAK GRIP TO KEEP THE FACE OPEN

Some of the world's greatest chippers play short, delicate chip shots with a weak left-hand grip. This technique helps keep the clubface open through the hitting zone – which promotes a higher and softer- landing ball flight – enabling the most delicate of chips. Using a weak left-hand grip is a technique that is well worth practising – give this routine a try next time you are working on your chipping.

1 Place about 12 balls on a good lie on the fairway. Play a standard chip shot with a pitching wedge using your regular chipping technique. Observe the way the ball travels through the air and the amount of roll there is after landing.

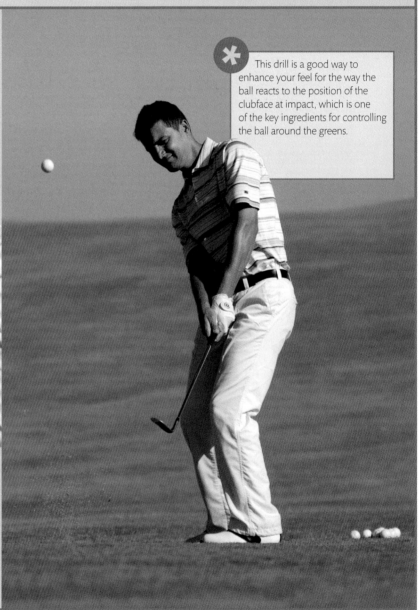

* This drill is a good way to enhance your feel for the way the ball reacts to the position of the clubface at impact, which is one of the key ingredients for controlling the ball around the greens.

2 Now weaken your grip by rotating your left hand, so that you can barely see the second knuckle on the back of your left hand.

3 Hit another chip shot. Since your weak grip effectively keeps the clubface more open through impact, this should translate into a slightly higher, floated trajectory with much less run on landing. Alternate between hitting some chip shots with your regular grip and others with a weak grip.

3·22 PLAY FROM A CIRCLE AROUND THE GREEN

Many players practise their short game by hitting a few chips from the same spot, but as you improve you should give yourself greater challenges to become truly "match fit". This is a particularly effective practice drill because it recreates some of the situations you might encounter during a round. Once you have practised this exercise, you will be better prepared for the real thing.

✱ Analyse your performance as you work through this exercise. How many balls finish within 2 m (2 yd) of the hole (therefore leaving you an achievable putt)? What is the general pattern of your poor chips: do they finish mostly short or long? It is important to learn from your mistakes and make improvements next time.

LEVEL THREE

1 Drop 10 balls around a green. Make a point of varying the quality of the lie. Place some on the closely mown apron of the green and others in the first cut of rough (with a few sitting up and some nestling down). If there are sloping lies, position one ball on a downslope and another on an upslope.

2 Work your way around the green, trying to chip each ball as close as possible to the hole. Have several clubs to hand so that you can visualize each shot and match the correct club to each situation (see Drill 7, pp.156–7).

LEVEL DRILL

3·23 TRY THE "BELLIED WEDGE" SHOT FROM THE COLLAR OF ROUGH

One of the most perplexing dilemmas for golfers is when the ball rests against the collar of rough bordering the apron of the green. Even though you are close to the putting surface, a putter does not seem to be the most appropriate club. But then again, neither does a wedge, since the grass behind the ball gives the impression that a clean strike will be impossible. The solution is a shot called the "Bellied Wedge", which involves striking the equator of the ball with the leading edge of the clubhead.

1 Take your pitching wedge and adopt your putting grip (see Drill 1, pp.234–5) and posture (see Drill 2, pp.236–7). Choke down on the club, as this brings your hands closer to the clubhead and enhances your control of the stroke.

2 Hover the clubhead so that the leading edge is level with the ball's equator (see the Key Checkpoint on p.183). This ensures that the clubhead will not become snagged in the rough.

3 Keep your head and body as still as possible, and make a firm-wristed stroke back and forth. Make sure your wrists barely hinge – this is known as a "dead-hands" technique.

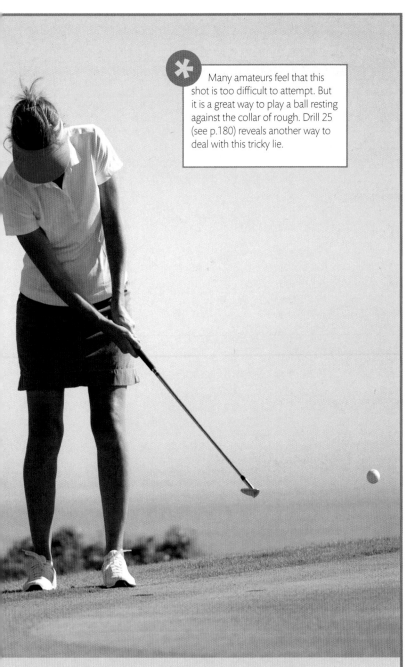

✱ Many amateurs feel that this shot is too difficult to attempt. But it is a great way to play a ball resting against the collar of rough. Drill 25 (see p.180) reveals another way to deal with this tricky lie.

4 Strike the middle of the ball with the leading edge of the clubhead. The ball might hop a little at the start of its journey, but it should roll much like a putt thereafter, making it relatively easy to judge distance. After a couple of tries, you will be amazed how well you can judge line and length.

(see p.180)

KEY CHECKPOINT

Practise holing every chip you hit

It is easy to be a little defensive on chip shots, which can mean leaving the ball short. Train yourself out of this tendency by practising an aggressive and positive outlook, aiming to hole every chip shot you hit. This attitude has two clear benefits. Firstly, if you get the ball running towards the hole, there is always a chance that it might drop in (the hole never comes back to meet the ball, remember). Secondly, if the ball misses the hole you can observe its progress past the hole, which will give you a clue as to whether your return putt will break or run straight.

Thinking positively gives you every chance to realize your potential, which will result in a higher standard of chipping. Often it is when you are overly defensive that you hit your worst shots.

THINK POSITIVELY *Aim to hole every chip you hit. Raising your expectations is often a great way to lift the standard of your overall game, too.*

LEVEL THREE

LEVEL DRILL

3·24 TRY CHIPPING USING YOUR PUTTING TECHNIQUE

Any idea that might make the short game easier is well worth considering. The technique described in the following drill is employed by some of the world's best players, which is reason enough to give it a try. It can be applied to a variety of clubs, from a pitching wedge down to an 8-iron, depending on the circumstances.

Chipping using your putting technique might improve your chips immeasurably.

1 Adopt your putting grip (see Drill 1, pp.234–5) instead of your regular full-swing grip.

Adopting your putting grip when chipping minimizes wrist action, which has three benefits: it simplifies the stroke, increases the consistency of the strike, and enhances your feel for distances. Because the ball receives very little backspin from this shot, as soon as it comes into contact with the green, it will roll just like a putt. The shot works best when you are faced with a delicate chip shot from short range: when there is up to about 7 m (7½ yd) between you and the flag. At first this technique will feel strange, but it will allow you to play a superb "feel" shot.

Grip
Choke down on the club's grip for extra control

Hands
Adopt your normal putting grip in a chipping stance

Takeaway
Sweep the club away with your hands and arms

2 Nudge your hands ahead of the clubhead and ball at address. The shaft of the club should now be leaning noticeably towards the target.

LEVEL THREE

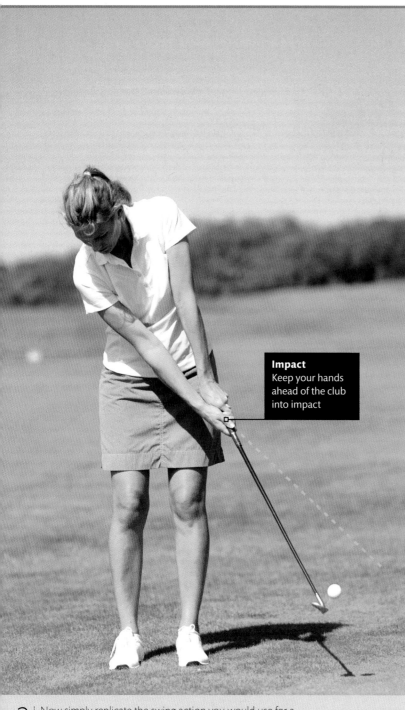

3 Now simply replicate the swing action you would use for a long putt. As you swing your arms back and through impact, it is important that your hands remain ahead of the clubhead.

Impact
Keep your hands ahead of the club into impact

KEY CHECKPOINT

Read the green when you prepare for a chip

Golfers have no hesitation in lining up a putt and assessing the amount of break. Curiously, very few do the same with chipping, even though it is no less relevant. So, when you visualize chip shots, take into account the effect slopes on the green will have on the ball's path to the hole. This sounds quite obvious but is often overlooked, and that can result in a perfectly played chip shot finishing off target. So make sure that you read a chip just as you would a putt.

SEE THE LINE *Let your actions reflect your intentions: you should read the green if you want to chip in or at least leave the ball extremely close to the hole.*

LEVEL DRILL

3·25 TRY THE "TOE-POKE" WITH A PUTTER

You might have seen a few tour professionals striking the ball with the toe-end of the putter when playing a shot from the collar of rough around the green. This technique might seem unorthodox, but there is considerable logic to the shot, which is known as a "toe-poke". Although it is close to the flag, the collar of rough creates a very awkward lie. The tendency is to play too delicate a shot from this position, leaving the ball well short. The toe-poke is a useful remedy for this dangerous inclination.

1 Place a ball against the collar of rough beside the apron of a green. Now, instead of reaching for your wedge, take your putter out of your golf bag.

2 Hold the putter so that the toe-end of the club is hovering behind the ball's equator. The end of the club should also be pointing towards the hole.

3 Make a short, sharp, stabbing stroke and aim to strike the centre of the ball. You will find that there is no interference from the grass behind the ball – the primary reason for playing the shot in this way. The ball will pop into the air before the topspin takes effect, allowing it to roll on to the putting surface.

* Drill 23 (see pp.176–7) highlighted the other way to deal with this situation. Should you prefer the toe-poke with a putter, the only reservations concern the distance the ball needs to travel – anything over 6 m (6½ yd) is too far – and the type of putter used. This shot only works with a putter that has a relatively flat toe-end. If the toe-end is rounded, the ball tends to come off in unpredictable directions. However, if you bear these considerations in mind, this shot is worth trying.

LEVEL THREE

PLAY A MINI-HOOK SHOT TO GIVE YOUR CHIPS MORE RUN

This advanced chip shot is best described as a miniature hook. The thing to understand about this shot before you attempt it is that a hook produces right-to-left spin, which makes the ball run further than normal.

This makes it a very useful shot to have in your repertoire when you have a lot of green between you and the pin. Work on the following three points to perfect the shot.

✳ With this chip shot, you only have to make a short swing to send the ball up a long green, and short swings are easier to control. It is basically an alternative to chipping with a 6-iron – the advantage being that the shorter shaft on an 8-iron helps to enhance your control. The additional run created by this technique may take you by surprise at first, but after a few attempts you will quickly learn to judge the extra distance.

1 Select a short iron, such as an 8-iron. Position the ball well back in your stance, opposite your right toe, and place your hands well in front of the clubhead (even more so than for a normal chip shot). Also, feel that you align your body a little right of the target, with the clubface aiming straight at the flag.

2 Take the club back on a path that is distinctly more on the inside than for a regular chip shot.

3 Then swing the club into impact on the same path, so that the clubhead travels right of the target through the ball. This in-to-out path – coupled with the fact that the clubface will be closed (relative to your swing path) – will impart the necessary right-to-left spin. The ball will fly a little lower than an ordinary chip with the same club, and will roll more.

KEY CHECKPOINT

Leave the pin in if you want to hole a chip

From a chip shot off the green, a ball is more likely to drop in the hole when the flag is still in place. This was proven beyond doubt by Dave Pelz, a former NASA space scientist who has chosen to apply his considerable intellect to the game of golf. Using scientific instruments, he has measured almost every conceivable aspect of a ball's behaviour, from the moment it is struck to the time it stops moving. His studies have entailed rolling thousands of balls at various speeds into different parts of the hole, both with the flag out and with the flag in. The results were conclusive: taking the flag out before you play a chip may do a lot for your ego, but it will do nothing for your chances of holing the shot. And remember, there is no penalty for hitting the flag if you are playing from off the green.

FLAG IN *Scientific research by one of the most intelligent men in golf has shown that the ball stands a better chance of dropping in the hole if the flag is left in.*

LEVEL 3·27 DRILL

PRACTISE THE CHIP WITH A LOFTED WOOD

A few years ago, chipping with a lofted wood was a rarity. But since the likes of Tiger Woods and Greg Norman have played this shot in major competitions, it has moved rapidly from obscurity to credibility. This practice drill demonstrates how you can use the lofted wood with surprising effectiveness for shots close to the green.

1 Take a 3- or 4-wood, and choke down on the grip so that your lower hand almost touches the metal of the shaft.

2 Adopt your normal chipping set-up, only stand a little taller to accommodate the longer club. You will also need to stand a little further from the ball than when using a wedge (otherwise your hands and arms become tucked into your midriff, giving you no room for movement).

3 Now make your regular putting stroke (see the "Putting" section, pp.232–79), swinging the clubhead back and forth low to the ground and with very little wrist hinge. It is principally an arms-and-shoulders swing, which means the clubhead will brush the ground through impact. The ball spends virtually no time in the air and rolls quickly over the green.

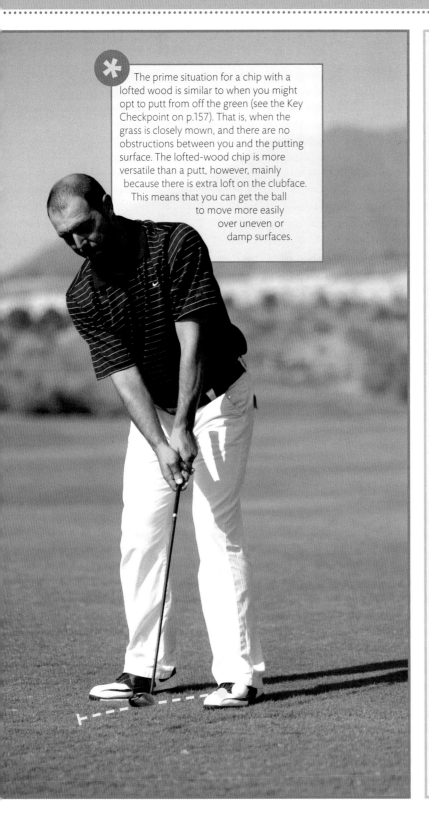

The prime situation for a chip with a lofted wood is similar to when you might opt to putt from off the green (see the Key Checkpoint on p.157). That is, when the grass is closely mown, and there are no obstructions between you and the putting surface. The lofted-wood chip is more versatile than a putt, however, mainly because there is extra loft on the clubface. This means that you can get the ball to move more easily over uneven or damp surfaces.

Hover the club on rough chips

In the section on pitching, the benefits of hovering the clubhead at address were discussed (see Drill 20, p.137). The same advantages exist when it comes to chipping. Hovering the club promotes an unimpeded takeaway and also enhances the quality of your strike. If the ball is lying in rough around the green, hover the blade of the club around the ball's equator rather than nestling it in the grass. In your takeaway you will notice how freely the clubhead moves away from the ball. It does not become caught up in the grass on the way back, which can so easily upset the rhythm of your swing. Also, by hovering the clubhead behind the ball at address, you will raise the base of your swing by just a fraction. This means that you are less likely to bury the clubhead in the grass behind the ball and should instead make a better strike. This technique might require a little practice, but it is well worth becoming accustomed to, as the benefits are significant.

RAISE YOUR GAME *Hovering the clubhead behind the ball in the rough promotes a smoother takeaway, as the clubhead does not become snagged.*

LEVEL THREE

THE PERFECT CHIP SHOT

Former Ryder Cup player, and multiple winner, Barry Lane is one of only a select few players to have competed in more than 600 events on the European Tour – an astonishing achievement. No surprise then, that Barry has a very tidy short game. Indeed, he has all the qualities of a great chipper, key ingredients that elevate him above the merely good: a wonderful imagination (in essence, the ability to visualize the right shot at the right time), super feel in his hands, and a correct technique. This enviable combination enables him to play all manner of chip shots, in this case a chip-and-run shot from 25 yards. Enduring talent such as this is well worth studying.

*

NOTE HOW RELAXED Barry is in this sequence – he is totally comfortable over the ball and has not an ounce of tension in his hands and arms. This gives him maximum feel for the clubhead and good judgement of distance on all chip shots.

1 ADDRESS

Earlier in this section we brought to your attention one sentence that sums up the essence of a good set-up for chipping: ball back, hands and weight forward. Here you see that theory put into practice as Barry prepares to play a chip. He has the ball back in his stance. The hands are ahead of the ball, with the shaft angled towards the target. His weight clearly favours his front foot, the left foot. All of this is designed to encourage a descending angle of attack into impact.

2 BACKSWING

The backswing is essentially a simple movement whereby the triangular relationship established at address between the arms and the shoulders is maintained as the club moves away from the ball. The weight distribution remains the same, still favouring the left side, to help promote a descending blow at impact. Trouble for the majority of golfers often starts here, when the backswing is either too short or, more commonly, too long for the shot in question.

3 COMING INTO IMPACT

As the arms and body begin the transition from backward to forward motion, a softness in the hands and wrists produces a slight lag in the wrists and a sense that the hands are leading the clubhead down towards the ball. It is a subtle move, but a decisive one, especially on a shot as short as this. It is an essential ingredient of a crisply struck chip shot, which is exactly the shot played here by Barry.

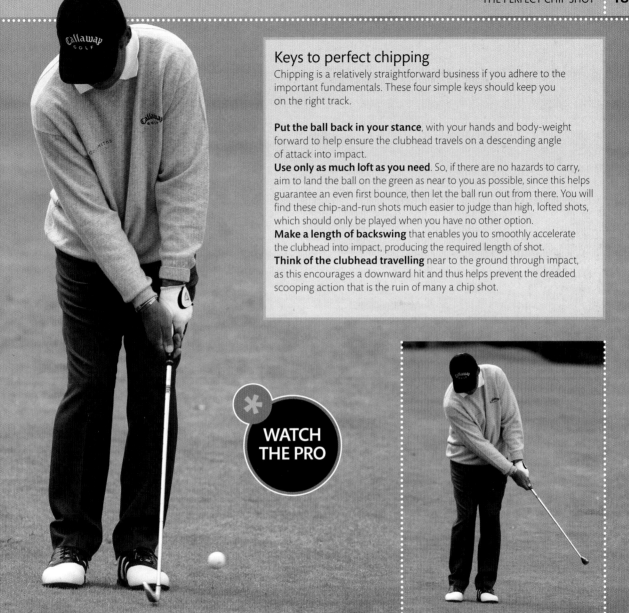

Keys to perfect chipping

Chipping is a relatively straightforward business if you adhere to the important fundamentals. These four simple keys should keep you on the right track.

Put the ball back in your stance, with your hands and body-weight forward to help ensure the clubhead travels on a descending angle of attack into impact.

Use only as much loft as you need. So, if there are no hazards to carry, aim to land the ball on the green as near to you as possible, since this helps guarantee an even first bounce, then let the ball run out from there. You will find these chip-and-run shots much easier to judge than high, lofted shots, which should only be played when you have no other option.

Make a length of backswing that enables you to smoothly accelerate the clubhead into impact, producing the required length of shot.

Think of the clubhead travelling near to the ground through impact, as this encourages a downward hit and thus helps prevent the dreaded scooping action that is the ruin of many a chip shot.

WATCH THE PRO

4 THROUGH THE HITTING ZONE

Contact is ball-then-turf, the hallmark of all good players, and a skill that allows good control of spin and trajectory. Note that through impact Barry's hands stay ahead of the clubhead as the body turns through. This coordination is extremely important – if the body stops moving, the club tends to overtake the hands and it is easy to strike the ball poorly as a result.

5 FOLLOWTHROUGH

Looking up too soon is a common fault among club golfers, but Barry keeps his eyes down until the ball is well on its way. Note the economy of movement; almost perfect symmetry either side of the ball. It is such a tidy action with no wasted motion. With shots such as this there should always be a sense of natural acceleration through the ball, as Barry demonstrates perfectly.

BUNKER PLAY

THERE IS LITTLE DOUBT that for most club golfers, bunker play creates more fear and problems than any other type of shot. This cannot be attributed to the degree of difficulty involved because, ironically, the standard bunker shot is one of the most forgiving strokes in golf. For one thing, you do not even have to hit the ball. With a sound technique you can hit the sand between 2.5 cm (1 in) and 6 cm (2½ in) behind the ball and still produce an acceptable result. You cannot get away with anything like this margin for error with other clubs. If this does not comfort you, the even better news is that in no other department of the game can you go from poor to good, or from good to excellent, in such a short time.

DEVELOPING NEW SKILLS

As you work your way through this section, your fear of bunker play will evaporate. Praying to get the ball out of the sand first time will soon become a distant memory. You will learn that long-range bunker shots are no harder than normal iron shots, and from short range you will start expecting to finish the hole in two strokes almost every time (unless the lie is terrible). To approach bunker play in this way may seem an impossible dream, but as you perform the following drills, you will see how achievable good sand performance actually is.

TEST YOUR SKILLS

THE BUNKER-PLAY TEST

Getting out of the sand first time might be the sole ambition for many of you reading this, but that does not represent a worthwhile test. As with chipping (see pp.148–9), you have to judge your performance with accuracy in mind. However, because you probably find bunker shots tougher than chips psychologically at the moment, for this test the radius of the target circle is trebled.

1 Find a greenside bunker where the flag is between 6 m (6½ yd) and 7.5 m (8 yd) away. Because bunkers are uncommon at driving ranges, perform this test on a golf course at a quiet time (so that you will not be interrupted).

2 Make a circle of tee-pegs – with a 3 m (3 yd) radius – around the flag. As a rough guide, 3 m (3 yd) is approximately three times the length of your sand wedge.

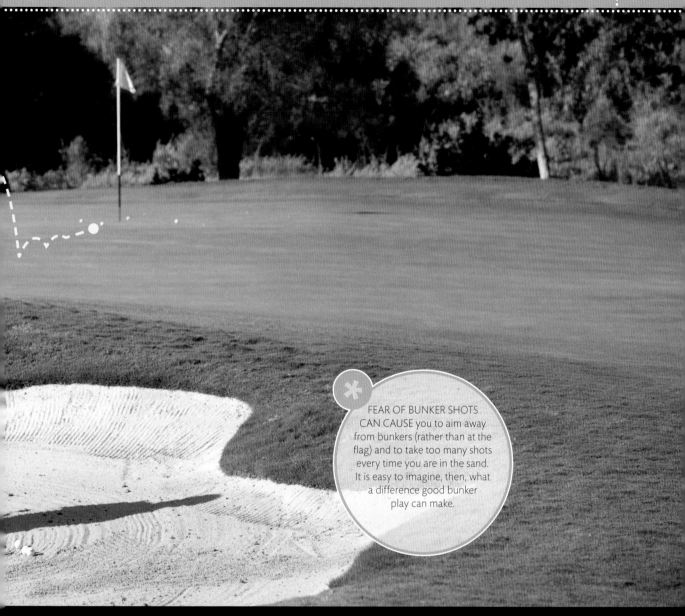

FEAR OF BUNKER SHOTS CAN CAUSE you to aim away from bunkers (rather than at the flag) and to take too many shots every time you are in the sand. It is easy to imagine, then, what a difference good bunker play can make.

3 Take your sand wedge and 15 balls into the bunker. From a good lie, try to get as many balls as possible inside the circle of tee-pegs. Once you have completed this exercise a total of three times, average your scores, and check your results against the performance chart (right).

PERFORMANCE CHART

1
1–5 =
LEVEL ONE
(pp.188–203)

2
6–10 =
LEVEL TWO
(pp.204–217)

3
11–15 =
LEVEL THREE
(pp.218–229)

LEVEL   DRILL

1·01   OPEN YOUR FEET, HIPS, SHOULDERS, AND THE CLUBFACE

In golf there is nothing more futile than trying to hit good shots from a poor address position, and this is never more so than when you are playing from sand.

Next time you practise your bunker play, use the following drill to rehearse and become familiar with the perfect set-up for a greenside bunker shot.

1 Stand in a greenside bunker, and address a ball as you would any ordinary iron shot, with your stance parallel to the ball-to-target line, and the clubface square to the flag. The ball should be opposite your left heel.

2 Take your right hand off the club, and loosen your left-hand grip. Hold the bottom of the club's grip with your right hand, and turn the club clockwise (so that the clubface opens). Imagine that the flag is at 12 o'clock on a clockface, and stop turning when the clubface is aiming at 2 o'clock. Reapply your left hand, and place your right hand back on the grip.

3 Now move into an open stance, so that the alignment of your feet, hips, and shoulders aims at 10 o'clock (to the left of the flag). Make sure that the clubface remains open, however (aiming right of the target).

4 Shuffle your feet down into the sand. This not only gives you a secure footing on an insecure surface but also gives you a feel for the sand's texture.

❋ If you perform badly in bunkers, the simple process of organizing your set-up is probably the single most significant step forward you can take. It will promote the correct shape of swing and allow the bounce on the sand wedge (see the Key Checkpoint on p.191) to work to maximum efficiency.

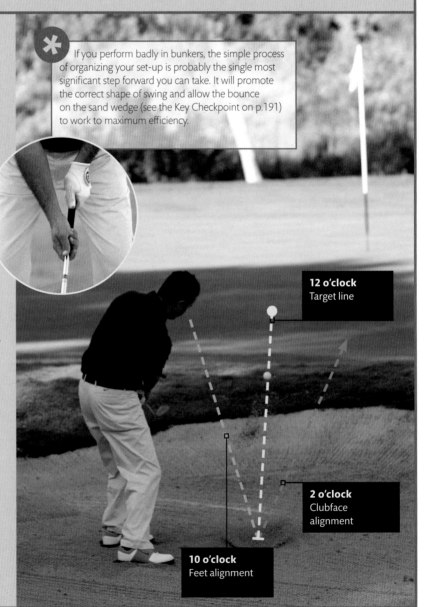

12 o'clock Target line

2 o'clock Clubface alignment

10 o'clock Feet alignment

LEVEL   DRILL

1·02 MAKE RIGHT-HANDED SWINGS TO FEEL THE SPLASH

As noted in the Key Checkpoint on page 191, one of the most important things to understand about bunker play is that the bounce on your sand wedge is designed to help you but can only do so if your technique is correct. Drill 3 (see pp.190–1) helps you appreciate how the sand wedge moves through the sand. The following practice drill has a similar theme and also introduces some freedom into your technique.

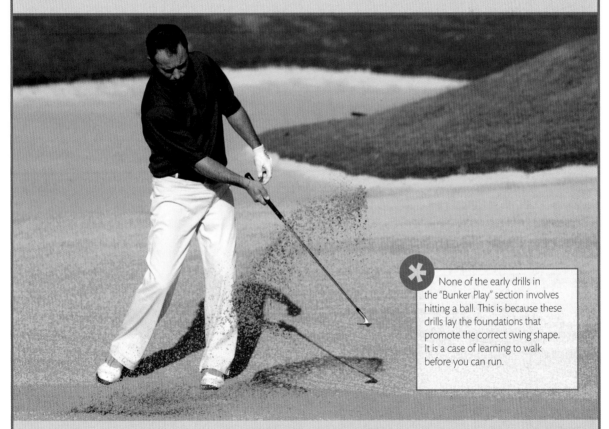

LEVEL ONE

* None of the early drills in the "Bunker Play" section involves hitting a ball. This is because these drills lay the foundations that promote the correct swing shape. It is a case of learning to walk before you can run.

1 Step into a bunker with your sand wedge. For now, do not worry about a ball.

2 Assume a good address position (see Drill 1, left), but hold the club with your right hand only.

3 Make one-handed swings, and almost "throw" the clubhead into the sand. Allow your right arm to straighten, and your wrist to unhinge. Try to make the clubhead slide through the sand (utilizing the bounce on the club), rather than letting it dig too deep. You should be left with a shallow cut of sand, about 30 cm (12 in) long.

LEVEL **1** DRILL **03**

LISTEN TO THE SOUND OF GOOD BUNKER PLAY

If you struggle to escape from a bunker in one shot, then you have to go right back to basics. This exercise, which is performed as much by sound as by feel, does just that by examining the correct and incorrect clubface positions for greenside bunker shots.

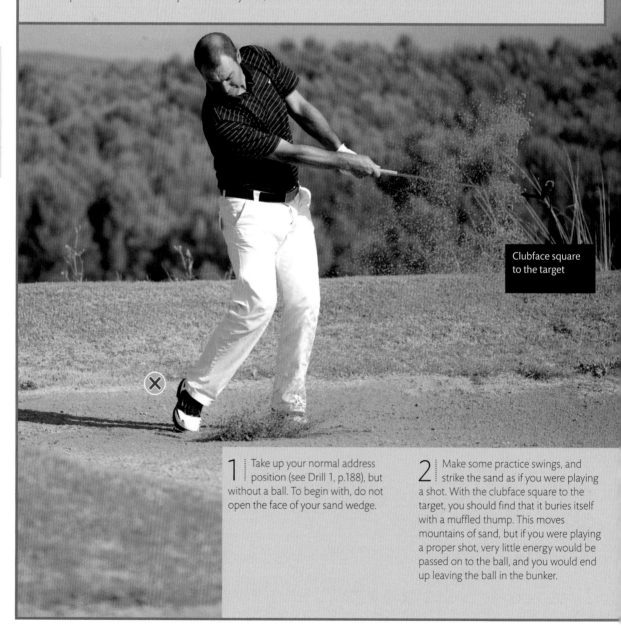

Clubface square to the target

1 | Take up your normal address position (see Drill 1, p.188), but without a ball. To begin with, do not open the face of your sand wedge.

2 | Make some practice swings, and strike the sand as if you were playing a shot. With the clubface square to the target, you should find that it buries itself with a muffled thump. This moves mountains of sand, but if you were playing a proper shot, very little energy would be passed on to the ball, and you would end up leaving the ball in the bunker.

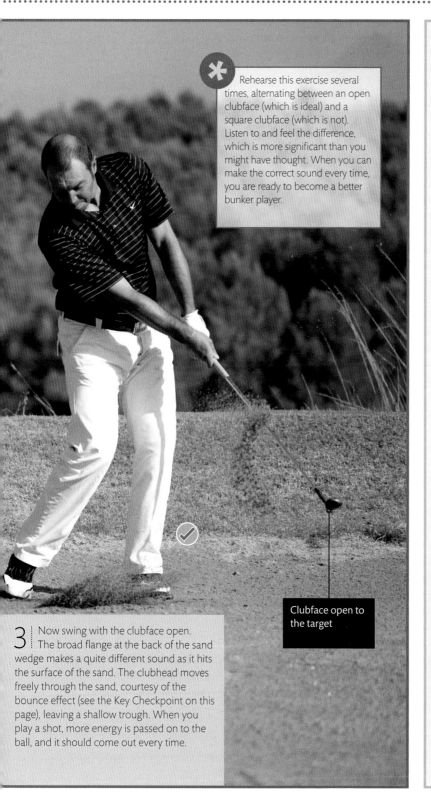

Rehearse this exercise several times, alternating between an open clubface (which is ideal) and a square clubface (which is not). Listen to and feel the difference, which is more significant than you might have thought. When you can make the correct sound every time, you are ready to become a better bunker player.

Clubface open to the target

3 Now swing with the clubface open. The broad flange at the back of the sand wedge makes a quite different sound as it hits the surface of the sand. The clubhead moves freely through the sand, courtesy of the bounce effect (see the Key Checkpoint on this page), leaving a shallow trough. When you play a shot, more energy is passed on to the ball, and it should come out every time.

KEY CHECKPOINT

The "bounce" is all important

Up until the early 1930s, golf clubs were not designed to cope well with shots from sand. The sole of the club was too thin, like the 3-iron in your bag today, which meant that the clubhead cut deeply into the sand at impact. This made bunker play much harder than it is now – a sobering thought if you already struggle in the sand. But Gene Sarazen (the first man to win all four of golf's majors), who thought bunker play was more difficult than it should be, filed the sole of his sand wedge. This made the sole more rounded, introducing a wide flange (as seen on today's sand wedges). His invention completely transformed bunker play.

When the rounded sole of the clubhead (the "bounce") makes contact with the sand, it does not bury itself like the clubs of old but instead bounces back up leaving a shallow trough of sand where the ball was. This is known as the bounce effect. The rounded sole acts in the same way as a tennis ball, for example, thrown on a low trajectory into a bunker. The ball does not bury itself in the sand, but instead skims off the surface at the same angle it came in. The sand wedge only reacts in this way, however, if your technique is sound.

THE BOUNCE *The wide, rounded sole of a sand wedge, known as the bounce, encourages the clubhead to travel more easily through the sand.*

LEVEL 1·04   DRILL

DRAW A LINE IN THE SAND TO GUIDE YOUR PATH

It is now time to hit some proper greenside bunker shots. This practice drill involves drawing a line in the sand to indicate the ideal swing path through impact. Remember that you cannot do this during a round of golf because touching the sand with your club before playing the shot is against the rules (see the Key Checkpoint on p.209).

1 Place a ball in the sand and address it (see Drill 1, p.188).

2 Use the butt-end of the club to draw a line in the sand along the line of your toes. Then draw another line that extends about 20 cm (8 in) either side of the ball, parallel to the first line.

3 Swing the clubhead back along the second line, hinging your wrists a little earlier than you would for a chip shot. This will set the club on a slightly more upright swing plane. Do not forget to turn your body as you swing the club upwards.

4 Splash the clubhead into the sand behind the ball (see Drill 5, pp.194–5), again swinging the clubhead along the line in the sand through impact. This means that in essence you are swinging the club along the line of your toes, to the left of the target, with the clubface open. This will help you propel the ball out of the sand and towards the flag.

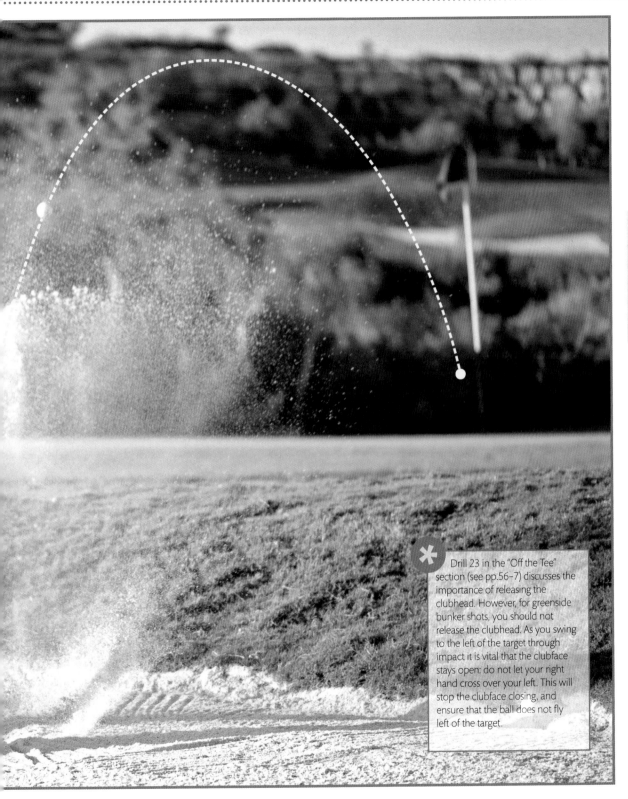

* Drill 23 in the "Off the Tee" section (see pp.56–7) discusses the importance of releasing the clubhead. However, for greenside bunker shots, you should not release the clubhead. As you swing to the left of the target through impact it is vital that the clubface stays open: do not let your right hand cross over your left. This will stop the clubface closing, and ensure that the ball does not fly left of the target.

LEVEL   DRILL
1·05

DRAW A LINE IN THE SAND TO FOCUS YOUR STRIKE

Just like Drill 4 (see pp.192–3), this drill involves drawing a line in the sand. But rather than assisting your alignment and swing path, it helps in the development of another important element of bunker play: learning to consistently hit the right spot in the sand behind the ball.

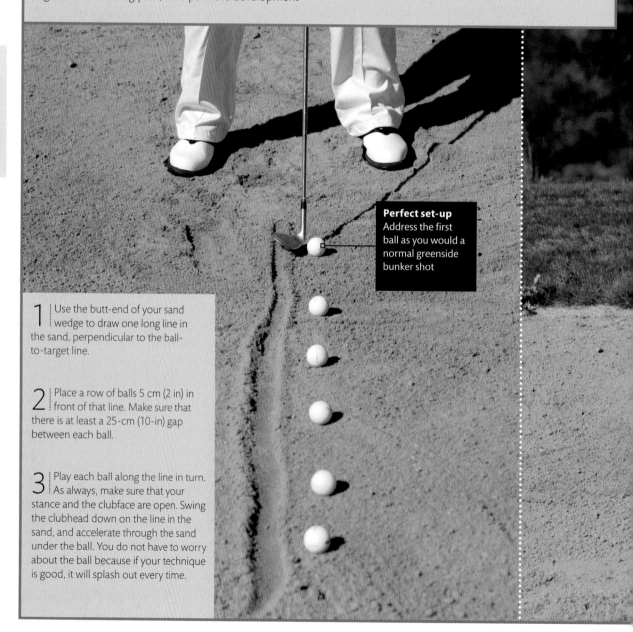

Perfect set-up
Address the first ball as you would a normal greenside bunker shot

1 | Use the butt-end of your sand wedge to draw one long line in the sand, perpendicular to the ball-to-target line.

2 | Place a row of balls 5 cm (2 in) in front of that line. Make sure that there is at least a 25-cm (10-in) gap between each ball.

3 | Play each ball along the line in turn. As always, make sure that your stance and the clubface are open. Swing the clubhead down on the line in the sand, and accelerate through the sand under the ball. You do not have to worry about the ball because if your technique is good, it will splash out every time.

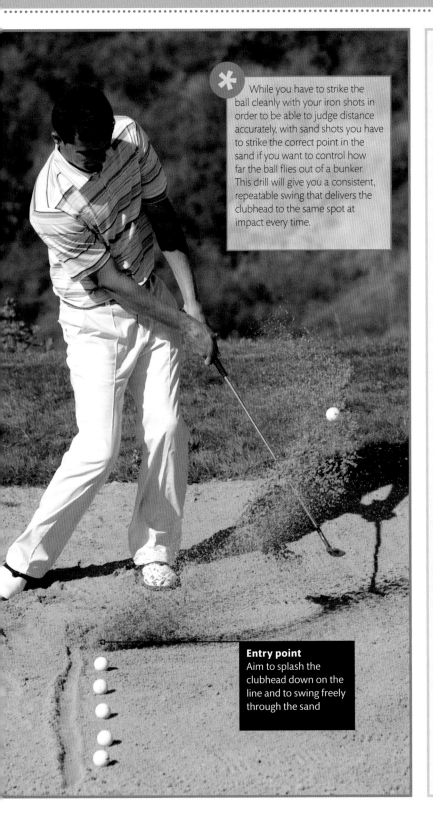

While you have to strike the ball cleanly with your iron shots in order to be able to judge distance accurately, with sand shots you have to strike the correct point in the sand if you want to control how far the ball flies out of a bunker. This drill will give you a consistent, repeatable swing that delivers the clubhead to the same spot at impact every time.

Entry point
Aim to splash the clubhead down on the line and to swing freely through the sand

KEY CHECKPOINT

Put the ball further forward than you think

Most golfers who struggle with bunker play almost always have the ball in the middle of their stance. Although this is appropriate for pitch shots and chips, in a bunker it is too far back – the clubhead will travel down too steeply and dig deeply into the sand. This means that you will lose all the energy in your swing, and there will not be enough force to propel the ball up and out. In view of this, always have the ball forward in your stance – opposite your left instep (as you do with the driver and long irons). This ball position will allow you to swing the clubhead into the sand on a shallower angle of attack, which encourages it to slide through the sand under the ball. This creates a splash that sends the ball upwards and forwards over the front lip of the bunker.

As is so often the case, a small adjustment to your set-up can have a major effect on your swing. Whenever you practise your sand play, make regular checks on this and the other address fundamentals.

BALL POSITION *If the ball is forward in your stance, this promotes a shallower angle of attack, which helps create a wave of sand that propels the ball outwards.*

LEVEL DRILL
1·06 THROW A STONE TO RECREATE THE RIGHT-HAND ACTION

Drill 4 (see pp.192–3) explained that you should not release the club when playing a bunker shot so as to ensure that the clubface stays open through impact. Here is a practice drill that will help you become accustomed to how your right hand should work when playing a bunker shot. It involves a movement apparently unrelated to golf yet which comes naturally to almost everyone.

Like throwing a stone
When playing a bunker shot, the movement of your right arm should mirror the action of throwing a stone. In your followthrough, your right shoulder turns under your chin

*This practice exercise encourages not only the correct right-hand action but also good acceleration of the clubhead into and through the sand. These are two factors that will stand you in good stead as you work your way through this section.

1 Take a small stone, and throw it as if trying to skim it across a body of water. Notice that after drawing your throwing arm backwards, your right shoulder then turns down and under your chin as your body opens up, and your right hand swings through to throw the stone on a flat trajectory. Repeat this action a few times, and be aware of how your right hand moves and your body turns.

2 Step into a bunker with your sand wedge, and make a practice swing. Try to imagine your right hand moving as it did to throw the stone. In your downswing, your right shoulder should again turn down as your body opens up, and your right hand should swing flat so that the clubhead slides through the sand on a shallow trajectory.

3 Now hit some shots, recreating the sensations experienced in step 2. Let the clubhead splash freely through the sand under the ball.

LEVEL DRILL
1·07 FOCUS ON THE SAND, NOT THE BALL

Walter Hagen, a flamboyant figure from the first half of the 20th century (and one of the greatest golfers of all time), used to say that bunker shots should be the easiest shots in the game because you do not even have to hit the ball. This thought can make playing a good bunker shot more straightforward, as this drill will illustrate.

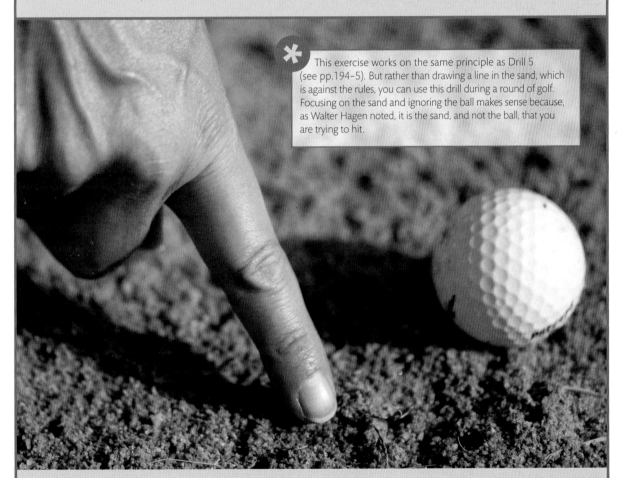

*This exercise works on the same principle as Drill 5 (see pp.194–5). But rather than drawing a line in the sand, which is against the rules, you can use this drill during a round of golf. Focusing on the sand and ignoring the ball makes sense because, as Walter Hagen noted, it is the sand, and not the ball, that you are trying to hit.

1 Step into the sand and set up for a regular greenside bunker shot from a good lie.

2 Instead of looking at the ball, which is something you instinctively do on every shot, focus on a spot in the sand 5 cm (2 in) behind the ball (above). Although this might seem a little strange at first, resist the temptation to look at the ball.

3 Keep focusing on the sand as you swing: do not even worry about the ball. If you make a good swing, and accelerate the clubhead into the right spot in the sand, the ball will naturally fly out of the bunker every time. Hit several balls using this technique.

LEVEL 1 · DRILL 08

DOUBLE YOUR SWING-LENGTH FROM GRASS TO SAND

LEVEL ONE

Golf is not an exact science. The way to approach a shot cannot usually be determined using special formulas. However, the following drill will show you a simple equation that will help you judge the distance of your greenside bunker shots.

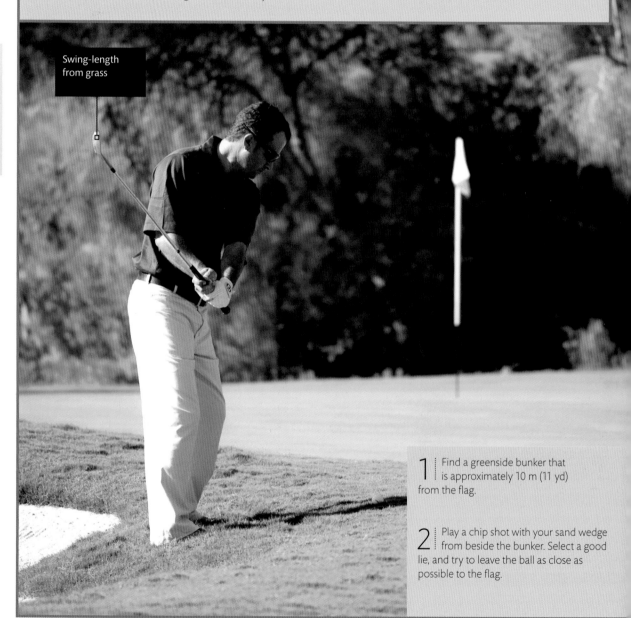

Swing-length from grass

1 Find a greenside bunker that is approximately 10 m (11 yd) from the flag.

2 Play a chip shot with your sand wedge from beside the bunker. Select a good lie, and try to leave the ball as close as possible to the flag.

Swing-length from sand

* Although it is impossible to play golf by numbers, doubling the length of your swing from sand compared to a shot from the same range on grass is a useful piece of mental imagery that will promote better judgement of distance out of greenside bunkers.

3 Now step into the bunker, and double the length of swing that you just made from the grass. Try to feel that your rate of acceleration through impact, and the overall tempo of your swing, is the same as for the previous shot. The cushioning effect of the sand trapped between the clubface and the ball should ensure that the ball travels the same distance as the chip.

LEVEL **1** DRILL **·09**

EXPERIMENT WITH TWO METHODS OF VARYING YOUR DISTANCE

Opinion is divided when it comes to recommending the ideal way to vary the distance you hit a bunker shot. Most golf instructors say it is best to take the same amount of sand every time and vary the length of swing to generate more or less distance. The previous drills in this section have been based on this theory. A few experts, however, say you should make the same length swing every time and vary the amount of sand you take at impact: not much sand for longer shots; more sand for short shots. That was the way the great Bobby Jones used to play bunker shots. Because each method has its merits, the best way to decide which you prefer is to rehearse this drill, and then make up your mind.

A shorter swing means less distance

1 Push three tee-pegs at random into any green that features a bunker.

2 Select your sand wedge, step into the bunker, and separate six balls into two batches of three.

A longer swing means more distance

Repeat this exercise several times to see which method gives you the best distance control. Once you have made your decision, it should form the basis of your approach to bunker play, and you should practise accordingly.

Close to the ball
Hit 1 cm (⅜ in) behind the ball, and see how far it flies

Further behind the ball
Hit 8 cm (3¼ in) behind the ball, and see how far it flies

3 Firstly, hit one ball to each of the three tee-pegs using the method whereby you take the same amount of sand every time. Vary the length of your swing to control distance. Start with the tee-peg closest to you, and make progressively longer swings to send the remaining two balls further each time.

4 Now, hit the remaining three balls using the technique whereby you make the same length swing every time and vary the amount of sand you take at impact to control distance. Take lots of sand to send the first ball to the nearest tee-peg, slightly less sand to make the next ball fly to the middle tee-peg, and even less sand still to reach the furthest tee-peg. Experimentation is the key here.

LEVEL 1 · DRILL 10

MATCH YOUR BACKSWING AND FOLLOWTHROUGH

When playing a greenside bunker shot you must accelerate the clubhead through impact to ensure that there is sufficient energy to create a wave of sand big enough to propel the ball from the bunker. This drill will help you accelerate the club through the sand every time.

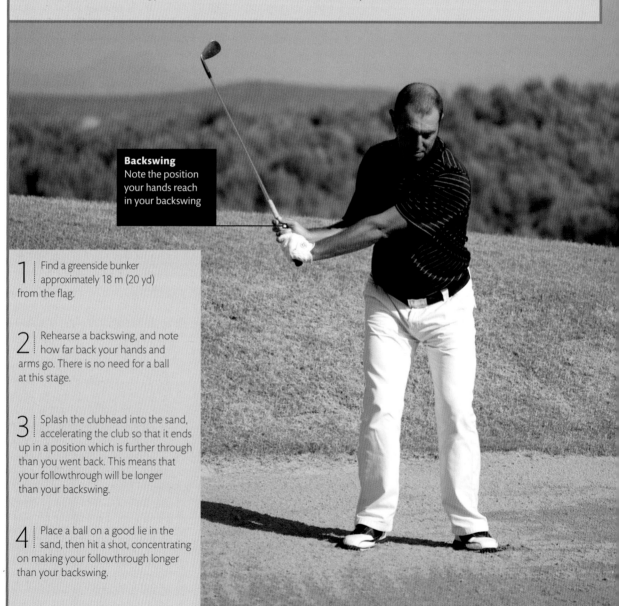

Backswing
Note the position your hands reach in your backswing

1 Find a greenside bunker approximately 18 m (20 yd) from the flag.

2 Rehearse a backswing, and note how far back your hands and arms go. There is no need for a ball at this stage.

3 Splash the clubhead into the sand, accelerating the club so that it ends up in a position which is further through than you went back. This means that your followthrough will be longer than your backswing.

4 Place a ball on a good lie in the sand, then hit a shot, concentrating on making your followthrough longer than your backswing.

Followthrough
Swing the club so that your followthrough is longer than your backswing

It is worth stressing again that decelerating the clubhead in the downswing is a serious mistake in bunker play. The sand easily soaks up what little speed is left in your swing, virtually guaranteeing that the ball will stay in the bunker. Making sure that your followthrough is longer than your backswing means that every bunker shot you play will be a positive strike.

KEY CHECKPOINT

Always cover your tracks

Once you have finished playing a bunker shot, always use the rake provided to smooth over your footprints and the trough left by the clubhead splashing through the sand at impact. Try to leave the bunker in a state in which you would wish to find it. This is a simple matter of etiquette (see pp.334–7) that ensures that every golfer has an equal chance of ending up with a good lie in the sand. You deserve this; and so too does the golfer playing in the group behind you. Although this advice is located in Level One, it does, of course, apply to golfers of all standards.

RAKE THE SAND *It is part of the etiquette of golf to leave a bunker just as you would hope to find it. There is nothing more disheartening than finding your ball has come to rest in the middle of a deep footprint.*

Re-test yourself

Before moving to Level Two, take the test on pp.186–7 again. If you have not improved, it is worth revisiting the Level One drills. However, if the performance chart shows that your bunker play has progressed sufficiently, then you are ready to tackle the more advanced drills in Level Two.

LEVEL 2·11 DRILL

BUILD A CLEANER STRIKE FOR LONG-RANGE BUNKER SHOTS

The following practice drill is designed to improve your long-range bunker shots. The exercise will teach you how to strike the ball cleanly, with no interference from sand between the clubface and the ball, which – unlike in the case of greenside bunker shots – is exactly what you should do in fairway bunkers. The benefits gained from this drill are just as great for your general iron play, too.

1 Find a fairway bunker without a major front lip, and with plenty of space to hit shots from a flat lie.

2 Draw a narrow line in the sand, and place as many balls as possible along that line. The back of each ball should just be touching the line.

3 Take your 7-iron and address the first ball in the line. Use the same set-up you would for an iron shot (see pp.20–3).

4 Shuffle your feet into the sand to secure your footing. As this lowers the base of your swing, choke down on the grip by about 2.5 cm (1 in) to compensate.

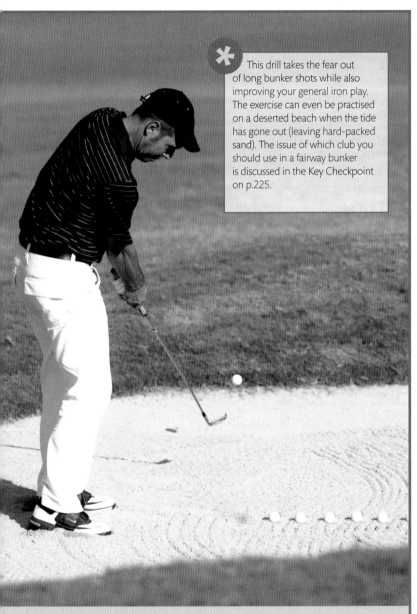

※ This drill takes the fear out of long bunker shots while also improving your general iron play. The exercise can even be practised on a deserted beach when the tide has gone out (leaving hard-packed sand). The issue of which club you should use in a fairway bunker is discussed in the Key Checkpoint on p.225.

5 Now hit shots with a full swing. Do not worry about a target – the object of the exercise is to strike the ball cleanly. To do this you need to strike the ball first, then the sand, which requires a descending blow. The principles are the same as for producing a good iron shot (see the Key Checkpoint on p.75). If you are playing the shot correctly, there will be a small mark in the sand after the spot where the ball was, indicating ball-then-sand contact. If the clubhead touches the sand before the line, you will know you have hit the shot "heavy". Try placing the ball a fraction further back in your stance to promote clean contact. Do not try to scoop the ball out of the sand.

LEVEL TWO

KEY CHECKPOINT

These are touch shots: choke down on the grip

Choking down on the grip is recommended for almost every short shot, and bunker shots are no exception. By all means experiment to see what suits you best, but, as a rule, about 5 cm (2 in) down the grip is ideal. This change is helpful because the closer your hands are to the clubhead, the more control you will have. If you were to hold the top end of a pen, for example, you would find it difficult to write neatly and would grip the pen nearer to the nib for extra control. The same applies when playing a bunker shot. Choking down on the grip gives you better feel for, and increased control over, what the clubhead is doing in your swing.

The only time it is not a good idea to choke down is when the ball is well below the level of your feet. In this situation you need all the length of your sand wedge just to reach the ball at the moment of impact (see Drill 18, pp.216–7).

HANDS DOWN *Choking down on the grip enhances your touch from close range, and bunker shots are certainly no exception to this rule.*

LEVEL 2 · DRILL 12

MAKE LIGHT OF THE INTERMEDIATE BUNKER SHOT

This drill answers one of the most commonly asked questions about bunker play: should you strike intermediate-length bunker shots – those in the 40–50 m (44–55 yd) range – cleanly or with a bit of sand at impact? As these bunkers are neither truly greenside bunkers nor fairway bunkers, most golfers become caught in two minds and make a mess of the shot. The following exercise will eliminate all confusion.

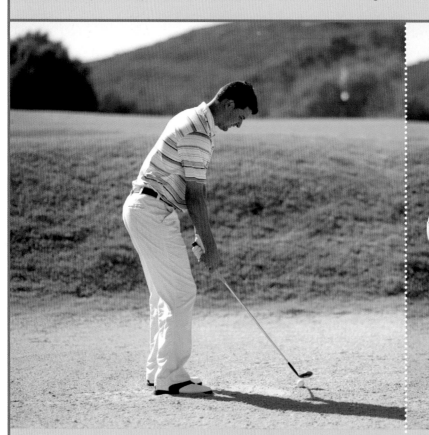

1 Find a bunker 40–50 m (44–55 yd) from a flag. Give yourself a good lie in the sand.

2 Use your pitching wedge rather than your sand wedge. Imagine that the flag is at 12 o'clock on a clockface (see Drill 1, p.188), and stand slightly open, with your feet, hips, and shoulders aligned to 11 o'clock (left of the flag). Open the clubface so that it is aiming between 12 and 1 o'clock (right of the flag).

3 Take less sand than you would from a greenside bunker – aim to strike the sand about 1 cm (⅜ in) behind the ball. Remember that for most greenside bunker shots you should strike the sand 5 cm (2 in) behind the ball (see Drill 5, pp.194–5), and for fairway bunker shots you should strike the ball then the sand (see Drill 11, pp.204–5).

4 Now imagine that your head is at 12 o'clock and that the ball is at 6 o'clock (see Drill 24 in the "Pitching" section, pp.142–3). Swing your hands back to 10 o'clock and aim to strike the sand in the spot identified in step 3. Your open stance will produce an out-to-in swing path (see pp.26–7) through impact, which, combined with an open clubface, produces a shot with a touch of sidespin. You can therefore anticipate some left-to-right movement through the air and a kick to the right when the ball pitches on the green.

✳ Another way to deal with intermediate-length bunker shots involves taking a shorter swing and playing a cleanly struck shot with a pitching wedge, a technique that will be explored towards the end of Level Three (see Drill 25, p.226). For the meantime, the current drill will give you a method that is easier to use and is simple to repeat.

LEVEL 2·13 DRILL

TAKE A PITCHING WEDGE ON HARD-PACKED SAND

The bounce on your sand wedge (see the Key Checkpoint on p.191) is what enables you to play good greenside bunker shots: the clubhead slides freely through the sand under the ball, rather than digging down too deep. When the sand is hard-packed, however (perhaps after a prolonged spell of rain), bounce is the last thing you want because the sand wedge will tend to skid off the surface into the middle of the ball, which could send your shot into the face of the bunker or beyond the green. Next time you are in wet or hard-packed sand, try this drill to get you out of trouble.

Difficult shot
When the ball is on hard-packed sand, you should use your pitching wedge, which will cut through the sand more easily

* As you practise this shot you will notice distinct differences between this and a regular greenside bunker shot. Because you are taking a less-lofted club, and not opening the face as much as you would normally, the ball will come out a bit lower than it would with a sand wedge and will therefore have more run. Bear this in mind when you are selecting a landing spot on the green.

Shallow mark
Aim to take a little less sand than you would when playing a regular bunker shot, therefore leaving a shallower mark in the sand

1 Instead of your sand wedge, select your pitching wedge, which has a sharper leading edge. This will help the clubhead cut into the hard-packed surface of the sand, slide underneath the ball, and create the all-important "splash" that makes a good bunker shot.

2 Stand a little squarer to the target than you would for a normal bunker shot (instead of opening your stance), and have the clubface only slightly open.

3 As you swing, hinge your wrists a little earlier in your backswing to create a slightly steeper arc. Aim to hit a spot in the sand about 2.5 cm (1 in) behind the ball. As always, accelerate the clubhead down and through impact.

LEVEL DRILL
2·14 STAGGER YOUR TARGETS TO IMPROVE YOUR RANGE

Several of the Level One drills concentrated on the important subject of judging distance out of sand. The following exercise continues this theme and takes it a stage further, training you to make an even better job of different-length greenside bunker shots.

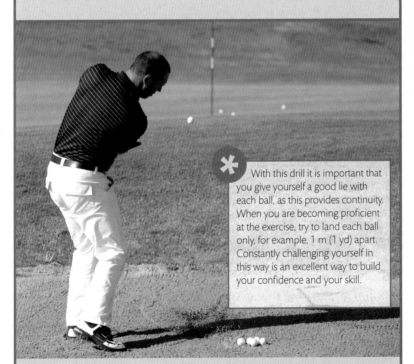

✳ With this drill it is important that you give yourself a good lie with each ball, as this provides continuity. When you are becoming proficient at the exercise, try to land each ball only, for example, 1 m (1 yd) apart. Constantly challenging yourself in this way is an excellent way to build your confidence and your skill.

1 Armed with at least 12 balls, set yourself up in a greenside bunker. The bigger the putting green, the more value you will gain from this drill.

2 Hit your first shot on to the green with the object of making it land as near to you as possible. Try to strike the shot so that the ball lands only 6–7 m (6½–7½ yd) away.

3 Aim to hit your second ball a little further up the green, perhaps 2–3 m (2–3 yd) beyond the first.

4 Try to hit your third ball 2–3 m (2–3 yd) further still, and so on until you run out of room on the green. The more balls you can land in a line before you run out of putting green, the better your bunker play and judgement of distance will become.

KEY CHECKPOINT

Hover the clubhead to avoid breaking the rules

Although there is a section dedicated solely to the rules of golf later in the book (see pp.338–45), it is relevant now to examine the rule that represents the biggest difference between bunker play and other areas of the game. The benefits of hovering the clubhead at address were discussed in the "Pitching" (see Drill 20, p.137) and "Chipping" (see the Key Checkpoint on p.183) sections. However, in a bunker this is essential: you must hover the clubhead above the sand as you address the ball. If you allow the clubhead to touch the sand, either at address or in your backswing, you incur a one-stroke penalty. Always be aware of this when you are playing bunker shots.

Be particularly vigilant if your ball comes to rest on a severe downslope, as it is all to easy for the clubhead to touch the sand during your takeaway. How to play bunker shots from a downslope is discussed in Drill 16 (see pp.212–3).

BE CAREFUL IN SAND *It is an essential requirement in bunkers to hover the clubhead at address so that it does not touch the sand. A one-stroke penalty results if the club comes into contact with the sand.*

LEVEL 2 · DRILL 15

BE BOLDER ON AN UPSLOPE

More often than not your ball settles into a reasonably flat lie in bunkers. But there are occasions, especially on courses that use soft, powdery sand, where your ball will cling to a slope. At times, your normal bunker technique will not suffice: you have to be creative with your set-up, and adapt your swing in order to counteract the effects of the slope. This drill will show you how to do this.

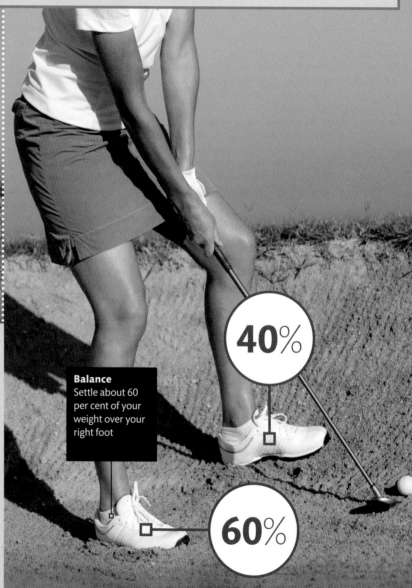

40%

Balance
Settle about 60 per cent of your weight over your right foot

60%

1 Place a ball on the upslope at the front of a greenside bunker. Take your sand wedge from your bag, and address the ball.

Although your first instinct will be to lean into the slope, absorb the majority of your weight on your lower foot, which in this case is your right. Flex your knees to anchor your weight in place – this will provide a stable foundation from which to swing. Once you have effected this weight-distribution change, your shoulders will be more level with the slope, as they would be on a flat lie in the sand. This position enables you to swing the clubhead through the sand on the ideal angle of attack.

2 In your backswing, it is important to focus on keeping your knees flexed and your head steady. Do not sway backwards or forwards because this will upset your balance, making it extremely difficult to strike the correct spot in the sand.

Backswing
Maintain your original weight distribution during your backswing

3 As you change direction from backswing to downswing, keep your weight on your right foot, and focus on swinging the club up the slope through impact. If you let your weight shift towards the target in the downswing, you will bury the clubhead too steeply into the face of the bunker and the ball will not receive enough energy.

60%

40%

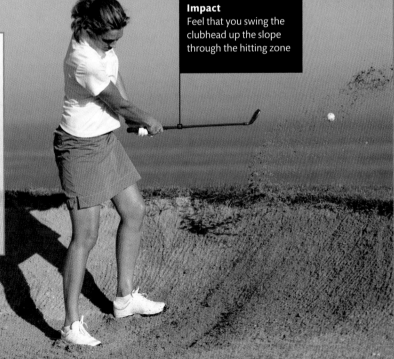

Impact
Feel that you swing the clubhead up the slope through the hitting zone

❋ Because an upslope adds loft to the clubface (see Drill 14 in the "Chipping" section, p.165), the ball may pop out with too much upward momentum and too little forward flight, which means you end up leaving the ball well short of the flag. To avoid this, be much more positive. Aim to land the ball on top of the flag. You can be comforted in the knowledge that the ball will land softly and not run too far. One final note on playing from an upslope: if the ball is resting right under the front lip of the bunker, you may want to consider playing the ball out to the side, rather than aiming for the flag.

KEY CHECKPOINT

Hit from the high foot

Here is a useful rule of thumb that takes some of the mystery out of playing from sloping lies in the sand: always play the ball towards your higher foot. The reason for this comes down to basic impact mechanics. On a downslope, the clubhead comes into contact with the sand earlier in the downswing, which means that you need the ball back in your stance in order to obtain the correct contact. On an upslope, the clubhead meets the sand much later in its downswing arc, which means that you need the ball further forward in your stance to ensure a good strike.

SIMPLIFY SLOPING LIES *Always remember to address the ball towards your high foot: your right on a downslope (top); your left on an upslope (above).*

LEVEL 2·16 DRILL

CHASE THE BALL DOWN A DOWNSLOPE

The previous drill (see pp.210–1) covered one of the least demanding sloping-lie shots. This drill covers a more difficult option – when the ball comes to rest on a downslope. You cannot afford to ignore practising these shots – however difficult they might seem. If you do, a potential nightmare awaits you on the course.

40%

60%

1 | Take your sand wedge and place a ball on a downslope.

2 | Address the ball, distributing most of your weight on to your lower foot (your left). Introduce lots of knee flex to stabilize your balance, put the ball back in your stance, and keep your hands well forward. As with the upslope, your shoulders should be almost level with the slope, which enables you to swing the club into the sand on a descending angle of attack.

While the ball will emerge on a high trajectory from an upslope, it comes out much lower from a downslope, which creates plenty of run on landing. In view of this, be sensible with your target area. You may need to go for the main part of the green, rather than aiming at the flag, just to make sure your next shot is a putt. This is a good result from a downslope lie in a bunker.

LEVEL TWO

3 Hinge your wrists early to send the club upwards on a steep arc. This enables you to strike down steeply into the sand behind the ball. Keep your weight steady.

4 Keep your hands ahead of the clubhead, and hit down into the sand behind the ball. You need to feel as if the clubhead is chasing the ball down the slope so that it stays low to the surface well into the followthrough.

LEVEL 3 · DRILL 19
KEEP EVERYTHING SQUARE WHEN THE BALL IS BURIED

Drills 24 and 27 (see p.225 and pp.228-9) stress the fact that you should be prepared to play bunker shots with clubs other than the sand wedge should the situation call for it. The following practice exercise, which will show you how to play a ball in a plugged lie, focuses on another departure from standard bunker procedure. However, this time the change is to your technique, rather than your selection of club.

1 Recreate a lie in the sand where the ball is plugged (submerged in its own pitch mark). This often happens when the ball lands in the sand from a great height, such as when a lofted-iron shot finds a bunker.

2 Take your sand wedge and, instead of opening your stance and the clubface, stand square to the target, with the clubface aiming at the flag. Put the ball in the middle of your stance, and keep your hands well ahead of the clubhead.

3 Hinge your wrists almost as soon as you start your takeaway, as this promotes a more upright swing and a steep angle of attack into impact, which is essential from a plugged lie. Also make a longer backswing than you would from a good lie in the sand, so that you can build up plenty of clubhead speed in your downswing.

4 Now concentrate on a spot 5-7.5 cm (2-3 in) behind the ball, and bury the clubhead into the sand at that point. Thump the club down with plenty of aggression – try to knife the leading edge of the clubhead down powerfully into the sand. There is so much resistance from the sand that you can use more force than you might imagine. In a severely plugged lie, you might even have to swap your sand wedge for a pitching wedge to ensure that the clubhead digs deep enough into the sand. The ball will fly out of the bunker on a lower trajectory than in a normal greenside bunker shot. It will also run much further, so make sure you have plenty of green to work with if you attempt to play this shot during a proper round.

* A plugged lie is quite common, yet few golfers know how to deal with it correctly. For this reason it is one of the most poorly played shots in the game. Even when you know how to play from a plugged lie, absolute precision is impossible because you are hitting the sand with considerable force. But practise for just 30 minutes, and you will at least be able to knock the ball out of the bunker and keep it on the green virtually every time.

LEVEL 3 · DRILL 20

LOWER YOUR HANDS FOR EXTRA TOUCH

Any bunker shot of less than 5 m (5½ yd) demands great delicacy of touch. It is ironic that, although the ball is very near to the flag, it is nevertheless extremely difficult to land the ball close to the pin. This drill will give you the finesse necessary to play these very short bunker shots.

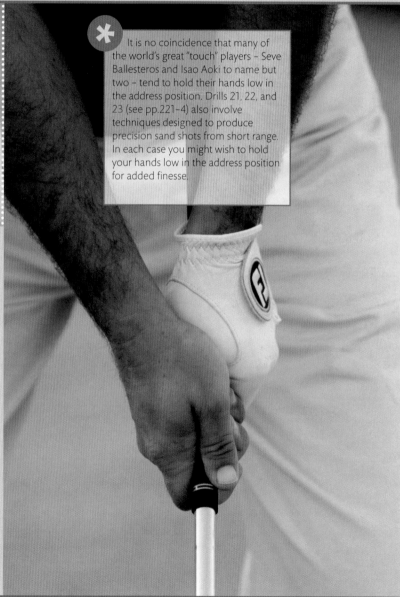

* It is no coincidence that many of the world's great "touch" players – Seve Ballesteros and Isao Aoki to name but two – tend to hold their hands low in the address position. Drills 21, 22, and 23 (see pp.221–4) also involve techniques designed to produce precision sand shots from short range. In each case you might wish to hold your hands low in the address position for added finesse.

1 Take your sand wedge, and adopt your normal address position (see Drill 1, p.188) in a greenside bunker.

2 Choke down on the grip so that your right hand almost touches the metal of the shaft, and then lower your hands by about 7.5 cm (3 in). This set-up has two effects that should help you play good short bunker shots. Firstly, it pushes the toe of the club into the air more, which encourages the heel to come into contact with the sand first. This helps the clubhead slide through the sand more easily. Secondly, lower hands at address promote a more "wristy" swing, which puts the club on a more upright plane in the backswing.

3 From the address position outlined in steps 1 and 2, accelerate the clubhead through the sand to make the ball climb quickly and land softly.

OPEN WIDE FOR A VERY SHORT SPLASH

Although long-range and intermediate-length bunker shots are tricky, the toughest sand shots of all are those where you need to carry the ball only 3–5 m (3–5½ yd).

This drill shows you a more effective technique than taking a normal-length backswing and decelerating into impact to stop the ball flying too far.

✱ You will soon realise that you can make a long swing, and accelerate the clubhead through the sand, yet see the ball travel only a small distance. This extremely useful skill will improve the quality of your short bunker shots.

1 Open your stance so much that your chest virtually faces the target, and spread your feet 30 cm (12 in) further apart than you would for a normal greenside bunker shot. This set-up will probably feel odd, but it is necessary.

Open the clubface to a greater degree than for any other shot. In fact, the clubface should be so open that you could almost rest a glass of water on it. Swing the club back along your body line. Your backswing will be way outside the normal swing path but totally appropriate for this type of shot.

2 Accelerate the clubhead down on the same path as your backswing, so that the clubhead travels on a severe out-to-in path (see pp.26–7). This swing path, combined with the massively open clubface, means that the club will slice through the sand, and the ball should rise sharply, with more upward than forward momentum.

LEVEL   DRILL

3·22

TAKE A SHALLOW CUT FOR EXTRA SPIN OUT OF SAND

This drill introduces another method designed to produce a delicate bunker shot from very close range. This is a difficult shot, but the rewards are in direct proportion to the difficulty. When played correctly, this technique generates impressive levels of backspin, which is essential for short bunker shots.

1 Open your stance and the clubface – a little more than you would for a standard greenside bunker shot.

2 Focus on a spot only 2 cm (¾ in) behind the ball. The key to the success of this shot is taking less sand than normal (see Drill 5, pp.194–5) at impact.

3 Now make your swing, and try to hit the spot identified in step 2. Take a shallow cut of sand from under the ball: the shallower the cut, the more the ball will spin (a thin layer of sand acts like sandpaper when it is trapped between the clubface and the ball). Keep your weight evenly spread throughout the stroke, as this promotes the desired (shallow) angle of attack.

You will probably hit the first few shots too far, due to the fact that less sand means less resistance, and therefore more force is imparted to the ball. Experiment with clubface positions and the relationship between swing length and acceleration through impact to see how much spin you can apply to the ball. This shot requires lots of practice.

LEVEL THREE

LEVEL 3 · DRILL 23

CUP YOUR LEFT WRIST TO OPEN THE CLUBFACE

When playing sand shots, if the clubface is open, the flange on the sand wedge's sole can bounce and slide through the sand under the ball, promoting a high flight and a soft landing. Drills 20, 21, and 22 (see pp.220–3) suggested ways of increasing the height and spin of a bunker shot. Here is a more advanced method, which involves "cupping" your left wrist in your backswing.

1 Take your sand wedge, and address a ball as you would normally for a greenside bunker shot (see Drill 1, p.188).

2 As you move the club away from the ball, rotate your forearms to the right to open the clubface even more. Also hinge your wrists so that when you reach the top of your backswing (with your hands at about 9 o'clock), the back of your left hand almost arches back on itself – you should be able to see creases in your skin where your thumb meets your wrist. This is described as a "cupped" left wrist. Pause at this point, and look at your hands and the clubface, which will be wide open. Rehearse this backswing a few times to become familiar with the movements and feelings.

3 Now hit some shots. Having set the clubface into a very open position in the backswing, it will stay that way through impact.

✳ If the clubface is wide open through impact, it will slide easily through the sand and cause the ball to climb steeply. You will soon find that you can make a very aggressive swing and generate lots of height but little distance.

TRY PUTTING FROM SAND

You might think that putting from a bunker is a cowardly last resort for golfers who are terrified of "proper" bunker play. However, if there is no front lip to speak of, and the lie is good, then a putt might be a sensible option. You should never be afraid to play an unconventional shot if it suits the situation.

* There is no question that this is unorthodox. But if you have never attempted the shot before you may be surprised how easy it is to play and how effective it can be. If the sand is firmly packed, a putt is even more appropriate because the ball will run over the surface with less resistance. However, it is essential that the front lip of the bunker is low enough to act as a ramp for the ball to roll up. If the lip is not sufficiently low, do not even contemplate playing this shot.

1 Take your putter from your bag, and find a shallow bunker with a low front lip. Place a ball in the sand on a good lie. Position the ball in the middle of your stance, and stand with your feet and shoulders parallel to the ball-to-target line, as you would for a normal iron shot on the fairway. Do not forget to hover the putterhead above the surface of the sand, otherwise you will incur a one-stroke penalty (see the Key Checkpoint on p.209).

2 Make a stroke that is controlled by your shoulders and arms, allowing for a little softness in your hands and wrists. Make a positive stroke, and aim to strike the middle of the ball. The putterface should meet the ball cleanly with a slightly descending blow. If you strike the ball correctly, there should be a shallow trough in the sand after impact. The ball should then skip along the surface of the sand, hop over the insubstantial front lip, run on to the green, and roll like a normal putt.

KEY CHECKPOINT

"Club up" from a fairway bunker

When the ball lands in a fairway bunker, use a slightly less lofted club than you would otherwise from the same distance on the fairway. If, for example, the ball were to land 150 m (165 yd) from the flag, you would probably use a 6-iron if you were on the fairway. But from a similar distance in sand, "club up" to a 5-iron (assuming, of course, that the lie is good). The main reason for this concerns the swing arc when playing from a bunker.

Drill 11 (see pp.204–5) explained that for a long bunker shot you should choke down the club an inch or so to allow for the fact that your feet shuffle into the sand, effectively lowering the base of your swing. Therefore, if you do not choke down on the grip you can easily hit the shot heavy. However, choking down, even by as little as 2.5 cm (1 in), reduces your swing arc and, therefore contributes to a shorter ball-flight. Also, with your feet buried in the sand, your leg action will be slightly restricted, which leads to a less powerful swing. This again takes some distance off the shot.

However, before you finally commit to playing the shot, you must be certain you have sufficient loft on the club to clear the front lip of the bunker. If there is any doubt in your mind, it is as well to remember that your first priority is to get out of the sand and on to the grass in one shot. There is nothing worse than hitting the ball into the face of the bunker having tried for too much distance and not allowed enough loft. In this situation, the ball usually stays in the sand, leaving you with yet another bunker shot. Remember this important maxim: "if in doubt, just get it out".

KEY CHECKPOINT

Match bounce to the texture of the sand

The Key Checkpoint on page 191 describes how Gene Sarazen reinvented the sand wedge by introducing bounce into the sole of the club. Things have moved on considerably since the 1930s, and you can now buy sand wedges with a variety of degrees of bounce. This is something you need to be aware of when making a purchase, as your requirements will depend on the type of sand used on the course at which you play most often. As a rule, the softer the sand the more bounce you need on the sole of the sand wedge; on heavier sand you need less bounce. Equipment requirements are looked at in greater detail in the reference section (see pp.326–31), but this is a point worth making before leaving the bunker and moving on to the putting green.

MORE OR LESS BOUNCE *The bounce on your sand wedge should suit the sand in the bunkers on your home course: less bounce (left) suits heavier sand; more bounce (right) is best for soft sand.*

LEVEL DRILL 3·25

TRY PLAYING THE "PUNCH-AND-SPIN" BUNKER SHOT

The following exercise is one of the last of the featured drills on bunker play because you need skill and confidence in equal proportions to pull off this shot. It is an intermediate-length bunker shot (see Drill 12, pp.206–7), which involves striking the ball first, not the sand.

1 Give yourself a good lie in a bunker that is approximately 40–50 m (44–55 yd) from the flag. Instead of using a sand wedge, reach for your pitching wedge.

2 Position the ball in the middle of your stance, rather than opposite your left foot. Then place your hands well ahead of the ball, so that the shaft of the club leans towards the target. Now aim the clubface straight at the flag, rather than opening it.

3 Make an arms-and-shoulders swing, keeping leg action to a minimum. You also need to keep your weight slightly favouring your left side throughout the swing, as this promotes a ball-first strike. Keep your hands ahead of the clubhead as you swing into impact, and focus on the back of the ball. The aim of this shot is to strike the ball cleanly with a descending blow, leaving a shallow trough in the sand after the point of impact. If you play the shot just right, the ball will fly half the height of a normal bunker shot, then will bounce once or twice across the green before backspin checks its progress.

* This shot is fun to try out in a practice session. However, during a round you need to be sure that the conditions are right for playing the shot: the front lip of the bunker must be relatively insubstantial (because the ball flies on a low trajectory), and you need lots of green to work with.

LEVEL 3 · DRILL 26
PRACTISE IN PREPARATION FOR THE WORST

The drills in this section have covered the skills required to make you a better bunker player. Now for the ultimate practice drill – one that enables you to apply your imagination and technique to a variety of different shots.

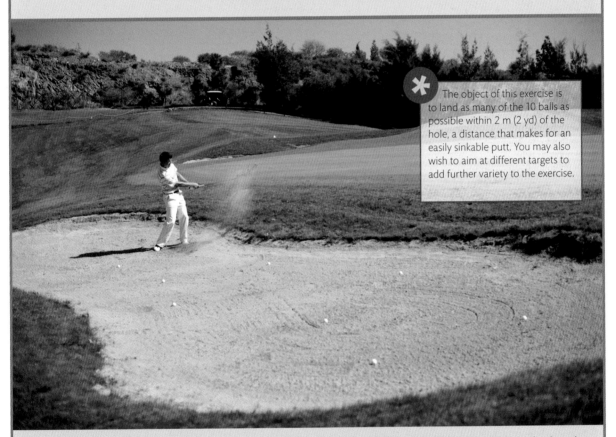

The object of this exercise is to land as many of the 10 balls as possible within 2 m (2 yd) of the hole, a distance that makes for an easily sinkable putt. You may also wish to aim at different targets to add further variety to the exercise.

1 Take 10 balls, and place them in a bunker. Position the first ball at the left edge of the bunker, below the level of your feet, and the tenth ball at the right edge of the bunker, above the level of your feet. Give each of the other balls a different lie. Make sure some have a good lie, while others are either partially buried, completely plugged, or stuck on upslopes or downslopes.

2 Work your way along the line, playing each ball in turn. You will find that the sand wedge is best for most shots, but have other clubs, such as a pitching wedge and a 9-iron, within easy reach should you wish to experiment as you go along.

3 Size up each lie, visualize how the ball will come out of the sand, and try to match your technique and club selection to suit the shot.

LEVEL DRILL

3·27

EXPERIMENT WITH DIFFERENT CLUBS FROM SAND

The sand wedge did not get its name by accident: it is designed to make bunker play as easy as possible. But it is not the only club you can use from sand around the green. With a little skill and know-how, using other clubs can increase your options and flexibility in the bunker. Practising this drill will enhance your repertoire of shots and make your short game more complete.

1 Step into a greenside bunker with a sand wedge, a pitching wedge, a 9-iron, and 12 or so balls.

2 Start with your sand wedge, and hit a couple of normal greenside bunker shots. Observe the way the ball flies and how far it runs.

3 Now switch to your pitching wedge. Remember, every club other than a sand wedge has a relatively thin sole, which in sand is not necessarily what you want. Therefore, make sure that you use the same technique as when using your sand wedge. Open the clubface, which will help it slide through the sand, and commit to making a positive swing to stop the clubhead becoming buried. You will find that the ball flies from the bunker on a lower trajectory than a shot with a sand wedge and also runs more.

4 Finally, take your 9-iron. Open your stance and the clubface again. You will find that the same swing produces an even flatter trajectory with even more run on landing.

✱ Obviously the lower-flying shots do not work when the front lip of the bunker is high. But a 9-iron or pitching wedge is a useful tool when you need to play a running bunker shot across a long green – a situation where a high-floated sand wedge often leaves the ball short.

LEVEL THREE

THE PERFECT BUNKER SHOT

There was a time when a couple of names stood out from the crowd when it came to bunker play, but not any more. These days all top tour professionals display exceptional skills from the sand. Sweden's Freddie Jacobsen is no exception. To him, a greenside bunker shot is no more challenging than a chip shot from the side of the green. Indeed, from a good lie such as this he would be looking to hole his share from this range. Freddie makes it look easy and indeed it is, providing you follow a few key fundamentals.

*GARY PLAYER, the greatest bunker player to ever set foot in the sand, has always maintained that the single most important fundamental to successful bunker play is making sure that you accelerate through the sand and into a balanced and full followthrough position.

1 ADDRESS
Freddie has adopted perfect alignment for a greenside bunker shot; his feet, hips, and shoulders are aligned slightly to the left of the flag, while the clubface aims to the right of that. This stance promotes the desired out-to-in swing path, while the open clubface helps the wide flange on the sole of the sand-wedge to slide through the sand. These elements combine to produce a straight shot.

2 HALFWAY BACK
Freddie has a slightly unorthodox means of taking the club away from the ball, but there is still much to observe and admire in this image. The key point is that as Freddie's hands and arms swing the club upwards, his body continues to turn – an essential combination, even on short shots such as this.

3 TOP OF BACKSWING
Although perhaps unorthodox halfway back, Freddie's technique is perfect at the top of the swing. The clubface is still wide open, an essential requirement of good greenside bunker play. The club-shaft points to the left of the flag, across the line, which makes it easy to swing the club down on the correct path and plane for optimum contact in the sand.

Keys to better bunker play

Successful sand play, which is not as difficult to achieve as many golfers think, makes a big difference to your scoring potential. The following keys form the core of a good bunker technique.

Open your stance so that your feet, hips, and shoulders aim at least 10 m (11 yd) left of the target. Open the clubface so that it aims at least 10 m (11 yd) right of the target.

Place the ball opposite your left heel so that you can swing the clubhead into the sand on a shallow angle of attack.

Take the clubhead back parallel to the line of your feet, to establish an out-to-in shaped swing path. Swing left through impact with the clubface open (aiming right).

Except when the ball is plugged, always followthrough in sand to ensure that you achieve the proper acceleration in the hitting zone.

WATCH THE PRO

4 | **IMPACT**
Notice how Freddie swings the clubhead freely through the sand under the ball. This image again highlights the importance of the correct address position. The open stance facilitates the out-to-in swing path, while the open clubface ensures that the clubhead slides through the sand and "splashes" the ball out of the bunker and towards the flag.

5 | **FOLLOWTHROUGH**
Despite the feel inherent in this type of shot – the ball floats upwards and forwards on a "soft" trajectory – the positive and accelerating swing is evident in the length of Freddie's followthrough. It is an aggressive yet controlled motion; there is certainly nothing tentative about this swing, and that is a good lesson to take into the sand.

PUTTING

ALTHOUGH THE PUTTING STROKE is very short in comparison to the full swing, it is open to greater personal interpretation than any other shot. You only have to watch the green-play in a professional event to appreciate the variety of styles that are used. One characteristic that all great putters share, however, is a consistent, repeatable stroke where all the moving parts complement one another perfectly. With this type of stroke, the ball will travel along the chosen line at the required speed relative to the length of the putt.

As putting accounts for about 40 per cent of the total shots played in a round, it would be a terrible mistake to neglect this department of the game. The following section will give you a thorough understanding of the mechanics of putting, which will enable you to incorporate the essential ingredients of an effective stroke into your personal style. You will also develop the two vital attributes of touch and confidence.

TEST YOUR SKILLS

THE PUTTING TEST
To fully assess your putting ability, this test is split into two parts: short-range holing-out skills (steps 1–3) and long-range putting (steps 4–5).

1 Find a green that does not feature significant slopes: the flatter the better. Place seven tee-pegs in the ground to form a circle around the hole. Each tee-peg should be about one putter-length from the hole – approximately 1 m (1 yd).

2 Place a ball next to each of the seven tee-pegs. Then work your way around each of the balls, trying to hole each one (above). Empty the hole whenever necessary to make room for other falling balls.

4 | Now move about 10 m (11 yd) away from the hole. Place a batch of eight balls on the ground.

5 | Putt as many of the eight balls as possible into the circle of tee-pegs (right). If any drop in the hole, so much the better, but for the purposes of this exercise a holed putt counts the same as a putt that finishes inside the circle. You may find that a ball occasionally strikes a tee-peg, in which case you must be honest with yourself and assess whether or not it would have finished in the circle.

Total your short- and long-range results to give you a score out of 15. Then repeat steps 2–5 another two times, and calculate an average score out of 15.

✱

SUCCESSFUL PUTTING IS ABOUT BALANCING two crucial ingredients: pace and line. One without the other is no use to you on the greens.

3 | Make a note of your score out of seven, and leave the tee-pegs where they are, as these form an integral part of the long-range putting test.

PERFORMANCE CHART

1 **1–5 =** LEVEL ONE (pp.234–247)

2 **6–10 =** LEVEL TWO (pp.248–269)

3 **11–15 =** LEVEL THREE (pp.270–277)

LEVEL   DRILL
1·01 FORM YOUR PUTTING GRIP

While there are three main types of recommended grip for the full swing (see p.18), with putting there is much more choice. That said, however, conventional wisdom suggests that using the grip known as the "reverse overlap" is the best way to control the putter as you swing. Use this drill to form the reverse overlap.

1   Place your hands either side of the club's grip, with your palms facing, and each hand square to the target.

2   Place your left hand on the club, with your thumb pointing straight down the middle of the grip; keep your forefinger off the grip for now.

✳ These rules for the ideal putting grip are not set in stone, but the reverse overlap does offer tangible benefits to your putting stroke. Primarily, it binds the hands together, encouraging them to work in harmony throughout the stroke, which is one of the fundamentals of a successful putting technique. The reverse grip also helps maintain the wrist angles into and through impact. This means that you are less likely to upset the path, pace, and aim of the putter head at the crucial moment: impact.

3 Place your right hand on the club, again with your thumb pointing straight down the grip. Wrap the fingers of your right hand around the grip, and put your left forefinger over them. This is the reverse overlap. (Note: according to personal preference, the left forefinger can either extend directly down the grip, as shown in this image, or it can be tucked slightly behind, as in the image accompanying step 4.)

4 Finally, extend the forefinger of your right hand down the side of the grip, as this enhances your control of the putter. Exactly how far this finger reaches down the grip is again determined by personal preference. Hold the club at least as softly as in the full swing. Putting relies on delicate touch – softness is the key to the optimum grip pressure.

LEVEL   DRILL

1·02 TAKE UP THE IDEAL PUTTING POSTURE

Good posture is very important if you are about to make a full swing. But it is critical to the success of your putting stroke, too. Ideally, you should adopt a posture at address that allows your arms to hang down – not totally straight, but free from tension to promote a smooth action back and forth. This simple routine will help you establish a good putting posture.

This drill shows you how to assume excellent posture for putting. Your alignment, on the other hand, is more a matter of personal taste. However, most experts recommend that your shoulders be parallel to the ball-to-target line, whereas your feet can be slightly open to the target.

1 Stand up straight with the putter resting against your left leg. Flex your knees a little and bend from your hips so that your arms hang limp from your shoulders. Jiggle your hands to relax your arms. Form your putting grip in the normal way (see Drill 1, pp.234–5)

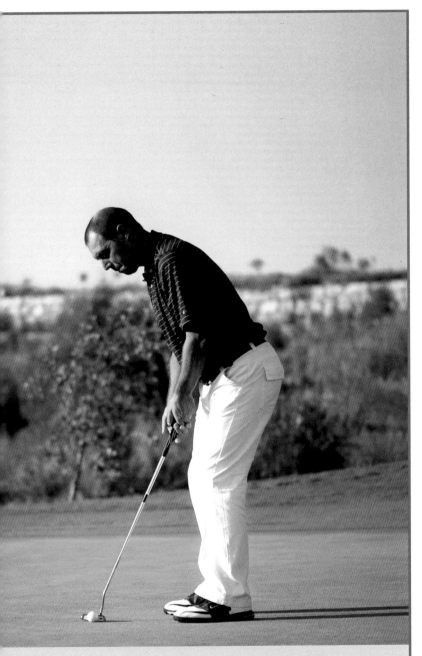

KEY CHECKPOINT

The geometry of a good putt

From a worm's eye view, the putting stroke is saucer-shaped. The putterhead sweeps away from the ball on a very gradual upward curve and comes down on the same angle. At the bottom of its arc, the putterhead travels horizontally before following an upward curve through impact. One of the secrets to a good putting stroke is making sure that ball-contact occurs just after the putter has reached the bottom of its swing arc (use a mirror to identify the exact position of the flat spot at the bottom of your putting stroke). This means that the putter is travelling slightly on the up when it meets the ball, which helps give the ball a smooth roll. The followthrough, which mirrors the backswing in shape, should be slightly longer than the backswing. This promotes the correct amout of acceleration through impact.

As for the path of the putter, it should be straight back and through impact for close-range putts – up to about 2 m (2 yd). As the stroke becomes progressively longer, the putterhead should follow this path: inside on the way back, square at impact, then inside again on the followthrough. This swing path is just the same as for the full swing (see pp.26–7) but on a much smaller scale.

2 Now take a minute or two to take note of the key elements of this posture. There should be a slight bend in your arms, with your elbows pointing in towards your ribcage. If you think of your arms and shoulders as a triangle (see Drill 5, pp.240–1), it will help you to produce the correct stroke. You should also feel comfortable and relaxed, with your weight evenly balanced between both feet.

Perfect swing *In all the best putting strokes, the putter works in much the same way as a pendulum, swinging freely back and forth. The ball should merely get in the way of the putter as it swings through.*

LEVEL 1·03 DRILL CHECK YOUR BALL POSITION

Putting allows you more individuality than any other aspect of the game. But, whatever method you decide to employ, you should always ensure that your eyes are directly over the ball while you are in your address position. The following exercise enables you to fulfil this key requirement.

✳ With your eyes over the ball, you have the best possible view down the line of the putt. If your eyes are either side of this line, your view is distorted, which can upset your aim. Try to find time to monitor ball position on a regular basis. In fact, it is a good idea to go through this routine each time you start a practice putting session, whether it is before a round or not. If you play the ball from the correct position, bad habits are less likely to infiltrate your technique.

1 Assume your putting posture (see Drill 2, pp.236–7), but do not place a ball on the ground. Take your right hand off the club, and hold a golf ball against the top of your nose, right between your eyes.

2 Let the ball drop (you might have to move the club slightly). Take careful note of where the ball first strikes the ground. This spot is where you should position the ball in your putting stance.

LEVEL 1 · DRILL 04

CHECK YOUR PUTTERFACE ALIGNMENT AT ADDRESS

Drill 5 (see pp.240–1) touches on aiming the putter correctly, which is not as easily done as you might imagine. A test carried out at a tour event produced some startling results: from a distance of 3 m (3½ yd), over half the professionals failed to aim the putterface within a 2.5 cm (1 in) margin either side of the hole. This drill will ensure that you are always aiming at the target.

1 Crouch down about 3–4 m (3½–4½ yd) away from the hole on a green. Line up the face of your putter so that it is square with the hole.

2 Stand up very slowly and take up your address position. Make very sure that you do not allow the putter to twist at all.
    Study the position of the putterface in relation to the hole. Look back and forth from the putter to the hole several times. Try to memorize the position of the putter in relation to the hole.

3 Hit a putt. If the ball does not travel straight to the hole, you know it is not a problem with your aim and must, therefore, be caused by a crooked stroke. If this is the case, work through Drill 5 (see pp.240–1) to get your stroke back on track.

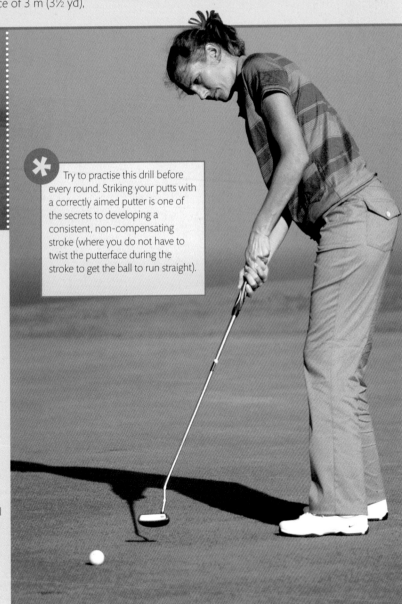

✳ Try to practise this drill before every round. Striking your putts with a correctly aimed putter is one of the secrets to developing a consistent, non-compensating stroke (where you do not have to twist the putterface during the stroke to get the ball to run straight).

LEVEL ONE

LEVEL   DRILL

1·05

FIND THE CORRECT ALIGNMENT TO DEVELOP GOOD STROKE REPETITION

In a professional tournament, you will notice that those at the top of the leaderboard will seem to be sinking every putt within 2 m (2 yd) of the hole. Similarly at club level, in your best rounds, you are likely to have holed your putts like a professional. The following drill focuses your attention on the three key elements of successful short-range putting: putterface alignment at address, swing path, and putterface alignment at impact.

1 Find a straight putt on the green no more than 2 m (2 yd) from the hole. Place two clubs on the green on a straight path to the hole, with about 2.5 cm (1 in) to spare either side of the heel and toe of the putterhead. These two clubs will give you an invaluable visual reference to help you aim the putterface squarely at the hole and will also allow you to monitor the putter's swing path.

2 Place a ball directly between the two clubs, and take up your address position. If the putterface is at 90 degrees to the two parallel clubs, as it should be, you will be aiming straight at the hole. Make sure that the putter tracks a neat path between the rails in your backswing.

* Repeat this drill as often as you can: it allows you to see the correct alignment of the putter and trains you to produce the ideal swing path. If you can, set up two clubs on the carpet at home, both pointing towards a target 60 cm (24 in) away. Then, whenever you have a spare 10 minutes, stroke some putts between the rails to develop a repeatable and well-honed stroke.

3 Swing the putter into the back of the ball, again making sure that it stays within the rails. If the putterface is square at impact, the ball will roll into the hole. Your shoulders, arms, hands, and the club should all be moving together. Try to maintain the triangle formed by your arms and shoulders at address, and adopt a soft grip pressure. Also, try to feel some "lag" (softness in the wrists) as you change direction from backswing to downswing.

LEVEL ONE

KEY CHECKPOINT

The art of reading greens

To read a green proficiently means taking into account a number of factors.

Study the green as you approach it to establish the predominant slope: this will give you a clue as to which way the ball will break. Once on the green, look from behind the ball down the line of the putt. If you crouch down, you will see subtle slopes more easily.

A good place to obtain another reading is from the low side of the hole. Stand a few paces back, midway between the ball and the hole. From this position you can assess how the ball will break as it rolls down the slope. Also look for unevenness close to the hole. The ball will be most affected by undulations when it is rolling at its slowest speed (when it is close to the hole).

Finally, bear in mind that the ball will break more on a fast green than on a slow green: you should generally read more break into your putts in summer, when the greens are most closely mown.

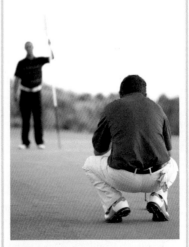

READING THE SLOPE *There are many areas on the green where you can read a putt. Crouching behind the ball is one of the most effective positions.*

LEVEL 1 · DRILL 06

MATCH YOUR BACKSWING TO THE DISTANCE

When you watch good putters in action, it is almost as if there is no "hit" as such; instead, the ball simply gets in the way of the swinging putterhead. This is a useful way to think of a putt, but you can only achieve such a smooth strike if your backswing is of a length appropriate to the length of putt. This drill will help you match the correct length of backswing to whatever putt you are faced with.

1 Stand about 6 m (6½ yd) away from a hole, drop three balls, and address the first. Make a very short backswing: no more than 10 cm (4 in) from the ball. To hole the ball from this position, you will have to jab the putter into the ball with an abrupt movement.

2 With the second ball, make an exaggerated backswing of approximately 50 cm (20 in). To hit the ball the correct distance you will find you have to slow down in the hitting area.

LEVEL ONE

The backswing lengths suggested in this drill relate only to a putt of about 6 m (6½ yd). Try this exercise from various distances around the green, using backswings that are too short, too long, then perfect. In doing so you will learn to recognize the correct backswing-length.

Backswing too long

Backswing too short

3 With the final ball, split the difference between the two backswing lengths employed in steps 2 and 3. You should find that you are able to accelerate the putter smoothly through the hitting area and send the ball the required distance. This movement should feel like a swing, rather than a hit.

KEY CHECKPOINT

Tell yourself: "This putt to win the Open"

It is easy to lose concentration when you practise your putting. The best way to stop this happening is to try to recreate some pressure by simulating a "real life" situation. To do this, tell yourself that the next putt you hit is to win the next competition at your club. Many of today's top professionals have told stories about when they were younger and dreamed of holing a putt "for the Open Championship". A few of them, such as Nick Faldo (in 1987, 1990, and 1992), had the opportunity to do it for real.

As you practise, if you imagine playing an important putt in a major tournament, the pressure is greater, and there is more satisfaction when you hole it. And, if in a competition you are on the last hole with a putt for victory, you have more chance of making it because you will have mentally rehearsed just such a shot.

OPEN WIN *Nick Faldo used to practise his putting telling himself: "this putt to win the Open". He successfully put the theory into practice on three occasions.*

LEVEL DRILL
1·07 LEARN TO HIT THE SWEET SPOT CONSISTENTLY

This drill, like Drill 8 (right) examines the importance of striking the ball consistently out of the sweet spot on the face of your putter. The theory is just the same as in, for example, tennis: if you do not hit the ball out of the centre of the racket, performance is impaired.

1 Take two tee-pegs and use sticky tape to attach them vertically to the face of the putter, so that each is about 2 cm (¾ in) either side of the sweet spot. This spot is clearly marked on almost all modern putters, either by a dot or a line on the top-edge of the putterhead.

2 Hit some putts of no more than 2m (2 yd), trying to strike the ball without making contact with the tee-pegs. If you can do that, you have successfully hit the sweet spot. However, if one of the two tee-pegs becomes trapped between the ball and the putterface, the ball will shoot off at a strange angle (you should feel and hear that something is wrong with the strike, too). Such indications mean that you have hit the putt out of the toe- or heel-end of the putterhead.

3 As you become proficient from short range, gradually increase the length of your stroke, with the sole aim of striking the ball out of the sweet spot – right between the tee-pegs.

* The longer your stroke becomes, the harder it is to avoid hitting the tee-pegs. However, if you can consistently strike the sweet spot, this will have a dramatic effect on your judgement of distance because you can more accurately predict the pace at which the ball will come off the putterface.

LEVEL 1 · DRILL 08

KEEP YOUR EYES DOWN FOR A PERFECT STRIKE

The old adage "keep your head down" has caused more faults in golfers' full swings than any other piece of advice because it prevents a good body pivot and free swing of the arms through impact. But with putting, keeping your head down is an excellent idea. It ensures that your body is steady, which helps keep the putter on a true path back and forth; this in turn promotes a controlled, confident strike. The following practice drill will help you keep your head down as you putt.

✱ Although this drill is great for the practice ground, you cannot place a coin under the ball during a round (it is against the rules). But that does not mean you cannot benefit from the principle learned. When you are on the course, try to think in terms of keeping your head down as you swing the putter through the ball. If you can discipline yourself to do this on every putt, you will strike more putts out of the sweet spot and will send the ball off on the correct line more consistently. Drill 12 in Level Two (see p.249) shows you another way to help keep your head down when you putt.

1 Place a coin under a golf ball, and take up your address position. Make a comfortable-length backswing (the length of putt you hit is not important), keeping your eyes firmly fixed on the top of the ball.

2 As you strike the ball, focus on the coin. Doing so will ensure that your head remains still until the ball has started its journey towards the hole.

LEVEL · DRILL
1·09 STAND AGAINST A WALL TO PRACTISE YOUR STROKE

If there are long intervals between each round you play, your game can become a little rusty. Often it is the short game, especially your putting, that is worst affected. This need not be the case, however. Between games, perform this simple indoor exercise based on the key subjects covered so far in this section: five minutes per day will be of enormous benefit to your game. You will soon notice a difference on the greens.

Head
Practising against a wall trains you to keep your head steady during the stroke

* By regularly rehearsing this exercise between games, your eyes become accustomed to seeing an on line stroke, and your muscles will remember how to produce such a shot. When you do eventually return to the course, you will not spend the first 10 holes struggling to recover your putting stroke.

Ball's path
The ball should travel parallel to the wall

1 Take your putter and adopt your normal address position, with your head resting gently against any of the interior walls in your home. Drop a ball from the bridge of your nose. Wherever it lands is where you should position the ball in your stance (see Drill 3, p.238).

2 Now hit some medium-length – about 4 m (4½ yd) – putts along the wall. Keep an eye on the path of the putter relative to the straight line of the wall or skirting board. The putterhead should initially travel straight back, gradually arcing inside as the backswing becomes longer. It should then return to square at impact, before again tracking an inside path as the putter swings through. If the path of the putterhead is correct, and if the putterface is square at impact, the ball should set off on a line parallel with the wall. If it does not, you know there is something wrong with either the path of your stroke or the alignment of the putterface.

LEVEL DRILL
1·10 HIT A BULL'S-EYE AT THE BACK OF THE HOLE

Rolling the ball in very slowly from short range is a risky business because even the slightest imperfection or subtle slope on the putting surface will knock the ball off course. For putts up to 1 m (1 yd), a firm strike, hitting the ball into the back of the hole, is often the best option. This will help stop the ball from breaking left or right, enabling you to treat most short putts as straight putts, which saves a lot of bother. The following drill will give you the confidence to hole-out from short range with authority.

When you are on the course, faced with a tricky short putt, imagine that there is a tee-peg in the back of the hole. Focus on that mental image, and try to hit the imagined tee-peg. On all but the most severe downhill slopes, this positive approach will usually work far better than trying to dribble the ball softly into the hole. A bolder strike is almost always better.

1 Find a relatively straight short putt on the practice putting green. Stick a tee-peg into the back of the hole. Angle it upwards slightly so that the cup of the tee-peg faces you, like a miniature bull's-eye, as you address the ball.

2 Hit a putt, and try to strike the ball with sufficient force to make it hit the tee-peg before dropping into the hole. Imagine you are using the ball to hammer the tee-peg further into the back of the hole. Repeat with at least 10 balls, so that you become accustomed to hitting your short putts firmly. If you previously "dribbled" short putts into the hole, you should now be striking the ball more firmly.

KEY CHECKPOINT

The hole is wider than you think

When your confidence on the greens is low, the hole can seem half its actual size. You may feel that no putt is short enough to be an easy tap-in. In desperate situations, try to find a new perspective. If you examine the photograph of a standard-size hole shown below you will see that the hole is almost three balls in width (no trick photography is involved). If you visualize the hole in this way, it eases the pressure because you know that there is a margin for error.

HOLE SIZE *When you are putting, it is worth remembering that the hole is much bigger than you might think – almost three-ball widths, in fact.*

Re-test yourself

Before moving to Level Two, take the test on pp.232–3 again. If you have not improved, it is worth revisiting the Level One drills. However, if the performance chart shows that your putting has progressed sufficiently, then you are ready to tackle the more advanced drills in Level Two.

LEVEL 2 · DRILL 11

BECOME ACCUSTOMED TO HOLING PUTTS

If your putting is a little shaky from 1.5–2 m (1½–2 yd), the worst possible way to start your practice routine is by trying to hole putts of this length. This is because you will most likely miss more than you hole, which only serves to lower your confidence. Therefore, before you play your next round, make sure that you work on holing putts, not missing them. The following drill will help you achieve this aim.

*Initially, it may seem that this exercise is too easy. However, the progressive nature of the drill is the secret to its effectiveness. By starting from close range and seeing the ball hit the back of the hole (rather than putting from further back and becoming accustomed to the ball slipping past the hole), you will start to believe that you are a solid putter.

1 Start at a distance from which you feel absolutely confident about holing every putt. Although this distance will vary from one golfer to the next, you will probably want to start about 30 cm (12 in) from the hole.

2 Hit five or six balls into the back of the hole (see Drill 10, p.247). Build a strong mental image of the ball going into the centre of the hole, and let your confidence grow.

Move back another 15cm (6in). Use the same number of balls and work on repeating a positive stroke. Repeat until you are about 1m (1yd) from the hole. Any further back and you run the risk of missing too many putts.

2·12 LISTEN, BUT DO NOT LOOK

LEVEL DRILL

Drill 8 (see p.245) suggests one way to help you keep your head down when you putt. This can be quite easy in practice, but psychologically it is very different during a proper round. Anxiety over a short putt (a frame of mind which simply does not occur in practice) can cause you to look up too soon to see if the ball is going in the hole. But your desperation to see the path of the ball can upset your stroke and usually results in a missed putt. Here is a method guaranteed to stop you looking up too soon.

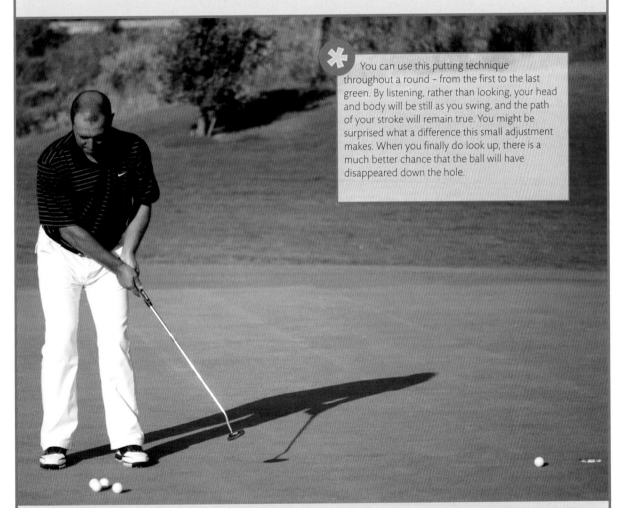

You can use this putting technique throughout a round – from the first to the last green. By listening, rather than looking, your head and body will be still as you swing, and the path of your stroke will remain true. You might be surprised what a difference this small adjustment makes. When you finally do look up, there is a much better chance that the ball will have disappeared down the hole.

1 Set up a short, straight putt of approximately 2 m (2 yd). Make a stroke, and ensure that you do not look up until you hear the sound of the ball dropping into the hole (or the ominous silence of a miss).

2 Work your way through as many balls as time allows. If you are putting well, you will find that you have to empty the hole regularly to make room for more balls to drop in.

LEVEL 2·13 DRILL

PUTT WITH A MIRROR FOR BETTER RESULTS

Having your eyes directly over the ball at address is one of the most important aspects of a good putting action (see Drill 3, p.238). From this position you can swivel your head for the perfect view down the intended line of the putt. If you can see down this line, you will more easily hit along it. This practice drill will not only ensure that your eyes are directly over the ball when you putt but will also give you visual feedback on the alignment of the putter and its path as you swing.

Eye position
As you look down at the ball, you should not be able to see your eyes in the mirror

1 Use a thick, black marker pen (or black tape) to draw two lines on a small mirror: one vertical and one horizontal, so that they form a cross in the centre.
   Place the mirror on a flat portion of a green (or on the carpet at your home). The horizontal line should point directly at the target. Position a ball on the mirror, in the centre of the cross.

2 Address the ball, and check your reflection in the mirror. Your eyes should be hidden by the ball.

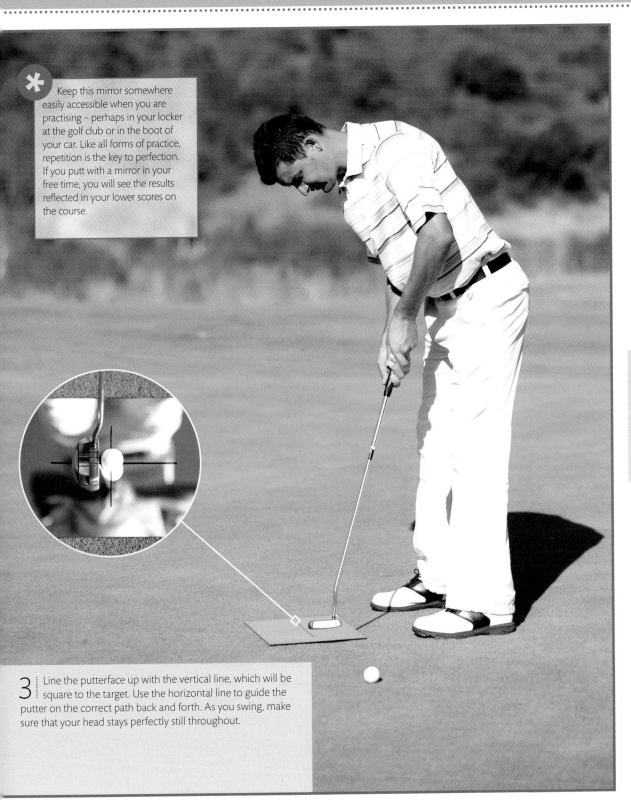

✳ Keep this mirror somewhere easily accessible when you are practising – perhaps in your locker at the golf club or in the boot of your car. Like all forms of practice, repetition is the key to perfection. If you putt with a mirror in your free time, you will see the results reflected in your lower scores on the course.

3 Line the putterface up with the vertical line, which will be square to the target. Use the horizontal line to guide the putter on the correct path back and forth. As you swing, make sure that your head stays perfectly still throughout.

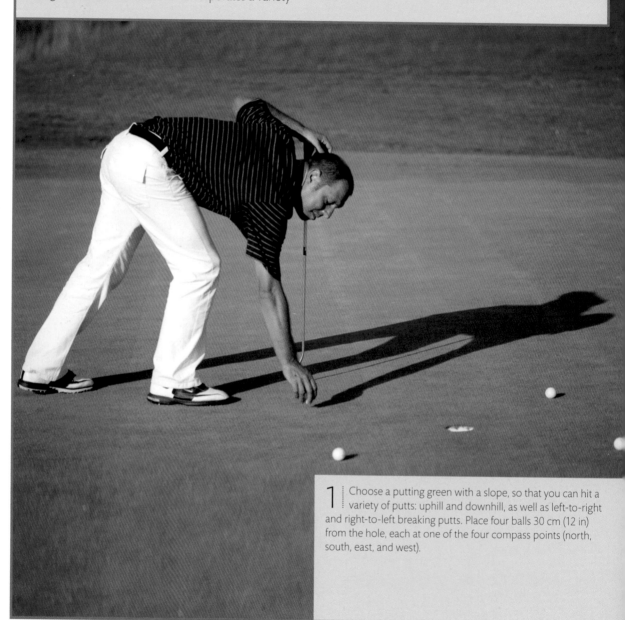

LEVEL DRILL
2·14

WORK YOUR WAY AROUND THE COMPASS

This is a more advanced variation on Drill 11 (see p.248), and is also designed to improve your holing-out skills. As this exercise incorporates a variety of different breaking putts, it is one of the best ways to improve your short-range putting skills.

1 Choose a putting green with a slope, so that you can hit a variety of putts: uphill and downhill, as well as left-to-right and right-to-left breaking putts. Place four balls 30 cm (12 in) from the hole, each at one of the four compass points (north, south, east, and west).

* You can add a competitive edge to this drill by keeping track of the number of consecutively holed putts, and striving to beat your record. If you can get into the mid-teens without missing you are doing well. Any number in the 20s is exceptional.

2 Putt each ball into the hole. Having started at such close range, you will immediately develop the confidence that comes with hitting the ball into the back of the hole every time. Complete one "set", move back 15 cm (6 in), place four balls at the compass points around the hole, and again try to hole each putt. If you succeed, move another 15 cm (6 in) further from the hole, and repeat the process.

LEVEL DRILL

2·15

GIVE YOURSELF A DECENT BREAK

The most common problem with putts on slopes is not so much reading the amount of break, which is a talent within everyone's grasp (see the Key Checkpoint on p.241), but in actually trusting what you see and committing yourself to striking the ball along your chosen line. The following exercise addresses both of these problems, and will give you extra confidence when tackling breaking putts.

1 Take eight or nine balls and your putter to a green with a slope. Place the balls at regular intervals in a gentle arc away from the hole. Start from about 2 m (2 yd) and go back as far as the edge of the green.

2 Beginning with the ball closest to the hole, carefully read each putt before hitting the ball. As the ball rolls towards the hole, take note how much the putt breaks. Because you are always working along an extension of the same line, as you hit the balls, you will start to see the break more clearly in your mind's-eye.

This practice exercise improves your ability to judge the pace and line of a breaking putt by encouraging you to form a clear mental picture of the slope and its effect upon the ball. This means that your confidence will grow, and you will become accustomed to making a committed stroke that sets the ball off along your chosen line. Although you may not hole every putt you look at, if you trust your judgement you will at least make a good, positive stroke. This in itself will significantly improve your performance on the greens.

LEVEL TWO

LEVEL **2**·**16** DRILL

TREAT EVERY PUTT AS A STRAIGHT PUTT

Drill 15 explained that missing a breaking putt often results from not committing yourself to the line you chose. The slightest doubt or indecision usually manifests itself in a tentative stroke. The following drill should help avoid this tendency. It is based on the principle of treating every putt as a straight putt.

✱ When you practise this drill, you are effectively treating every putt as a straight putt, allowing the contours of the green to sweep the ball towards the hole. This simplifies the whole business of break putting.

1 With your putter in hand, find a green with obvious slopes on it. Set yourself up with a putt about 5 m (5½ yd) from the hole. Read the green to see how much break there is on the putt (see the Key Checkpoint on p.241).

Decide on the line along which you want the ball to start. Visualize a secondary target on an extension of that line. Therefore, on a putt where you see 30 cm (12 in) of right-to-left break, imagine that there is a target 30 cm (12 in) to the right of the hole.

2 Make a few practice putting strokes, and focus on the imaginary target. Hit the putt at that target: the hole becomes of secondary importance.

LEVEL DRILL
2·17 BRUSH FORWARD TO CHECK YOUR AIM AND STROKE

The following exercise will reveal two key pieces of information about your putting stroke: whether the face of the putter is aimed correctly, and if the path of your stroke is on the correct line. Many of the world's leading tour professionals have been known to rehearse this exercise – Nick Faldo went so far as to credit it as one of the secrets behind his 1992 Open Championship victory, one of the finest putting weeks of a long, successful career.

✱ Where the ball goes when you brush it forward will tell you much about your putting action. If the ball travels into the middle of the hole, you know that the putterface was square at address and that your stroke was on line in the through swing – two key elements in a successful putt. If the ball goes to the left of the hole, either the putterface was closed at address, or you pulled the shot by swinging the putter to the left in the through swing. If the ball finishes right, the face was open at address or you swung the putter to the right.

1 Locate a green, and set up a straight putt about 1 m (1 yd) from the hole. Address the ball as you would normally, with the putterface sitting behind the ball, square to the hole.

2 Now brush the ball towards the hole with a smooth forward motion. Do not make any backswing at all.

LEVEL 2·18 DRILL PUTT ONE BALL PAST THE NEXT

Most golfers are quick to blame their short putting when they frequently three-putt, but, more often than not, the real problem lies in not getting the long-range approach putt close enough to the hole. The following drill will help solve this irritating problem, training you to be a better judge of the running speed of the ball across a green.

1 Take 12 or so balls and putt the first one about 5 m (5½ yd) across the green.

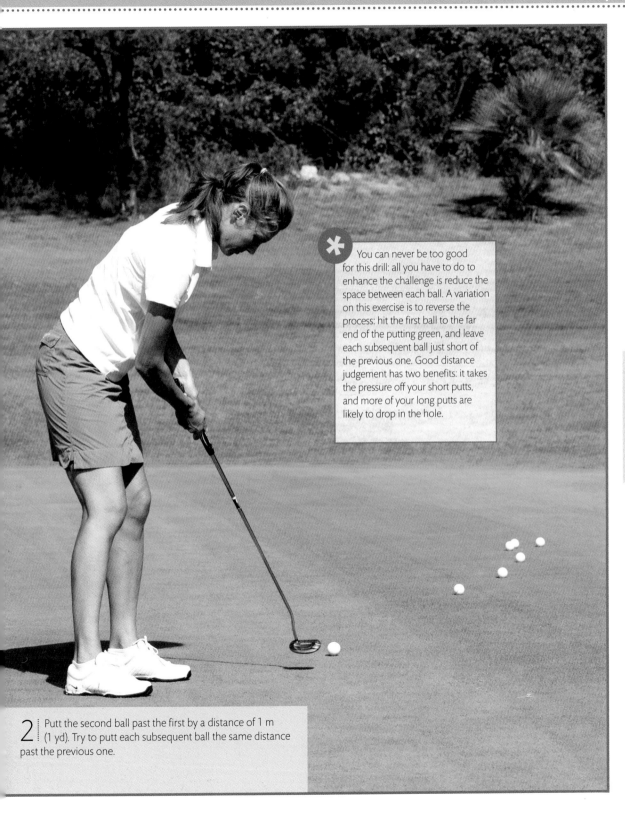

* You can never be too good for this drill: all you have to do to enhance the challenge is reduce the space between each ball. A variation on this exercise is to reverse the process: hit the first ball to the far end of the putting green, and leave each subsequent ball just short of the previous one. Good distance judgement has two benefits: it takes the pressure off your short putts, and more of your long putts are likely to drop in the hole.

2 | Putt the second ball past the first by a distance of 1 m (1 yd). Try to putt each subsequent ball the same distance past the previous one.

LEVEL **2**·DRILL**19**

TRY A "DRESS REHEARSAL"
OF THE IDEAL STROKE

For too many golfers, the practice putting stroke is little more than a casual, almost aimless, waft of the putter back and forth. Often it has no purpose or resemblance to the actual stroke. Make your practice putting stroke really count by rehearsing the following exercise and making it a permanent fixture in your putting routine.

1 Drop a ball anywhere on the green, and go through your usual process of reading which way the putt is likely to break (see the Key Checkpoint on p.241).

Once you have decided on a line, assume your normal posture, but do not address the ball just yet.

2 Make a few practice swings while all the time looking at the hole. Try to match what you feel will be the ideal length of stroke with the visual messages received from your view of the hole. Your backswing should be of a length that enables you to smoothly accelerate the putter through the hitting zone (see Drill 6, pp.242–3).

* As you work on this drill you should develop a much better feel for distance. If you think of your practice strokes as "dress rehearsals" for the actual stroke, you are more likely to putt well when it matters most.

3 When you are happy with your practice swing, address the ball, repeat the stroke you were rehearsing, and let the ball get in the way of the swinging putter (you should be looking at the ball now, not the hole).

4 Repeat this routine several times, but for each putt, drop the ball at a different distance from the hole.

LEVEL   DRILL

2·20   HIT UP-AND-DOWN PUTTS
TO IMPROVE YOUR SPEED

As was indicated in Drill 18 (see pp.258–9), the main reason for three-putting is a poorly judged approach putt from long range. This is exacerbated when slopes come into play because golfers often struggle to adjust their stroke accordingly. The following exercise is designed to improve your judgement of speed but, unlike Drill 18, it has the added difficulty of uphill and downhill putts.

1   Find a green with a pronounced slope right across the putting surface. You will need only three balls, your putter, and two tee-pegs.
     Place one of the tee-pegs in the green 1 m (1 yd) short of the top of the slope and the other the same distance from the bottom of the slope. To make this exercise truly effective, there should be at least a 12 m (13 yd) gap between the tee-pegs (otherwise the drill is not demanding enough).

2   Place three balls at whichever end you wish to start from, and putt towards the tee-peg at the opposite end of the green. Take your time over each putt, and try to leave the balls as close as possible to the target.

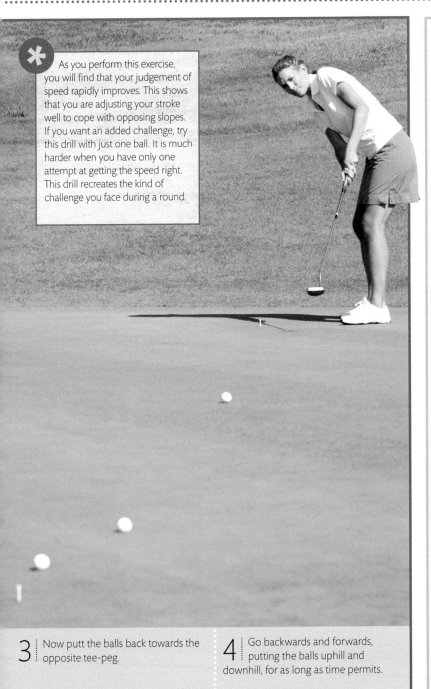

✳ As you perform this exercise, you will find that your judgement of speed rapidly improves. This shows that you are adjusting your stroke well to cope with opposing slopes. If you want an added challenge, try this drill with just one ball. It is much harder when you have only one attempt at getting the speed right. This drill recreates the kind of challenge you face during a round.

LEVEL TWO

3 Now putt the balls back towards the opposite tee-peg.

4 Go backwards and forwards, putting the balls uphill and downhill, for as long as time permits.

KEY CHECKPOINT

Speed is everything

To give your ball the optimum chance of dropping into the hole, irrespective of the putting distance, scientific research has shown that the ball should be moving fast enough to travel 45–60 cm (17½–24 in) past the hole. This ideal "running speed" ensures that the ball holds its line as it approaches the hole, when subtle breaks can all too easily knock the putt off line. Bear this in mind next time you size up a putt. It is a good idea to visualize an imaginary hole beyond the actual hole. This technique will encourage you to get the ball running at the perfect speed.

RUNNING SPEED *The ideal pace for holing a putt is such that if the ball did miss, it would travel 45–60 cm (17½–24 in) beyond the hole.*

LEVEL DRILL

2·21

AVOID EXCESS WRIST ACTION IN YOUR PUTTING STROKE

The conventional putting method involves a stroke controlled primarily by the shoulders and arms, with a small amount of wrist action – referred to as "lag" (see Drill 5, pp.240–1). This wrist movement is desirable because it promotes good rhythm and a smooth acceleration of the putter through the hitting zone.

However, excessive wrist action is sometimes the cause of erratic putting, as it can upset the alignment of the putterface and disrupt your ability to control the distance of your putts. This exercise will help keep your wrist action within sensible limits.

1 Address a ball as normal, and trap another ball between your right wrist and the top of the grip on your putter.

2 Hit some putts of about 8 m (8½ yd), making sure that the ball remains in place throughout the stroke. This prevents excessive wrist movement, which should promote a smooth, on line stroke. If the ball falls to the ground, there is too much wrist action in your putting stroke.

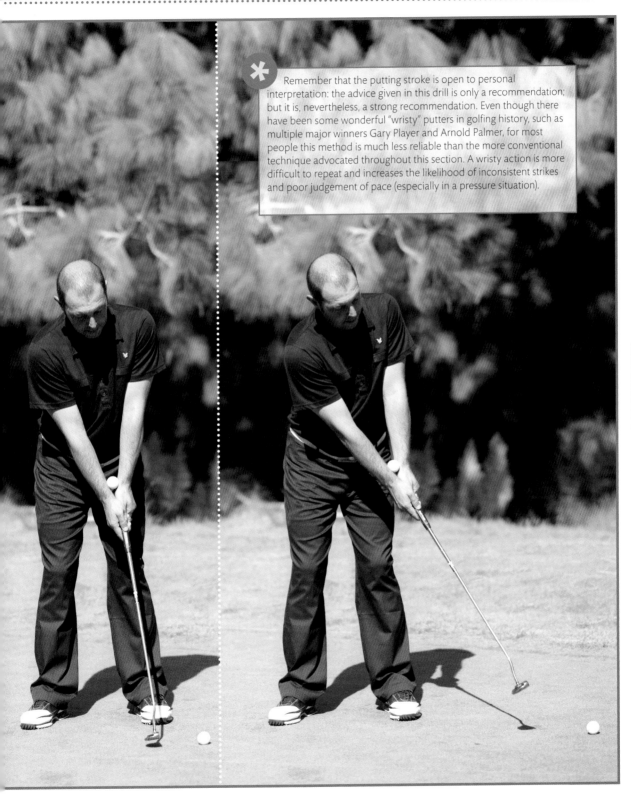

Remember that the putting stroke is open to personal interpretation: the advice given in this drill is only a recommendation; but it is, nevertheless, a strong recommendation. Even though there have been some wonderful "wristy" putters in golfing history, such as multiple major winners Gary Player and Arnold Palmer, for most people this method is much less reliable than the more conventional technique advocated throughout this section. A wristy action is more difficult to repeat and increases the likelihood of inconsistent strikes and poor judgement of pace (especially in a pressure situation).

LEVEL TWO

LEVEL   DRILL

2·22 TRY THIS LONG-RANGE TEST

This section has already introduced two exercises devoted to improving your long-range putting: Drill 18 (see pp.258–9) and Drill 20 (see pp.262–3). As this part of your game is so important, here is another, in the form of a mini-test. The results will give you an honest assessment of your long-range putting skills.

(see pp.258–9) and Drill 20 (see pp.262–3).

LEVEL TWO

This drill trains you to impart the correct pace to the ball, which gives you the best chance of not three-putting – your first priority when you are a long way from the hole. You will also stand a better chance of holing the occasional long-range putt.

1 Place any club 65 cm (26 in) behind a hole, and retreat to a distance from which you feel confident that you will not three-putt. From this position, putt five balls towards the hole.

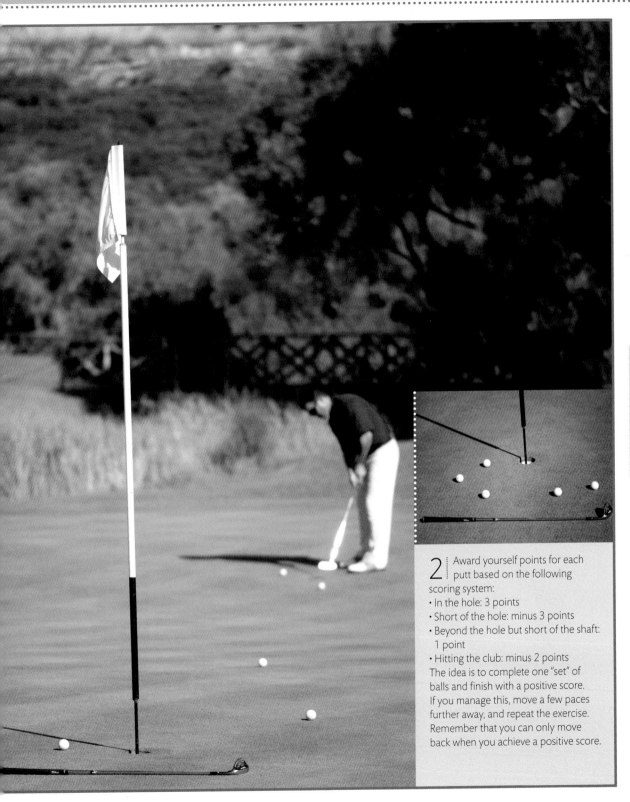

2 │ Award yourself points for each putt based on the following scoring system:
• In the hole: 3 points
• Short of the hole: minus 3 points
• Beyond the hole but short of the shaft: 1 point
• Hitting the club: minus 2 points
The idea is to complete one "set" of balls and finish with a positive score. If you manage this, move a few paces further away, and repeat the exercise. Remember that you can only move back when you achieve a positive score.

LEVEL 2·23 DRILL

HIT TO A SMALLER TARGET TO PUT THE HOLE INTO PERSPECTIVE

Visualization can have a wonderful effect on your game, as the following practice drill will illustrate. The exercise, which will give you a new perspective on holing-out, has maximum benefit if it is performed just before you start a round.

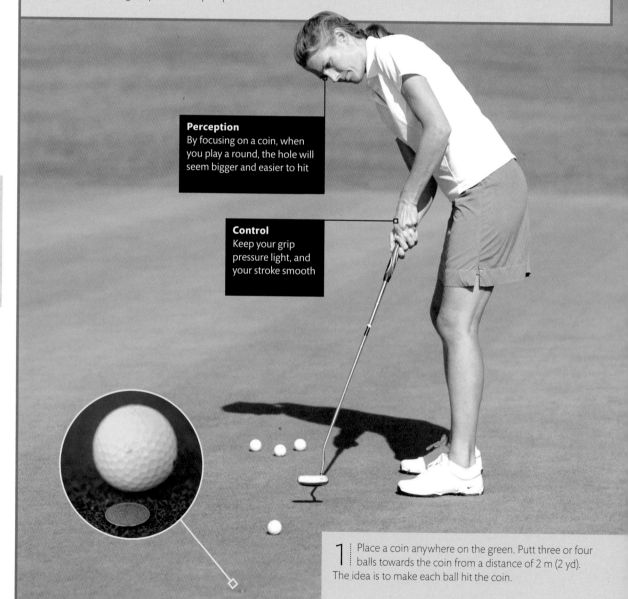

Perception
By focusing on a coin, when you play a round, the hole will seem bigger and easier to hit

Control
Keep your grip pressure light, and your stroke smooth

1 Place a coin anywhere on the green. Putt three or four balls towards the coin from a distance of 2 m (2 yd). The idea is to make each ball hit the coin.

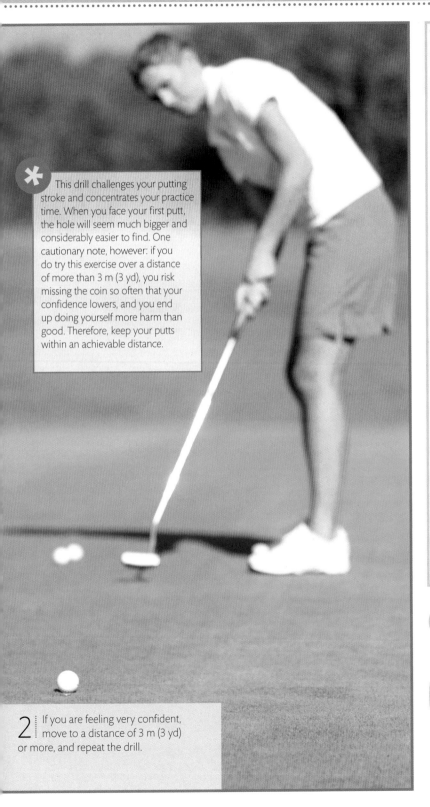

* This drill challenges your putting stroke and concentrates your practice time. When you face your first putt, the hole will seem much bigger and considerably easier to find. One cautionary note, however: if you do try this exercise over a distance of more than 3 m (3 yd), you risk missing the coin so often that your confidence lowers, and you end up doing yourself more harm than good. Therefore, keep your putts within an achievable distance.

2 If you are feeling very confident, move to a distance of 3 m (3 yd) or more, and repeat the drill.

KEY CHECKPOINT

"Tunnel vision" provides a clearer focus

Seeing things in your peripheral vision can distract you when you are trying to focus on reading the line of a putt – a time when you want to be completely concentrated. To rectify this problem, shield your eyes by placing your hands around your face to create a "tunnel vision" effect. This will help you read the green and will lessen the danger of distractions upsetting your concentration. If you find that your mind is wandering, try narrowing your field of vision: many professionals do just the same.

FOCUS *If you blinker your eyes when you are reading a putt, it will help block out unwanted distractions. This green-reading technique will also aid your concentration.*

LEVEL TWO

* Re-test yourself

Before moving to Level Three, take the test on pp.232–3 again. If you have not improved, it is worth revisiting the Level Two drills. However, if the performance chart shows that your putting has progressed sufficiently, then you are ready to tackle the more advanced drills in Level Three.

LEVEL 3·DRILL 24 MAKE YOUR STROKE FLOW

Here is one of the best ways to promote a free swing of the putter in your stroke: a prerequisite for good judgement of distance. Although this exercise relates to one of the fundamental putting issues, because it requires you to putt with one hand only, a reasonable level of skill is needed.

*After a few attempts you will be pleasantly surprised at the quality of your strike and how well you are judging distance – all using only your right hand. When you reintroduce your left hand and putt as normal, you will find that your stroke is less inhibited and not restricted by the tendency to guide the putter back and forth (which is a very damaging fault).

1 Grip the putter with your right hand, and let your left hand hang down by your side (or put it in your pocket).

2 Stroke some balls across the green. Keep your grip pressure light, make a free swing with your right arm, and let your wrist hinge slightly in response to the momentum of the putter changing direction from backswing to followthrough. This softness in your wrist encourages the putter to flow back and forth, whereas a stiff-wristed action tends to lack fluidity and makes it difficult to control the pace of the putt.

3 Think about pace rather than concentrating on a specific target. Have in mind an approximate distance, and try to group four or five balls as close together as possible.

FOR CLOSE-RANGE PUTTS
BE VERY PRECISE

Drill 11 in the "Pitching" section (see p.123) stressed the need for accurate approach shots. The same principle applies to close-range putts. Just as for pitch shots, where you need to aim for the flag rather than just the green, with short putts it can help to focus on a single point, not just the hole. This drill will teach you to narrow your focus to a very specific target.

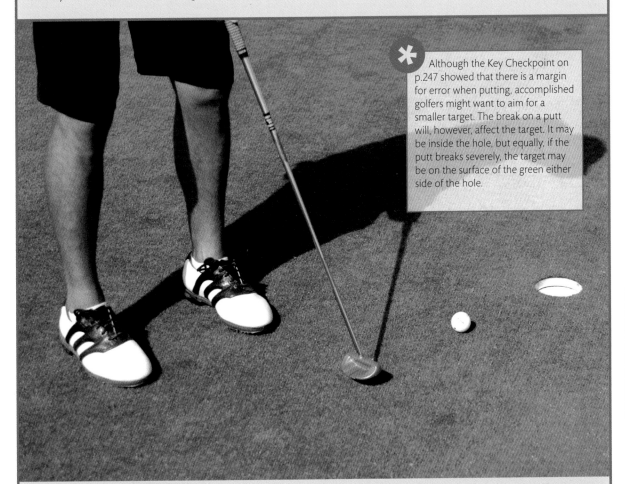

* Although the Key Checkpoint on p.247 showed that there is a margin for error when putting, accomplished golfers might want to aim for a smaller target. The break on a putt will, however, affect the target. It may be inside the hole, but equally, if the putt breaks severely, the target may be on the surface of the green either side of the hole.

1 Set yourself up with a straight putt no more than 2 m (2 yd) from the hole.
Address the ball. But rather than focusing merely on the hole, set your sights on a smaller detail within the hole, such as a slight imperfection on the rim of the cup.

2 With the specific target identified in step 1 fresh in your mind, switch your attention back to the ball and, without delay, make a stroke. Do not raise your head early to watch the run of the ball. Instead trust your stroke, and look up only to see if the ball has found your specific target.

LEVEL 3·DRILL 26

HOVER YOUR PUTTER TO PROMOTE A SMOOTH STROKE

Whenever you are under pressure or feeling nervous, it is extremely easy to lose the smoothness and rhythm of your putting stroke, which can be disastrous. Try the following exercise on the practice putting green, then use it on the course whenever you feel especially in need of a steady hand and a sure stroke.

1 Assume your putting posture, but without a ball on the ground. Raise the putterhead off the ground so that it hovers fractionally above the putting surface. Focus on maintaining a soft grip pressure.

2 Make a couple of practice putting strokes. Do not let the putter come into contact with the ground at any time.

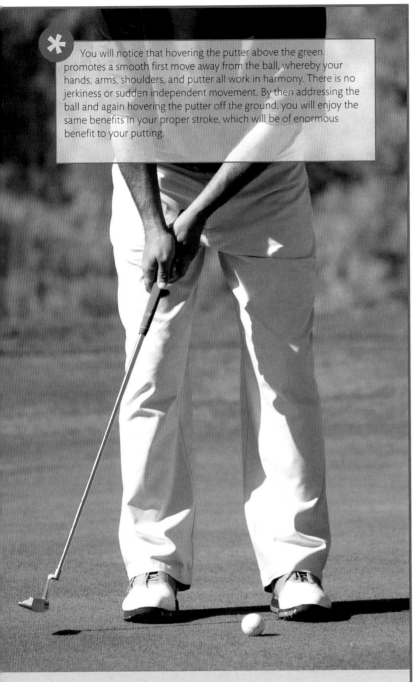

You will notice that hovering the putter above the green promotes a smooth first move away from the ball, whereby your hands, arms, shoulders, and putter all work in harmony. There is no jerkiness or sudden independent movement. By then addressing the ball and again hovering the putter off the ground, you will enjoy the same benefits in your proper stroke, which will be of enormous benefit to your putting.

3 Without altering your grip pressure, hover the putter behind the ball, and make a stroke from this position. Repeat this procedure – hover, practice stroke, hover, proper stroke – several times.

KEY CHECKPOINT

How to cope with fast putts

On fast greens or with downhill putts, you cannot afford to make an abrupt or jerky stroke. Every move has to be smooth in order to maximize your control and to improve your chances of trickling the ball into or near the hole. (For fast downhill putts, it is not advisable to give the ball enough force to travel beyond the hole, as with a normal putt.)

Although it would be unwise to remodel your stroke just to play one type of putt, there is a change you can introduce to your technique that will help with fast putts, without making your stroke feel strange. The alteration involves striking the ball from nearer the toe of the putter, rather than from the centre. This means that you can make your regular stroke (as if the green was flat) but, because you are not striking the ball from the sweet spot, less energy is produced at impact, and the ball leaves the face at a slower speed. If you try hitting the ball towards the toe, you will be better equipped to tackle fast putts.

LESS SPEED *On very quick putts, striking the ball towards the toe of the putter deadens the blow so that the ball does not race past the hole.*

LEVEL DRILL

3·27 WATCH YOUR HANDS, NOT THE BALL

Here is a great drill that will help if you have a tendency to freeze over short putts – an affliction caused by anxiety, which ruins any chance of making a smooth, on line stroke. Try this exercise to regain your confidence and composure.

Fresh focus
Look at your hands as you swing the putter back and forth

As a practice routine, this drill can be incredibly beneficial. It completely removes the tendency to hit at the ball, which is often at the root of short-putt problems. Instead, concentrating on your hands promotes a smooth, controlled stroke. It also has the added benefit of stopping you from looking up too soon, which is a sure-fire way to miss a short putt – see drills 8 (p.245) and 12 (p.249). But if you keep your eyes fixed firmly on your hands, you will regain your confidence and your stroke. You may even want to try this technique out on the course to help you during a round.

Smooth stroke
By not looking at the ball you stand a better chance of making a flowing putt

Swing, not a hit
This drill also promotes a swing, rather than a hit, and this produces a better roll on the ball

1 Stand on a green 3–4 m (3–4½ yd) from the hole. Practice your putting stroke before addressing the ball, and watch your hands as they swing smoothly back and forth (instead of looking at the putterhead or the ground as you would ordinarily).

2 Now address the ball, and when you are satisfied with your aim, posture, and alignment, switch your attention back to your hands. As in step 1, keep an eye on your hands as they swing back and forth in your stroke.

3 Repeat step 2 several times. Try to concentrate only on the quality of your swing, rather than thinking about the ball (holing the putt is not the principal aim of this drill). By not looking at the ball, it is easier to control the amount of force and acceleration in your stroke.

LEVEL DRILL
3·28 MAKE A CENTURY ON THE GREEN

The following drill is one that Colin Montgomerie used to practise every day without fail when he was at university in the US in the mid 1980s. It requires application, dedication, and concentration, but the rewards are tremendous.

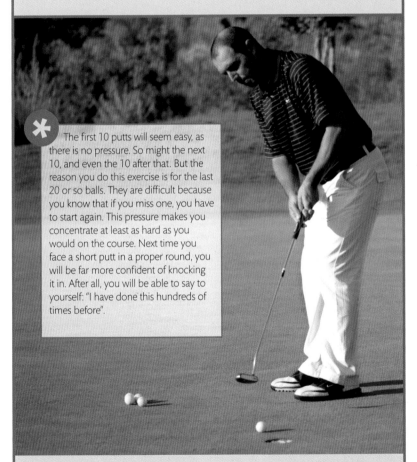

✱ The first 10 putts will seem easy, as there is no pressure. So might the next 10, and even the 10 after that. But the reason you do this exercise is for the last 20 or so balls. They are difficult because you know that if you miss one, you have to start again. This pressure makes you concentrate at least as hard as you would on the course. Next time you face a short putt in a proper round, you will be far more confident of knocking it in. After all, you will be able to say to yourself: "I have done this hundreds of times before".

1 Set yourself up with a putt you feel confident of holing. Just less than one club-length is a good distance for an accomplished player. If you lack confidence on the greens, place the ball a little closer to the hole.

2 Knock in one putt after another from the same spot, emptying the hole when necessary. Keep count as you go, and try to hole 100 consecutive putts. The twist is, if you miss a putt, you have to start again from one. The pressure intensifies greatly as you near the 100 mark.

KEY CHECKPOINT
The long putter is more than just a gimmick

If you decide to try a long putter – a club that caused a furore among traditionalists when it first came to prominence in the late 1980s – your level of success will depend on your address position. Firstly, anchor the butt-end of the putter either under your chin or against your chest. Then grip the club lightly between the thumb and forefinger of your right hand, which acts as the guiding hand. Many professionals work on the basis that the position of the right palm should mirror the putterface. This makes it easier to keep the stroke on line and also establishes a relationship between your hand and the putter – where your right hand goes the putterface follows. Your left hand should form a loose, "fist-like" grip at the top of the club's grip. Think of a grandfather clock, and imagine your left hand as the hinge and the shaft as the pendulum.

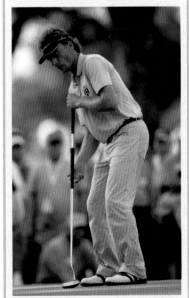

FREE SWING *When using a long putter, your right hand should guide the club back and forth like the pendulum on a grandfather clock.*

LEVEL 3·DRILL 29

CROSS YOUR HANDS IF YOUR STROKE IS NOT WORKING

If you are unhappy with your putting performance, do not be afraid to experiment with a less conventional stroke. The following exercise involves one of the most popular "alternative" methods of putting. Tour professionals such as Ireland's Padraig Harrington and Jim Furyk of the US have putted like this from an early age, and many other players have enjoyed success on the greens using this method.

1 Place your right hand above your left on the putting grip. The palms should still face one another, with each thumb pointing down the centre of the shaft. The reverse overlap (see Drill 1, pp.234–5) is also still apparent, only with this grip the forefinger of the right hand rests on the fingers of the left hand, rather than the other way around.

2 Start with a medium-length putt of approximately 6–7 m (6½–7½ yd). Rock your shoulders to move the putter back and forth. A soft grip is essential because, as you take the club back and then change direction into the downswing, you will experience that all-important "lag" (see Drill 5, pp.240–1). This softness in your wrists heightens the sensation of smooth acceleration into the ball and helps maintain the correct relationship between your hands and the putter as the club swings through the hitting area.

3 Continue to hit putts, and you should start to notice that your left wrist is more inclined to maintain its original angle through the hitting zone, which in turn helps maintain the alignment of the putterface. The putter is therefore less likely to open or close at impact, which means more of your putts will start on the desired line.

✱ In a sense, this technique involves more of a "pulling through" motion than the "swinging through" action of a conventional stroke. Although this grip will feel strange at first (your hands are in the opposite positions to every other golf stroke you play), it should not adversely affect the quality of your stroke. Indeed, many exponents of this method claim it is easier to rock your shoulders more naturally, which aids a consistent stroke. Also, the fact that this technique is very much arms-and-shoulders dominated, with the wrists moving barely at all throughout the stroke, means that it is simple to repeat. Although this technique will not be to everyone's taste, if you struggle on the greens you might find that, with a little practice, it works better for you than the conventional method. It is certainly worth trying.

Hands
The left hand is above the right

Hands
The left hand is below the right

Conventional method   **Crossed-hands method**

EXPERIMENT WITH PACE AND LINE

Drills 15 and 16 (see pp.254–6), as well as the Key Checkpoint on p.241, suggested that judging breaking putts is not an exact science. There is always more than one line into the hole, and which route you choose depends entirely on the amount of speed you apply to the ball (a softly struck putt breaks more than a putt struck firmly). Here is a useful exercise that will reveal the relationship between pace and line, enhancing your visualization and touch on breaking putts.

* This exercise will teach you what you can and cannot do with breaking putts, and will give you more confidence when dealing with breaking putts during a round. When faced with a breaking putt, use your imagination to pick whichever line you feel most comfortable with, and match that line with the right pace.

1 Find a 4-m (4½-yd) putt, where there is an obvious break from left-to-right or right-to-left.

2 Try to hole 3 or 4 putts from the same spot, hitting each ball on a different line and varying the speed of the stroke. For example, with the first ball, try to "straighten" the putt by striking it firmly so that there will be very little break. And with the next putt, stroke the ball so as to just trickle it into the hole, allowing for much more break than with the previous shot.

3 Continue in this fashion for as long as time permits. As you practise, keep trying to hole putts while always experimenting with different paces and lines.

THE PERFECT PUTT

There are no genuinely poor putters in the upper echelons of the professional game, but to win a European Order of Merit title and play Ryder Cup golf – as has Sweden's Robert Karlsson – you have to be an exceptional putter. His putting stroke is simple and contains three ingredients for success. The putterface is square at impact, swinging on a path that corresponds with the intended line of the putt, and at the absolute perfect speed. On top of that, Robert reads greens as well as any other top player, which means he produces a great stroke and invariably starts the ball on the correct line. It is a formidable combination, hence Robert's level of success.

* ONE THING these pictures cannot quite convey is the wonderful rhythm of a good putting stroke. The putter moves briskly but smoothly back and through. There is no hit as such, just smooth acceleration and letting the ball get in the way of the putter – a wonderful final thought.

1 ADDRESS
Robert is uncommonly tall for a golfer, standing at 1.96 m (6 ft 5 in), but there is nothing unorthodox about his address position. The grip is neutral, with the palms facing one another in the form of a very comfortable and correct grip. The stance is quite narrow, but that is typical of most top players. The key thing is that Robert positions his eyes directly over the golf ball. Finally, notice how comfortable Robert looks: there is no sign of tension in this, golf's ultimate feel shot.

2 TAKEAWAY
Robert's shoulders, arms, hands and the putter all move away together to produce a smooth and nicely synchronized start to the takeaway. The putter-head stays very low to the ground – perfect! A useful method of keeping the lower half of the body stable, as Robert does, is to keep the knees very still.

3 TRANSITION
Note that Robert's wrists do not hinge independently and his hands stay relaxed. This means that when he makes the transition from backswing to downswing, there is a softness in the wrists that causes the putter to momentarily lag behind the hands, rather like a mini-version of the chip shot played by Ian Poulter. This ensures that the putter does not overtake the hands at impact, which would cause the face to close and the ball to go left.

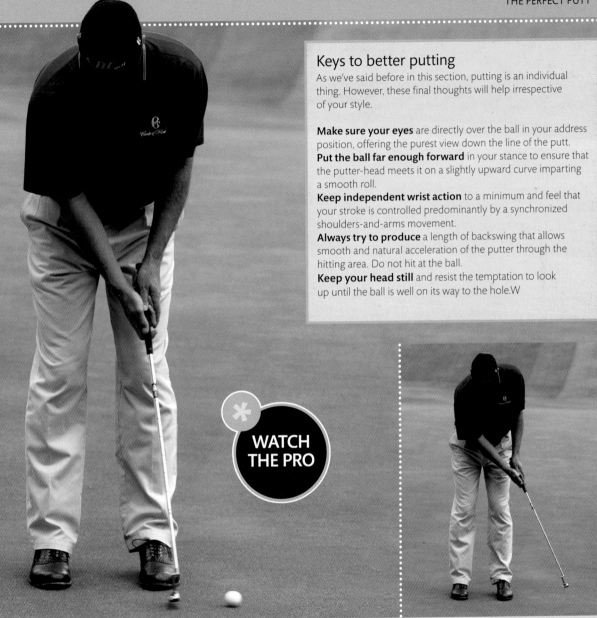

Keys to better putting

As we've said before in this section, putting is an individual thing. However, these final thoughts will help irrespective of your style.

Make sure your eyes are directly over the ball in your address position, offering the purest view down the line of the putt.
Put the ball far enough forward in your stance to ensure that the putter-head meets it on a slightly upward curve imparting a smooth roll.
Keep independent wrist action to a minimum and feel that your stroke is controlled predominantly by a synchronized shoulders-and-arms movement.
Always try to produce a length of backswing that allows smooth and natural acceleration of the putter through the hitting area. Do not hit at the ball.
Keep your head still and resist the temptation to look up until the ball is well on its way to the hole.W

WATCH THE PRO

4 | IMPACT

In putting, the impact position should be identical to the set-up. Study this image and you'll certainly struggle to discern any significant differences, save for the movement of the ball leaving the putterface. A point to note is that the putter has travelled just beyond the bottom of its swing arc at the moment of impact, which produces a slight upward strike that helps impart a good roll on the ball. Robert's head is steady as a rock, ensuring that no unwanted upper body movement can upset the perfect path of the putter into and through impact.

5 | FOLLOWTHROUGH

You can see that the putter-head finishes higher in the followthrough than it ever reached in the backswing, which is a product of smooth acceleration and an upward strike. Only now does Robert's head come up, affording a view of the ball heading inexorably towards the hole.

CHAPTER TWO

FAULTS AND FIXES

THE PREVIOUS CHAPTER encompassed just about every conceivable aspect of developing a repeatable, effective golf swing and a purposeful short game. However, no matter how hard you work on your technique, there are times when faults creep in, resulting in wayward shots. Such is the nature of the game at every level, from the bottom to the very top. Consequently, this chapter offers "trouble-shooting" advice that will provide useful fixes for those irritating faults. All the prime suspects come under the spotlight – essentially, ten of the most common problems. This chapter explains how and why such faults occur and, crucially, demonstrates a swift and effective way to cure them.

THE SLICE

This is the most common fault of all – the bête noire of thousands of golfers the world over. A slice is a shot where the ball starts on a course to the left of the target and swerves, often quite dramatically, from left to right through the air. Because the problem is made more acute by a lack of loft, the biggest slices are hit with straight-faced clubs such as the driver, 3-wood, and long irons.

Swing path
Maintain an inside line of attack in your downswing

Feet
Align your feet parallel to the target line

✱ An open clubface at impact is often the result of not releasing the club properly (see p.27). Soften the pressure in your grip to promote a free-flowing "swish" of the clubhead. This helps square the face at impact. But, if this does not work for you, an alternative is suggested in the "Off the Tee" section (see Drill 10, p.40).

FAULT: POORLY ALIGNED SET-UP
It is hard to say which fault comes first – an open clubface or an out-to-in swing path. One thing is certain, however: these problems arise from a poor address position. The typical slicer is aligned to the left of the target, and the swing path simply follows the lines established at address.

Out-to-in swing path

Sidespin

Open clubface

Target line

FIX: TRAIN AN ON LINE ATTACK
To cure a slice you must start by straightening your address position. Stand square to the target line, with your shoulders and feet in parallel alignment. This will promote a more correct path in your backswing. Then attempt to strike the ball so that it starts on a course to the right of the target line, encouraging an inside path of attack into impact. Also feel that you rotate your forearms through impact to promote an aggressive release of the club. Together, these measures will help to eradicate a slice.

WHAT CAUSES A SLICE?
The cause of a slice is an open clubface combined with an out-to-in swing path (see pp.26–7), whereby the club travels across the target line through the hitting area. This swing path causes the ball to travel left initially, and the open clubface delivers a glancing blow that imparts sidespin, which causes the ball to swerve to the right through the air.

THE HOOK

This shot is sometimes described as the "good player's bad shot" because the hands are very active through the hitting area. This is generally desirable, yet an incorrect swing path and closed clubface leave the ball flying well off line. With a hooked shot, the ball begins on a path to the right of the target and then moves right-to-left through the air. As with the slice, the problem is exaggerated by a lack of loft on the clubface, hence the biggest hooks occur with the driver.

* If, once you have aligned your swing path correctly, you see your first shots flying to the left, the clubface is still closed. Check your left-hand grip and make sure that you can see only two knuckles (see Drill 11, p.41). This should work the clubface into a more neutral position at impact, culminating in a straighter ball-flight.

Obstacle
Use an obstacle such as a headcover to encourage an on line swing path

FAULT: TRAPPED ON THE INSIDE
Typically with a hooked shot, the tendency is to slide your hips (instead of unwinding them) towards the target in your downswing. This leaves your hands, arms, and the club trapped too much on the inside. Instinctively, this feels as if the swing path will cause the ball to fly to the right; in an attempt to recover the situation, your hands become over-active, causing the clubface to close and the shot to hook.

In-to-out swing path

Sidespin

Closed clubface

Target line

FIX: CORRECT YOUR SWING PATH
To eliminate the excessive inside-the-line attack and to train a more on line swing path through impact, practise with an obstruction, such as a headcover, on the ground behind the ball and 15cm (6 in) inside the target line. The obstruction blocks the path on which the clubhead swings into impact for a hook, forcing you to deliver the club to the ball on the correct path. While re-establishing a better swing path, concentrate on unwinding your hips, clearing them out of the way in your downswing, rather than sliding them towards the target.

WHAT CAUSES A HOOK?
The ball-flight for a hook is the opposite of a slice, as are the impact conditions. The club approaches the ball from too far inside the target line, producing an in-to-out swing path combined with a closed clubface. The hooked ball tends to fly lower than it would normally and also runs a long way.

THE "HEAVY-CONTACT" CHIP

There is nothing in golf quite to match the ignominy of making a complete mess of a short shot, and the heavy-contact chip – a stroke in which heavy contact is made with the ground instead of the ball – ranks high in the embarrassment stakes. Somehow it is worse than missing a short putt and seemingly much harder to correct. However, the changes required to eliminate this shot are simple to apply.

✻ Make sure the ball is not too far forward in your stance, as this is often the cause of a poor strike. The ball should be opposite your right foot, with your hands forward. There should be a straight line formed by your left arm and the shaft of the club (see Drill 1, p.150).

Wrists
Make sure your hands lead, and stay ahead of, the clubhead through the hitting zone

FIX: KEEP YOUR HANDS AHEAD OF THE CLUB

The desired ball-then-turf contact (see Drill 5, p.154) can only be achieved if you keep your hands in front of the clubhead into and through impact. To do this, as you start your downswing, maintain the angle in your right wrist – it should remain constant through the hitting zone. The bottom of the swing arc should now coincide with the ball (see Drill 4, p.153), producing a clean strike and the smallest of divots after impact (instead of before).

FAULT: CLUB HITS THE GROUND BEFORE THE BALL

Heavy contact is the result of trying to help the ball into the air rather than letting the loft on the clubface do the work. Employing a scooping action causes the clubhead to pass the hands prior to impact and to strike the ground before the ball – hence, a "heavy-contact" chip. Generally, a divot is taken behind the ball, although this will not be the case if the ground is very hard.

Bottom of swing arc

WHAT CAUSES A HEAVY-CONTACT CHIP?

The cause of this shot lies in the clubhead's angle of attack into impact. The crux of the problem is that the bottom of the swing arc occurs before the ball. Therefore, the clubhead buries itself in the ground, which absorbs most of the power in the shot. This means that hardly any energy is passed on to the ball.

THE SHANKED IRON SHOT

The shank is probably the most destructive shot you can hit. The ball shoots off the club at an angle of at least 45 degrees to the target, often never to be seen again. You can hit a shank with any iron, but, whatever the club, once the damage is done it cannot be easily remedied.

*Ironically, taking the club back too far on the inside often causes you to loop the club outside the target line in your downswing. Slowly rehearse your backswing and make sure that the club travels inside but also upwards, as this promotes the correct downswing path (see Drill 15, p.129).

Clubface
With the club on the correct path, solid contact is made between the centre of the clubface and the ball

Obstacle
Place a ball-box just outside the ball-to-target line to prevent an out-to-in swing path

FAULT: POOR LINE OF ATTACK

With a shanked shot, the ball is hit from the hosel instead of the middle of the clubface. For that to happen, the clubhead must be further away from your body at impact than at address. This is caused by "throwing" the clubhead away from your body at the start of your downswing, so that it swings through the hitting zone on an out-to-in path.

Out-to-in swing path

Hosel

Target line

WHAT CAUSES A SHANK?

The shank occurs when the the hosel of the club (the point where the shaft joins the clubhead), rather than the clubface, strikes the ball. This happens when the clubhead travels into impact from way outside the ideal swing path. Because of the shape of the hosel, the ball flies almost sideways to the line of play – a highly destructive fault.

FIX: BLOCK THE PATH TO A SHANK

Curing a shank relies on eliminating the destructive path of attack into impact. Place a headcover or an empty ball-box just behind the ball, 8 cm (3 in) outside the target line. Then hit a shot with a short iron. The obstruction makes it necessary for you to swing the club towards the ball on the correct path, leading to solid contact between the centre of the clubface and the ball. If your old swing fault reappears, the club will hit the obstacle before it reaches the ball.

THE SKIED DRIVE

The skied drive is not the most damaging of shots – indeed, the ball tends to fly reasonably straight, which means you rarely lose a ball. You do, however, lose as much as 70 per cent of the normal distance for any given club. A skied drive occurs when the clubhead chops down steeply under a ball that is teed up (occasionally too high). The result is a ball-flight more reminiscent of a lofted pitch than a solid drive.

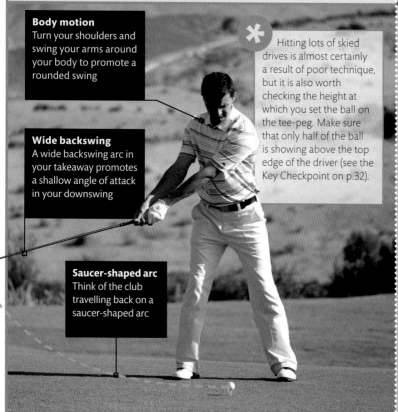

Body motion
Turn your shoulders and swing your arms around your body to promote a rounded swing

Wide backswing
A wide backswing arc in your takeaway promotes a shallow angle of attack in your downswing

Saucer-shaped arc
Think of the club travelling back on a saucer-shaped arc

* Hitting lots of skied drives is almost certainly a result of poor technique, but it is also worth checking the height at which you set the ball on the tee-peg. Make sure that only half of the ball is showing above the top edge of the driver (see the Key Checkpoint on p.32).

FAULT: STEEP DOWNSWING ATTACK
A skied drive is usually caused by an excessively upright backswing. This is the result of picking the club up too steeply with your hands in your takeaway – in essence, too much lift and not enough width. This establishes a narrow swing arc, and your downswing becomes a product of your poor backswing.

Steep angle of attack

Steep ball trajectory

WHAT CAUSES A SKIED DRIVE?
A skied drive occurs when the top-edge of the clubhead makes contact with the bottom portion of the ball. The ball then shoots up into the air quickly but with very little forward momentum. The shot is the result of a very steep angle of attack into impact, combined with the ball being teed up (sometimes too high), allowing the clubhead to make contact with the underside of the ball. The shot is most common with the driver and 3-wood.

FIX: START YOUR TAKEAWAY LOW AND SLOW
To promote a shallower angle of attack, widen your backswing arc. Concentrate on sweeping the club away "low and slow", turning your back on the target (see Drill 18, p.49), and swinging your arms and the club around your body more (see Drill 16, p.46–7). This promotes a backswing that is full and wide. In your downswing, try to focus on sweeping the ball away rather than hitting down on it. Create a longer flat spot at the bottom of your swing – the arc should be more saucer-shaped than tea-cup shaped.

THE TOP

The top is generally looked upon as a beginner's fault, but it also afflicts experienced players. In fact, even professionals have been known to hit this shot – a rarity, admittedly, but true nevertheless. Whatever your standard, it is an embarrassing shot because the outcome looks so pathetic. The clubhead just clips the top of the ball, sending it scuttling along the ground. The top occurs most with either a drive or a fairway-wood shot.

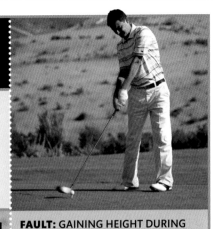

Impact
If you maintain your original height in the swing, you are more likely to generate solid contact

Posture
Maintain your spine angle from address until impact

✳ If you have a tendency to top your fairway wood shots, check that the ball is not too far back in your stance (see pp.22–3). This is sometimes the cause of a topped shot. Position yourself so that the ball is opposite your left heel. This set-up allows you to sweep the ball away in your downswing and followthrough.

FAULT: GAINING HEIGHT DURING YOUR SWING

If you top a shot, you are raising your posture in your swing, which brings up the bottom of your swing arc to the point whereby the clubhead is close to missing the ball altogether. This comes about because you fail to maintain the posture you established at address: you are either straightening your legs or lifting your upper body during your downswing.

Bottom of swing arc

FIX: MONITOR YOUR POSTURE FROM ADDRESS TO IMPACT

Whichever fault is causing you to top the ball, the conclusion is the same. You have to make sure you maintain good posture from address until the point of impact. Adopt a good posture (see pp.24–5) and address a tee-peg with your driver. Now make practice swings, trying to clip the tee-peg out of the ground while maintaining your spine angle throughout your backswing and through the hitting zone. Then tee up a ball and hit some drives, working on the same principles. Concentrate on solid contact rather than distance.

WHAT CAUSES A TOP?

With a top, the ball's behaviour painfully reveals what happens at impact. The bottom edge of the clubhead strikes the top third of the ball. This means that the ball ends up shooting along the ground. Although you will rarely lose a topped ball, neither will you progress very far down the fairway.

LOSS OF POWER

A towering drive is almost certainly the most admired shot in the game. Unless your name is Tiger Woods, you no doubt aspire to hit the ball further off the tee. Lack of power off the tee, which results in poor carry with the driver, is basically down to the ball spending too much time on the ground and not enough in the air.

Weight moving away from target

Correct weight transfer

Backswing
Your body should move away from the target in your backswing

Weight transfer
As the club is swung back, transfer your weight to your back foot

* Remember, at the top of your backswing, there should be a 90-degree angle between your right forearm and the shaft of the club. Any wider than that and there is insufficient wrist hinge, which will result in less power (see Drill 24, p.58).

Body turn
Turning your body in sympathy with the club promotes a good position at the top of your backswing

70%

30%

FAULT: REVERSE PIVOT WRECKS YOUR SWING
The most likely explanation for loss of power is an incorrect weight transfer during your swing, a move often called a reverse pivot. Instead of your weight shifting on to your right side in your backswing, then transferring to your left side during your downswing and through impact, the reverse happens. Your weight shifts towards the target in your backswing (above) and away from the target in your downswing.

WHAT CAUSES LOSS OF POWER?
Insufficient power off the tee comes down to a lack of clubhead speed through the hitting area and is often caused by a reverse pivot. In this situation your weight shifts on to your front foot in the backswing and on to your back foot in the downswing and hitting zone (above). Therefore, the shift in weight that helps provide power is moving the wrong way.

FIX: SHIFT YOUR WEIGHT TO PACK A PUNCH
To fulfil your potential power, transfer your weight in sympathy with the swinging club. Give yourself a head start by setting up with about 60 per cent of your weight on your right side. Shift at least another 10 per cent to your right side during your backswing, then transfer your weight on to your left foot in your downswing to maximize the force applied to the ball. Think of a boxer throwing a big punch: the weight briefly shifts to the back foot, then moves forward rapidly as the punch is thrown (see Drill 7, p.36).

WEAK SHOT FROM ROUGH

It does not take a terrible tee shot to find yourself in the rough; it could be that you have strayed from the fairway by only a few paces. The penalty is disproportionately severe, however, if you cannot produce a powerful strike and a decent ball-flight to put you back on track.

Take a close look at the position of the ball relative to your feet. Most golfers who struggle to hit short and mid-irons out of thick rough tend to have the ball too near their front foot at address, instead of further back as it should be (see pp.22–3).

Upright backswing
An upright backswing promotes a steep angle of attack

Point the tee-peg
The tee-peg stuck in the grip of the club should point towards the ball when your hands reach waist height

FAULT: SHALLOW ATTACK TRAPS TOO MUCH GRASS

Unless your lie is horrendous, you should be able to hit a good shot with all but the long irons. If you cannot, the clubhead's angle of attack into the ball is probably too shallow, which is often the result of an overly wide takeaway with insufficient wrist hinge (above). While a shallow attack is desirable with the driver, from thick grass a steeper angle is required.

Shallow angle of attack

Grass trapped between clubface and ball

FIX: POINT THE BUTT OF THE CLUB AT THE BALL

To hit strong iron shots from the rough, you have to create a steep angle of attack into impact. Use a mid-iron, and stick a tee-peg in the hole at the butt-end of the grip. As you make your backswing, try to point the tee-peg at the ball by the time your hands reach hip height. This pre-sets a more upright swing, which leads to a steeper angle of attack into impact. This means less interference from the grass around the ball, generating a more powerful strike.

WHAT CAUSES A WEAK SHOT FROM ROUGH?

A poor strike out of the rough is often caused by too much grass being trapped between the clubface and the ball. The result is a weak, cushioned blow, which takes the "sting" out of the strike and lessens the shot's distance.

THE PUSH SHOT

The end result of a push shot is much the same as a slice: the ball finishing way off to the right. But the cause is a different story. Whereas the slice begins on a leftward path and swerves from left to right through the air, the push shot starts on a path to the right and stays right. This can happen with any club from a driver to a wedge, and it is not necessarily caused by a poorly struck shot, either. Often, contact is solid.

* Although a push can happen with any club, if you are pushing your tee shots, it is probably because the ball is too far back in your stance. This means that the club fails to reach the on line portion of its arc. Put the ball opposite your left heel to help ensure that the club is travelling on the correct path at impact (see the Key Checkpoint on p.35).

Swing path
With your left side out of the way, it is easier to correct an in-to-out swing path

Open stance
Hit practice shots from a very open stance to encourage an on line swing of the club through impact

Normal feet alignment

FAULT: HITTING FROM IN-TO-OUT
The fault at the heart of a push is, in one respect, the same as for a hook (see p.283): the clubhead approaching the ball from inside the optimum swing path, and therefore travelling in-to-out through impact. The difference between the hook and the push is in the position of the clubface – for a hook, the clubface is closed to the in-to-out swing path, whereas for a push, the face is square to that same path. Hence the contrasting ball-flights.

In-to-out swing path

Clubface square to swing path

Target line

WHAT CAUSES A PUSH SHOT?
A push is the result of the clubhead swinging into the ball on an exaggerated in-to-out path, with the clubface square to that (incorrect) path. These factors cause the ball to fly in a direct line, albeit one that is off course. (Note: if the clubface is open to this path, a push-slice results, whereby the ball starts right and swerves further to the right in the air.)

FIX: TRAIN AN ON LINE ATTACK
The key to curing a push is to eliminate the excessive inside path of attack. Address the ball with your left toe in line with your right heel. Because your left side is already cleared out of the way (due to the very open stance), you have room to swing the club more to the left through impact. Once you have played a shot this way, try to recreate that swing from a normal stance. You should find that the ball sets off straight at the target, the sign of an on line swing path.

THE PULL SHOT

A pull is the opposite of a push. The ball starts on a leftward path, because of an out-to-in swing path. It then continues on that path because the clubface is square to the out-to-in line of attack. As with the push, it can happen with any club, from a driver down to a wedge.

Shoulders
Your shoulders should be parallel to the target line at address

If you are persistently pulling shots, check the alignment of your clubface at address (see pp.20–1). If it is closed (aiming left of target), this could be the reason for the fault.

Closed stance
Hit practice shots with your right toes aligned with your left foot's heel to promote an inside attack

Normal feet alignment

FAULT: "THROWING" THE CLUBHEAD OUTSIDE THE CORRECT LINE

A pulled shot means that your hands and arms are moving too far away from your body at the start of your downswing. You are "throwing" the club outside the ideal swing path, so that it meets the ball on an out-to-in path at impact. If the ball-flight were not evidence enough, another clue (at least with iron play) is the divot-mark, which will point to the left of the target (see Drill 9, pp.118–21).

Out-to-in swing path

Clubface square to swing path

Target line

WHAT CAUSES A PULL SHOT?

As with a slice, a pull shot is the product of an out-to-in swing path. But, whereas a slice occurs if the clubface is open, a pull occurs if the clubface is square to the out-to-in path. (Note: if the clubface is closed to this path, the result is what is known as a pull-hook. This shot starts left of the target and curves even further to the left in the air – a wild shot indeed.)

FIX: DEVELOP AN INSIDE ATTACK

In curing a pull, it is important to appreciate the sensation of the clubhead approaching the ball from inside the target line. Draw your right foot back from this line so that your right toe is level with your left heel (make sure that your shoulders stay square, though). This stance promotes a fuller body turn and, more importantly, creates space for the club to travel on an inside path during your downswing. Try to recreate the sensation of this stroke from a normal stance. This should promote an on line swing path.

THE ART OF SHOTMAKING

SHOTMAKING ENCOMPASSES two distinct areas of the game. There is the shot played out of necessity, as a result of a bad or unlucky previous stroke. The first part of the chapter (see pp.294–301) covers a number of ways to cope with these problem shots (particularly bad and awkward lies). And there is the shot played out of choice, where you call upon your golfing knowledge and powers of imagination and improvisation to shape your shots to suit the hole you are playing. The second part of the chapter (see pp.304–7) teaches you how to produce these shots, by altering either the ball's trajectory or direction. Sandwiched between the problem shots and the more creative shots is a section on wind play (see pp.302–3), an area of the game that combines both elements of shotmaking.

SLOPING LIES

THE ONLY PLACE on a course where you can guarantee a totally level lie is on the teeing ground. Once off that manicured turf, you have to accept that the ball may well come to rest on a sloping lie, whether it be an upslope, a downslope, or a sideslope lie (where the ball is awkwardly positioned either above or below your feet). An upslope effectively creates more loft on the club, generating additional height. This makes it a relatively easy lie to

deal with. The downslope, on the other hand, deprives the club of loft and places greater demands on your ability to strike the ball cleanly. It is a trickier prospect than an upslope lie, both psychologically and technically. Up- and downslopes each produce different flight paths. From an upslope, there is a tendency for the ball to move from right-to-left, whereas a downslope has the opposite effect,

PLAYING FROM A DOWNSLOPE

This is the tougher of the up- and downslope shots because the slope deprives the club of its normal loft (see p.295). Also, because the ground is effectively higher behind the ball than from a flat lie, it is easy to strike the turf before hitting the ball ("heavy" contact). Your first consideration is club selection. On even the slightest downslope you need to "club-down": use a more lofted club, which decreases distance and gives a higher trajectory. Change from a 6-iron to a 7-iron, for example, to make up for the lack of loft caused by the slope (on a severe slope you might find there is a two-club difference). The ball tends to fly low off a downslope, running further than usual on landing. Therefore, pitch the ball short of the target to avoid over-shooting.

Left side
Put more of your weight on your left side

Impact
There should be a descending blow into impact

55%

45%

Ball position
Position yourself so that the ball is further back in your stance

KEEP THE BALL BACK
Position the ball 5–10 cm (2–4 in) further back in your stance than it would be from a flat lie, to lessen the likelihood of heavy contact. Put slightly more weight on your front foot, and try to feel that your left shoulder is slightly lower than for a regular shot. This posture promotes a steeper swing, which will help you strike the ball cleanly.

CHASE THE BALL DOWN THE SLOPE
When the ball is on a downslope, the natural inclination is to lean back, in an effort to help the ball into the air. Resist this temptation. In your backswing, keep your weight distribution as it was at address. Then swing down the slope so that the clubhead chases after the ball through impact. Let your bodyweight go with the clubhead's flow. These factors encourage a steeper angle of attack, so that you can strike the ball cleanly (rather than leaning back and taking a large divot).

causing a left-to-right ball-flight. But do not be perturbed by such apparent difficulties. Once you have knowledge of the techniques outlined on these two pages, you will soon become accustomed to making informed club selections and allowances for the differences in ball-flight. Downslopes and upslopes will then hold no fear for you.

Now consider sideslope lies (see pp.296–7). In these situations, the ball will be either above or below the level of your feet, and each case places unique demands on your technique. Unless the slope is severe, having the ball above the level of your feet is not overly challenging. Indeed, your set-up should feel quite comfortable at address. However, when the ball is below the level of your feet, your set-up will probably feel terribly awkward at address and even more so in the swing – maintaining a balanced stance becomes a problem.

Coping with sloping lies is, in essence, a two-part strategy. Firstly, you must identify what you need to do to strike the ball properly; and secondly, you need to understand and make allowances for what the ball will do after impact.

PLAYING FROM AN UPSLOPE

This is considered the easier of these two up- and downslope lies. You can strike the ball cleanly without difficulty, and loft is added to the club (below right), which means that the ball will fly higher and shorter than from a flat lie. Again, club selection is important: you need to "club-up". For example, if the shot would call for a 6-iron from a flat lie, club-up to a 5-iron to regain the distance that is lost when playing from an upslope. Experience will teach you to match the right club to the degree of slope.

60%

40%

Impact
There should be a sweeping blow into impact

Narrow or widen your stance

Most golfers fail to realize that playing off a slope has a subtle effect on leg action in the swing. Because an upslope tends to restrict leg action, you might want to experiment with hitting shots from a slightly narrower stance (this gives you more mobility from the waist down). A downslope has the opposite effect, with your legs becoming more active. To counter this tendency, try widening your stance a little to promote a more stable leg action as you swing back and through.

Loft on slopes

When playing from an upslope, the clubface is effectively more lofted than if you were playing the same shot from a flat lie. A downslope effectively reduces the loft on the clubface, relative to the horizontal lie.

Upslope   Flat lie   Downslope

PREPARE FOR LAUNCH
Put the ball forward in your stance (exactly how far will depend on the severity of the slope). Settle your weight on your lower foot, with a little more flex than normal in your left leg to align your hips with the ground – as they are when playing from a flat lie. The ball will tend to fly right-to-left from an upslope – aim slightly right to compensate.

REMAIN STEADY
As with the shot off a downslope, any lateral shift of your body in your backswing makes it difficult to strike the ball correctly. Therefore, keep your weight firmly anchored over your right knee as you make your backswing – do not sway any further down the slope. Your head should be steady in your downswing and you should feel that you swing the club up the slope, almost sweeping the ball away.

KEY CHECKPOINT

Adjust the clubface aim

One of the effects of playing from above or below your feet is that the ball tends to deviate to the right or left through the air. As discussed, you can allow for this by altering your alignment. But an alternative is to change the aim of the clubface. When the ball is above your feet, open the clubface to counter the ball's right-to-left flight. And when the ball is below your feet, close the clubface to fight the left-to-right flight path.

BALL BELOW YOUR FEET

This is the toughest of the sloping lies because it necessitates a swing from such an uncomfortable address position. The keys to success are establishing a balanced address position, and then maintaining your height through the hitting area. If you can do these two things, you should strike the ball solidly. However, you will not be able to make as powerful a swing as from a flat lie, therefore use a less-lofted club to make up the extra distance.

Arms
Let your arms do the majority of the work in your swing

Legs
Flex your legs and stand a little closer to the ball to avoid overstretching

KEEP THE WEIGHT ON YOUR HEELS

When the ball is below your feet, adjust your posture to facilitate a solid strike. "Sit down" a little at address by flexing your knees, and widen your stance to further enhance your sense of balance. Because the ball is lower than usual, stand a fraction closer to it so that you are not overstretching. Because the ball will fly from left-to-right off this type of lie, aim left of the target to compensate.

SWING SMOOTHLY TO PROMOTE GOOD BALANCE

With sloping lies it is important that you swing smoothly and do not over-extend yourself – this is certainly the case when the ball is below your feet. Keep your knees flexed and make an "arms-dominated" swing to help you keep your balance. The slope tends to force your weight downhill, which can produce a shank (see p.285). To counter this problem, keep your weight back on your heels as you swing.

BALL ABOVE YOUR FEET

This is probably the easiest of all four sloping-lie shots, partly because the address position will feel comfortable but also because the slope does not hinder your ball-striking. What you do need to be wary of is the ball-flight, which can be quite "hot" (less backspin and lots of forward momentum) from this type of lie. The ball also travels on a powerful right-to-left flight path. Therefore, it is always wise to club-down to decrease distance and to aim right of the target.

Grip
Choke down on the grip effectively to reduce the length of the club

Stance
Stand more upright than for a flat lie, with your weight more on your toes

STAND TALL; CHOKE DOWN

With this sort of shot, the ball is effectively raised. Therefore, on a severe slope, shorten the club by choking down on the grip and standing more erect at address. To maintain your balance as you swing, settle your weight a little more towards your toes.

ALLOW FOR A ROUNDED SWING

From this kind of set-up and from this type of slope, your swing will be a little more rounded than usual. This means that your hands will not rise as high above your shoulders as with a regular swing. Other than that, there is nothing to worry about with this shot. Just make a smooth swing, maintaining your height and balance to produce a solid strike.

TACKLING PROBLEM SHOTS

IN GOLF'S EARLY DAYS, when the only greenkeepers were the sheep grazing on the land, virtually every shot bar the drive and putt might have been considered problem shots. Nowadays, modern greenkeeping equipment produces nicely manicured playing surfaces, and bad lies are less frequent. But inevitably they still occur, and it is important to be able to deal with these tricky situations. The process of playing a successful shot from a problem spot can be separated into three stages.

Firstly, assess the lie of the ball and decide what effect it might have on your club selection. For example, some lies in the rough are so bad that – in order to obtain the loft necessary to dig the ball out of thick grass – all but the short irons are ruled out. In such cases you have to forget distance and play for position instead. Ultimately, the shot you choose to play must reflect the limitations of the lie.

Secondly, picture the shot in your mind's eye. If the target is within range, think where you want to pitch the ball, and try to envisage how the ball will react on landing.

Or, if you are playing a lay-up shot (in which you want to find a position for a simple chip or pitch on to the green), focus on a spot that should give you a good lie for your next shot.

Thirdly, commit yourself to the shot you have elected to play, and trust the club you have chosen. Do not let doubt creep into your mind.

Here are three of the most common bad lies. But if you apply this three-part strategy, you should, with practice, find that such lies need not cost you dearly.

Rhythm
Maintain good balance by making a smooth swing with good rhythm

SHOT FROM A BARE LIE

This is one of the toughest shots in golf, and the closer you are to the green, the more difficult the task. Even the slightest mishit can be heavily punished from a bare lie. For this reason, the challenge is to produce a perfectly clean strike, trapping the ball between the clubface and the ground.

Clean strike
Do not try to help the ball into the air but rather trust the loft on the club to do the job for which it was designed

PRE-SET A CLEAN STRIKE
Never use a sand wedge from a bare lie, as the rounded sole tends to bounce off the ground into the middle of the ball. All other clubs have a sharper leading edge, which sits flush to the ground. To further promote a clean strike, position the ball roughly 2.5 cm (1 in) further back in your stance than for a normal fairway shot.

STEADY INTO IMPACT
As you make the shot, trust your set-up and swing to deliver the leading edge of the clubhead into the bottom of the ball. This should create a low trajectory but plenty of backspin because there is less interference between the clubface and ball at impact. This means that the ball will stop quickly on landing.

PLAYING OUT OF A DIVOT-MARK

When your ball lands in an old divot-mark, the chances are it is when you have just hit a nice shot down the middle of the fairway – such is the nature of the game. But unless the divot-mark is very deep, this is by no means a hopeless situation. Start by taking out a more-lofted club than if you were playing from the same distance with a good lie.

BALL BACK; HANDS FORWARD

Position the ball almost opposite your right heel and align your hands with your left thigh. This will promote an almost V-shaped swing, where the clubhead travels steeply into impact.

IT IS ALL IN THE WRISTS

To promote the necessary angle of attack in your downswing, hinge your wrists abruptly in your takeaway so that the club travels steeply upwards. Then hit down hard into the back of the ball. Imagine that you are trying to drive the ball down even deeper into the ground. You will need to keep a firm hold of the club, as the force of impact is severe. (The followthrough is kept short with this shot.) Expect a low trajectory with lots of run on landing. Because of this, be aware of trouble spots beyond the back of the green. Because the ball will tend to have a left-to-right flight path, aim a little left of the target to accommodate the swerving ball-flight.

IRON SHOT FROM THICK ROUGH

Light rough presents the accomplished golfer with very few problems, as all you need to do is allow for less backspin (as you cannot strike the ball cleanly) and, therefore, a little more run on landing. Thick rough, however, severely limits your options. Determine the longest club you can hit, and if you can reach the green with that, fine. But if you cannot, accept your fate and play a well placed lay-up shot instead. Either way, you should apply the following principles of successful deep-rough play.

ORGANIZE YOUR SET-UP

If your set-up is not correct, no amount of muscle will pull you out of trouble. Put the ball in the middle of your stance. Then aim the clubface at the target. Keep your weight evenly balanced, maybe even slightly favouring your left foot if the lie is terrible. Align your feet about 15–20 degrees left of the target (at 11 o'clock if you imagine the target at 12 o'clock). This type of stance goes some way to pre-setting a steep downswing attack, which is essential for decent contact.

PUNCH DOWN AND THROUGH

To further promote a steep attack, swing your hands up a little higher in your backswing. Then swing the clubhead steeply into the back of the ball. However, even if you achieve a perfect technique, you will still need to put a little bit more effort into this shot at impact – use a powerful strike and try to shift a sizeable chunk of grass from around the ball.

CONJURING EFFECTIVE ESCAPE SHOTS

HAVING HIT a ball into trouble, all too often the tendency is to opt for an inappropriate recovery shot, sometimes attempting wildly ambitious escapes that even a tour professional would think twice about playing. The result usually turns the situation from bad to worse. When in doubt, it is usually best to play safe.

However, there are occasions when it is necessary to take a calculated risk and play an attacking escape shot. You might, for example, be in a matchplay situation (see pp.332–3) in which taking a penalty drop would probably cost you the hole and maybe the match.

Or you might be playing a friendly game and testing the limits of your ability.

Here are three great escape shots for when you have a difficult lie close to a tree or near a cluster of bushes or trees. This is a common problem, and one that most golfers can, with a little practice, negotiate successfully. (Whereas playing from, for example, ditches or water are tasks best left to the professionals.) Even these three shots may seem tricky at first, but, if you follow the advice outlined on these two pages, you should soon become proficient.

AWKWARD OBSTRUCTION

This shot is handy when the ball comes to rest at the base of a tree-trunk in a position that makes it impossible for you to take up your usual stance – the tree is precisely where you would normally stand. A penalty drop may seem like the only option, but not if you learn how to play the back-handed chop.

Impact
Make sure that you accelerate the clubhead into the ball at impact

ADDRESS POSITION

Select one of your more lofted clubs, as they have a broader hitting area than a long iron. Turn your back on the target, and stand with the ball 15 cm (6 in) outside your right foot. Hold the grip with your right hand only, and twist the club around so that it sits on its toe-end, the clubface still looking at the target. Your arm should be relatively straight, hanging by your side.

A STRAIGHT-ARMED SWING

Swing your right arm back and through like a pendulum, and accelerate the clubhead into the back of the ball. The shot calls for a straight-armed swing, and wrist action should be virtually non-existent as it increases the likelihood of a miss. Do not swing your hand above waist height, and settle for a maximum range of 35–45 m (38–49 yd).

RESTRICTED BACKSWING

It is quite common on heavily wooded courses for a wayward ball to come to rest in a spot where your backswing is restricted by branches. Making a normal swing is out of the question as the club would become tangled, which often results in an air shot (where you miss the ball entirely). The following technique shows you how to avoid the branches and how to generate sufficient power, so that you will hit the ball well up the fairway.

A LOW ADDRESS POSITION

This shot revolves around the principle of dramatically lowering and reducing your swing arc. Start by taking a severely wide stance, spreading your feet at least double the distance of your normal set-up. Then choke down on the grip so that your right hand touches the metal of the shaft. These two factors ensure that the club will not be anywhere near as high as normal at the top of your backswing.

MAKE A NARROW SWING

To reduce your swing arc, use maximum wrist hinge. At the top of your backswing, your hands should be around chest height so that the clubhead does not rise too far. This enables you to make an unimpeded downswing. More lofted clubs, which have short shafts, are ideal for this shot.

IN THE TREES

If the ball has come to rest among a cluster of trees or in the clear behind a large copse, making a normal swing is usually not a problem. The difficulty you face is having to thread the ball through the tangle of branches in your path. As you eye the gaps, there are several factors to bear in mind.

USE A STANDARD TRAJECTORY

First and foremost, you should always try to find an approach that allows you to play a normal shot. Look for gaps that suit the natural loft of a particular club, rather than manufacturing a punchy low shot or a fantastically high lofted shot, which is riskier.

FRAME YOUR GAP

Take a moment to frame a gap in your mind's eye, and pick the club that will produce the required trajectory (see Drill 26, pp.102–3). Try to avoid tiny openings, and select a patch of fairway or green in the distance that does not place extra demands on the bounce and run of the ball. If you can take as normal a swing as possible, you stand a better chance of success.

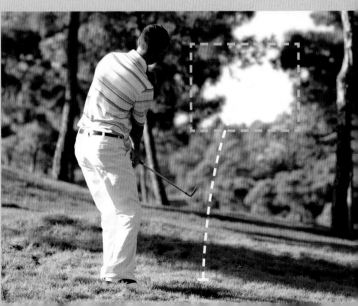

BETTER WIND PLAY

A ROUND OF GOLF in the wind presents a greater challenge than playing on a calm day, but breezy conditions need not blow you completely off course. Assessing the conditions – knowing which way the wind is blowing – is something you will need to re-check as you work your way around the turns and contours of the course. There are many clues all around you: glance up at the sky to see which way the clouds are moving; look at the treetops and note which way they are swaying; maybe even check the flag on an adjacent hole. Some tour professionals take a miniature map of the course, such as the one on the back of the scorecard, and draw an arrow across it indicating the wind direction. This gives them a broad reference throughout the round. Assessing the conditions is all very well, but hitting the right shots for the conditions is ultimately what counts. That is the area focused on here. Contained on this spread are a handful of ideas that will improve your performance when the wind blows.

Wide stance
When hitting into the wind, widen your stance for greater stability

Wind

SOLID FOUNDATIONS
One of the main problems when playing in a strong wind is being blown off balance. Widening your stance gives you a more stable foundation, which promotes a steadier stance.

KEEP THE BALL LOW
There is no joy in playing a high ball into a strong wind. You will struggle to judge distance, the ball is easily blown off line, and you will have little control over the outcome of your shot. For these reasons, you have to keep the ball low. This simply means opting for a less-lofted club than you would otherwise use. If, for example, you are 135 m (150 yd) from the flag and that represents a normal 7-iron shot, club-up to a 5-iron and swing more easily. Obviously the strength of the wind dictates how much you club-up, but experience will tell you the difference between a one-club, a two-club, or even a three-club wind.

COMPENSATING FOR WIND
When playing a shot into the wind, club-up to produce a lower ball-flight, and remember the old adage: "swing with ease into the breeze".

SWINGING SMOOTHLY OFF THE TEE
The temptation when you are hitting a driver into the wind is to swing harder than normal. This will probably cause you to lose your balance, leading to a poor ball-strike and loss of distance and accuracy. To achieve good balance, widen your stance, moving your feet 13 cm (5 in) further apart than normal. This also helps shorten your swing slightly, promoting a more compact movement and a solid strike. Do not tee the ball too low, as this often causes you to swing down more steeply into impact, causing the ball to balloon upwards into the wind. However, you should tee the ball a fraction lower than normal to promote a slightly lower flight (although it is important that you continue to focus on sweeping the ball away).

Hitting downwind, however, extends the ball-flight, and you might want to select a 3-wood off the tee, as the extra loft maximizes the height of the ball and, therefore, the wind's influence on it.

Wind

Club selection
Take a less-lofted club so that the ball's trajectory is kept low

SHAPE YOUR SHOT OR ADJUST YOUR AIM

In a crosswind you have two options. If you are proficient at shaping the ball with sidespin, work the ball into the wind. In a left-to-right breeze, for example, play a draw (see p.306), and in a right-to-left breeze go with a fade (see p.307). These measures should produce an almost straight shot, although distance is sacrificed for accuracy and control.

Alternatively, play a straight shot in which you make allowance for the crosswind by aiming left or right of the target, accordingly. The ball will carry about one club further on the wind, and will not sit down as quickly as a shot shaped into the wind.

CROSSWINDS

If, for example, the wind is blowing from right to left, you have two choices: you can play a fade, so that the ball holds its line, or you can aim right and let the wind blow the ball back towards the target.

Fade
A shot hit with fade fights against the wind, resulting in an almost straight ball-flight

Aim right
An alternative to the fade is to aim right and allow the wind to carry the ball leftwards

WIDEN YOUR PUTTING STANCE

The act of putting involves such a precise movement that even the slightest buffeting from the wind can upset the path and pace of your stroke. Widen your stance by up to 50 per cent more than normal – this gives you a solid foundation. Also choke down on the grip so that you are more crouched over the ball. This lowers your centre of gravity so that you are less susceptible to the effects of the wind. Hit a few practice putts to familiarize yourself with the new stance. Your stroke stays the same, so it should not feel too strange.

REMAIN STEADY

The main challenge when putting in a strong wind is to maintain a steady head and body position. If you are able to do this, you will be able to make a smooth, on line stroke. If you widen your stance and choke down on the grip, you will find it easier to hold constant body and head positions.

WIND INFLUENCES BREAK AND SPEED

Few golfers take into account the fact that a strong wind affects the ball's journey as it moves along the green. A crosswind either exaggerates or cancels out the break on a putt; a tail wind makes a putt run faster; and a headwind slows the ball down. You have to allow for these factors when you read each putt, even from short range. This becomes a bit of a balancing act, but, if you are aware of the wind's speed and direction, you can take steps to compensate for its effects.

WIND BREAK

It is a very good idea to take into account the wind's influence when you are putting. If you do not, your shot will probably miss. This is because a strong wind makes a difference to the break and speed of a putt, especially on fast, well-manicured putting surfaces.

HOW TO HIT HIGH AND LOW SHOTS

NOW THAT PROBLEM SHOTS have been covered, as well as the up and down world of wind play, it is time to move on to the more favourable string in a shotmaker's bow: creative shots. While a full set of clubs offers a wide array of lofts, all designed to generate shots of various trajectories, there are occasions when it is desirable to manipulate the natural loft of a club in order to work the ball into the flag on a higher or lower flight path. Sometimes this is a better option than changing to a more- or less-lofted club. Imagination plays a large part when it comes to fine-tuning trajectory: a good shotmaker can look from the ball to the target and visualize several different aerial routes, which offer up a host of attacking and defensive options. On the other hand, golfers who passively accept the constraints of the manufacturer's loft miss out on a range of shots that are fun and rewarding to play. These shots also help golfers reach the proximity of the flag or achieve a well-placed lay-up shot when a conventional stroke could not.

LOFTING THE BALL HIGH

Launching the ball high into the air towards the target is a useful skill in certain situations. One such example is when you are playing downwind and want to maximize distance with a long iron. Another scenario might be when the flag is placed close to the front of the green and is guarded by a bunker: then you would want to bring the ball down from a greater height to encourage it to sit down quickly.

Head back
Your head should stay behind the ball for a little longer than usual through the hitting zone

Hands finish high
Finish the stroke with your hands held high to reflect the intention of sending the ball on a high trajectory

ADD LOFT TO THE CLUB

In the situations outlined above, taking a more lofted club will not give you sufficient distance. Instead, use the club you would normally hit, and take these steps to effectively increase the loft. Firstly, put the ball a little more forward in your stance, as this has the effect of increasing the loft on the clubface by a few degrees. Also stand a little closer to the ball, with a more erect posture. This leads to a slightly more upright swing, which generates extra height on the ball-flight.

SWING NORMALLY AND FINISH HIGH

You can now make what feels like a regular swing, trusting your adjusted set-up to produce the desired impact factors. As you swing the club, ensure that your head stays behind the ball for longer than normal in the downswing and hitting zone. Also, let your followthrough reflect your intentions by finishing with your hands held high.

It is worth pointing out that the likes of Seve Ballesteros and Lee Trevino became such remarkable shotmakers and good all-round players because they started playing the game with less than a full set of clubs. Take their lead and play the occasional practice round with only three or four iron clubs in your bag. You may at first feel restricted by the lack of choice, but such an exercise teaches you a great deal about the game. It improves your imagination and skill for inventing shots, which will make you a more complete golfer. Aside from these benefits for your game, it is also great fun.

Followthrough
Keep your followthrough low to reflect your desire to produce a low ball-flight

Torso
You should sense that your torso is over the ball as you sweep the ball away through the hitting zone

PUNCHING THE BALL LOW

The "knockdown-punch shot", as it is often called, is suited to a variety of situations. As was mentioned in the section on wind play (see pp.302–3), this type of stroke is a great weapon to have at your disposal when playing into a strong headwind, helping the ball hold its line. It is also useful when you want to pitch a ball short of the green and let it run up to the flag.

REDUCE THE LOFT ON THE CLUB
The ball needs to go back in your stance by as much as three ball-widths, which has the effect of delofting the clubface by several degrees. Also push your hands even further forward than normal so that the shaft is angled towards the target. In doing so, you have to be careful that the clubface does not become open. Turn in the toe of the clubhead slightly to ensure that the face is looking at the target. Your weight at address should be evenly spread.

DRIVE THE BALL AND FINISH LOW
Try to sweep the club away low to the ground and make a shorter, more compact backswing than normal. Do not forget to turn your shoulders, though. Then, in your downswing, keep your torso over the ball at impact, and swing the clubhead low to the ground through the hitting zone. Again, your followthrough should reflect the ball-flight: your hands should stay low in the finish.

TWO SIMPLE WAYS TO SHAPE YOUR SHOTS

THERE ARE MANY FACETS to the shotmaker's art, and there are times when it can be helpful to shape the ball through the air. You might, for example, want to bend a ball around a dogleg fairway, avoid a tree blocking your path to the flag, or seek out a cunningly positioned flag. However, the majority of golfers view shaping shots as beyond their ability, regarding the techniques involved as for experts only. Indeed,

whenever a ball moves left or right through the air, many view this as a poor shot, failing to appreciate the potential benefits of a swerving ball.

The laws of physics explain why a ball flies through the air the way it does. Basically, ball-flight is determined by the clubhead's path in the swing and the aim of the clubface relative to this path. These two elements combine to impart sidespin on the ball, which in turn makes the

SHAPING SHOTS WITH A DRAW

A draw is the perfect shot when the flag is located in the left corner of the green. Aiming straight at the target is risky because there is so little margin for error left of the flag. But, if you aim to the right of the flag and "draw" the ball in towards the target, the risks are less. If the ball flies straight, you hit middle of the green – no disaster there – and, if the ball draws according to plan, you are looking at a short putt. Even if you pull the shot a little left of where you were aiming, the chances are you will still find the left edge of the green.

Aim

Feet alignment

ALIGN RIGHT; FACE SQUARE
The key to playing a draw lies largely in changing your set-up. If you want to swing the ball from right-to-left through the air, align your feet, hips, and shoulders right of the target. The more you want to draw the ball, the further right you stand. Then aim the clubface straight at the target. Also position the ball a little further back in your stance than is normal for whichever club you are using.

RELEASE THE CLUB AGGRESSIVELY
A draw requires an aggressive release of the club, whereby the right hand rolls over the left. The alignment of your stance encourages an in-to-out swing path through impact, parallel to the line of your feet. And the clubface (which is closed in relation to your stance at address) will be closed to this path at impact, imparting "draw-spin" on the ball. This causes the ball to start right of the target and drift from right-to-left through the air.

ball deviate one way or the other. Controlling these impact factors allows you to shape your shots.

So how do you exert control over a clubhead when it is swinging at speeds up to, and sometimes in excess of, 160 kph (100 mph)? Well, it largely comes down to what you do at address. Providing you introduce the necessary alterations, your swing is not that different from the norm. It does, however, take practice to reach a stage where you have the confidence to play these shots on the course. As you practise, bear in mind that the less

loft there is on the club, the easier it is to shape the ball. This is because a relatively straight-faced club, which has very little loft, will always impart more sidespin than backspin on the ball, therefore making it easier to bend the flight of the ball. A lofted iron, however, creates more backspin and less sidespin, reducing the bend on the ball. Also, you need a good lie to shape a ball. Out of the rough, therefore, it is nearly impossible to make a strike clean enough to impart the necessary sidespin.

SHAPING SHOTS WITH A FADE

A fade is useful when dangers lurk on the right-hand side of the green (a bunker or water hazard, for example) or if the flag is tucked away on the right side. If the penalty for missing the green on the right side is more severe than missing it on the left, aiming to the left of the flag and playing a fade is the smart shot. If the stroke goes according to plan, you will finish close to the hole. If you stray slightly one side or other of the perfect line, you will most likely still hit the green. Even in the worst scenario, the ball will probably land to the left of the green, forcing you to make a straightforward chip onto the putting surface.

Aim

Feet alignment

ALIGN LEFT; FACE SQUARE
To make the ball move on a left-to-right flight path, the address position is almost opposite to that required for a draw. You do aim the clubface straight at the target (as with a draw), but you must align your feet, hips, and shoulders slightly left of the target (essentially, an open stance). Also, position the ball a touch further forward in your stance at address – just one ball-width more than normal is usually enough.

USE AN OPEN CLUBFACE
Now make what feels like a regular swing. The path of your swing through impact reflects your alignment, and so the clubhead swings along the line of your feet on an out-to-in path. The clubface will return to its position at address (open to this swing path), imparting sidespin so that the shot starts left and then fades right. This shot travels about one club less than a draw and stops quickly on landing, which is useful when the greens are firm or the landing area is small.

PLAYING THE GAME

CONVERTING THE POTENTIAL you show on the practice ground into a low score on the course depends on many factors that go beyond the process of striking the ball. This chapter explores these fascinating areas. You will discover the key elements of successful course management, which is essentially the art of moving the ball from A to B with minimum fuss and maximum effectiveness. The chapter will also help you think more clearly on the course, which will improve your decision-making and will enable you to cope better with nerves and pressure situations. You will also learn about a host of other often overlooked ways of becoming a more consistent and competitive golfer, such as improving your psychological approach.

WARMING UP BEFORE A ROUND

JUST AS AN ENGINE needs to warm up before it can perform at its best, so too do your muscles, tendons, and joints. To avoid damaging these body parts, you must warm up in whatever way your schedule allows. Here are some stretching exercises and three routines of different lengths (designed to suit the time you have allowed before stepping on to the first tee). Apart from the threat of injury, walking on to the first tee cold can be bad for your score because the first two or three holes effectively become your practice range.

STRETCHING EXERCISES
The following stretches will loosen the tension in your muscles, increase the flow of blood around your body, and prepare you for the round ahead. Fit as many exercises into your warm-up as time permits, and repeat each ten times.

SWINGING WITH TWO CLUBS
When time is short, practising with two clubs is a valuable exercise that helps prepare your muscles and joints for a proper swing.

Hips
Bend from the hips to loosen your back and hamstrings

BODY-PIVOTS
Assume a good golfing posture (see pp.24–5), and hold a club across the back of your shoulders. Pivot your body to the right to simulate a backswing and then swing back to the left to simulate a downswing and followthrough. You should feel your upper body rotating over the resistance of your lower half.

SIDE-BENDS
With your arms above your head, grasp the ends of a club in both hands. Slowly bend from your waist to the left and then to the right, in each case pulling down with your lower hand and resisting with your upper hand. This will stretch the muscles in your torso and along your spine. It will also loosen your shoulders.

TOUCHING TOES
With your arms hanging straight down, hold the shaft of a club in both hands. Bend from the waist, and gently lower the club towards the ground while keeping your legs straight. You should feel some tension in your hamstrings. Go down as far as you can manage comfortably, then slowly return to a standing position.

BACK-ARCHES
Arching your back is an exercise that usefully complements touching your toes. Stand upright, hold a club above your head, and arch your spine backwards. Pause for a few seconds, and return to your original position. Slow repetition of this exercise will stretch the muscles in your lower back.

The one-minute warm-up

If you have left yourself very little time before the start of a round, use this quick routine to minimize the chances of muscle and tendon damage. With only a minute to go, the key is to loosen-up the most injury-sensitive areas of your body. Hold a club across your shoulders and rehearse some body-pivots. This stretches your back muscles, and has the added benefit of replicating the movement required in a golf swing. Then, make some rhythmical practice swings holding two clubs. Attempt to simulate a proper swing rather than half-heartedly swishing the clubs back and forth, and try to complete a balanced followthrough. If you can do that with two clubs, you can certainly do it with one.

The 10-minute warm-up

As you undoubtedly know, anything can happen with the first few shots of the day; therefore, it is wise to play some settling-in strokes before you go out on the course. Start with a little stretching – body-pivots, side-bends, and touching toes – if possible. Then hit some chip shots. The great teacher Harvey Penick believed that these were the ideal shots for a warm-up if time was short. They sharpen you up mentally and put you in tune with your game. And all the while you are playing your chips, you are improving your feel for the club.

CHIPPING
If facilities allow for it, practising your chipping is an excellent way to prepare for a round, especially if time is limited. Make sure that you vary your targets and the lie of the ball in order to promote good touch.

The 30-minute warm-up

Few golfers give themselves this much time for a warm-up, but 30 minutes can make a tremendous difference to your performance. Once again, start with some stretching exercises, and in this case you can work through all four laid out on the opposite page. Then hit some soft pitch shots to fine-tune the pace of your swing, focusing solely on solid contact and a smooth rhythm.

Do not fall into the trap of thinking that being ready is all about the number of balls you hit on the range. Make your practice sessions physically undemanding but mentally focused. Hit quality shots that mean something, thereby establishing good rhythm and boosting your confidence.

Having hit a few pitch shots, go on to play about a dozen mid-iron shots, and then turn your attention to the driver, hitting shots at about 70–80 per cent power. As with the pitch shots, focus on rhythm, balance, and making solid contact out of the centre of the clubface. Try to give each shot as much attention as you would during a round.

Then change down a few gears to hit some gentle chip shots. Follow that by taking three balls and hitting putts to different points around a green, developing your feel for speed. Finally, knock in a few putts from close range to bolster your confidence prior to going to the first tee (see Drill 10, p.247).

USE YOUR TIME WISELY
When practising, do not hit as many balls as possible. Instead hit half as many with twice the thought and application.

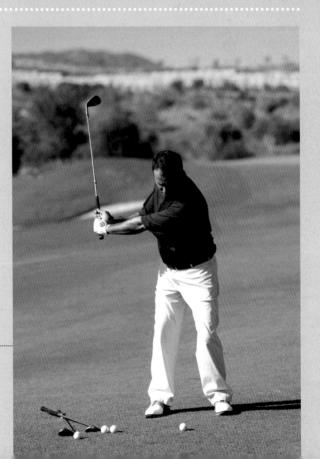

THE VALUE OF A PRE-SHOT ROUTINE

JACK NICKLAUSs, perhaps the greatest golfer who ever lived, had a perfect way of summing up the importance of the address position: "If you set up correctly, there is a good chance you will hit a reasonable shot, even if you make a mediocre swing ... If you set up incorrectly, you will hit a lousy shot even if you make the greatest swing in the world". The great man is, of course, absolutely right. And there is no better way to set up correctly than by developing a reliable pre-shot routine. Every tour professional uses such a ploy, whereas just about every club golfer does not.

Learning and repeating a routine gives you the best possible chance of addressing the ball correctly for every shot. Everybody's routine will vary in content and length, but the key point is to rehearse it so often that it becomes second nature to you. The elements that follow, which are taken from the pre-shot routines of the stars, may sound like a lot to remember prior to taking a shot. But, if you develop and rehearse a routine during practice, you will be amazed how soon it becomes habit. A routine, which should take no longer than 20–30 seconds, will help you apply yourself equally to every shot, which is one of the keys to playing well under pressure.

Swing rehearsal
Your practice swing should be as close as possible to the shot you intend to make

1 **PREPARING FOR A SHOT**
Building a mental picture of the shot you want to hit can greatly enhance your chances of correctly executing that shot. Stand four or five paces behind the ball, and take a few seconds to compose yourself while you picture the ball's flight to the target.

2 Make one or two smooth practice swings. As you do so, concentrate on your rhythm, and try to match the physical feelings throughout your body to your mental images of the shot. This has the effect of focusing your intuitive hand-eye coordination.

3 If you are under pressure or nervous, your heart rate will quicken, and adrenaline will start to flow. One negative aspect of these natural reactions is that you inevitably hasten your movements. And if your swing becomes hurried, you can lose the rhythm necessary for a decent shot. A useful device that many good players employ is to take a couple of deep breaths before addressing the ball. This relaxes the muscles in your body, and gives you a feeling of calm.

Role Models

When watching a tournament on television, it is easy to become caught up in the excitement of a spectacular shot – a soaring drive, a brilliant chip, or a long putt – but it is also worth paying attention to the way top golfers prepare to hit a shot. There is a great deal you can learn from them in this department of the game. Watch how the professionals approach the ball, and note how they never seem to rush. They stay calm and keep their movements smooth and unhurried. Also, if anything distracts them during their pre-shot routine, they start again. This ensures that they are always mentally ready to take on each shot.

Hands
To relieve tension in your hands, waggle the club back and forth at address

4 Aiming the clubface at an intermediate mark between the ball and the target (such as an old divot-mark a few paces away) is a better way of producing an accurate shot than concentrating solely on the distant target. It makes the task seem a little easier, and that helps to keep you in a positive frame of mind. This process is called "spot marking" and is discussed further on pp.20–1.

5 Step into your address position with your grip already formed on the club, alternately fixing your sights on the intermediate target and the target itself. Aim the clubface at your intermediate target and, assuming you want to hit a straight shot, build a stance that is parallel with the aim of the clubface. Your feet, hips, and shoulders should then be square to the ball-to-target line. Now you are ready to go.

STRATEGY OFF THE TEE

GOLF IS AS MUCH about strategy as execution. Every shot you face involves a decision of some kind, and that is as important as the swing you make. Arguably, it is the most under-estimated, under-practised aspect of the game. Yet there is no surer way to lower your average scores in a round than by exercising your grey matter before and during play.

The decision-making processes on the tee are vital to your chances of playing a good drive. Anyone who tees the ball up with little regard to placement and then merrily aims on a general path down the middle of the fairway is missing out on an opportunity to make the game easier. By adopting certain strategies and avoiding others, you can increase the average number of fairways you hit and, just as importantly, dramatically reduce destructive tee shots, which all contribute to a high score.

THE TEEING AREA
Knowing how to shape your shots (see pp.306–7) enables you to avoid danger on one side of the hole or the other. However, most golfers have a natural shape to their shots – either a slight fade or draw. If you are aware of this, you can make allowances. For example, if your natural shot is a fade, tee up on the right, and aim down the left side of the fairway. If the ball flies straight, you should still hit the fairway; if the ball fades according to plan, you will be right in the middle of the fairway. Even if the ball fades more than you planned, you should hit the fairway, or the light rough at worst. Similarly, if your natural shape is a draw, tee up on the left, and aim down the right side of the fairway. Smart thinking on the tee effectively widens your margin for error.

MAKE A GOOD FIRST IMPRESSION
Hitting the first tee shot of the day safely down the middle of the fairway is important for your mental well-being, and it also lets your opponent know that you will be a tough competitor. Try to select a club with which you are confident of striking a solid and straight shot. This helps you feel in control of your game. Your first priority should be keeping the ball in play, even if this means sacrificing distance. The last thing you want to begin the day is a wild drive into trouble. It is a stressful way to start a round and will almost certainly cost you a couple of shots. Remember, you cannot win a competition on the first few holes, but you can easily ruin your score if you make a horrendous start to the game.

SHAPE YOUR DRIVES AROUND DOGLEGS
Dogleg fairways are a common feature on many courses. A hole with a dogleg is an ideal opportunity to use your shotmaking skills to your advantage. If the fairway curves to the right, a drive hit with a hint of fade will hug the bend and run around the corner. On a hole that curves to the left, a drive hit with draw enables you to shape the ball around the opposite corner.

AVOID OUT-OF-BOUNDS
Any tee shot with an obvious threat of out-of-bounds is tough, mentally more than technically. With these tee shots you have to avoid taking risks, and should try to put your mind at ease. Firstly, play with a club you feel comfortable using. Even if this puts the green out of range for your next shot, you can still chip and putt for par, and

the worst score you might make is a bogey. Knock the ball out-of-bounds off the tee, however, and you could end up with a double bogey, or worse. Secondly, stick with your pre-shot routine (see pp.312–3). Remember, in golf, familiarity breeds confidence, and a pre-shot routine can put you at ease.

Finally, aim away from the trouble: if the out-of-bounds is on the left, tee-up on the left and aim right; and vice versa if the trouble spot is on the right. Commit yourself completely to the shot you have opted to play, and do not think about the out-of-bounds area. This might all sound too easy to be true, but that is often the nature of the game. Keeping things simple and playing with safety in mind can make all the difference.

TEE-SHOT STRATEGY

Multiple teeing areas are a common feature at most golf courses as they change the length of the hole, allowing players of different standards to enjoy a fair challenge. With careful thought you can use the teeing area to optimize your strategy on every hole, altering your angle of attack to seek out flags or avoiding trouble on one side of the fairway.

ON THE FAIRWAY AND IN THE ROUGH

MAKING A GOOD DECISION on the tee, and hitting a solid drive is an important start. But it is, nevertheless, only a start. Once the tee shot is away, you then have to turn your attention to the second shot. If you are on a par 3, your second shot should be a putt, but on the longer holes, you will be aiming to hit the green or find a good position further up the fairway with your second shot.

These two pages focus on some typical situations where using your brain can save you shots. As your game improves, you will realize more and more that shooting a low score is not about all-out attack. Indeed, a good round of golf can frequently be attributed as much to the overly ambitious shots you do not hit as to the terrific shots you do. Golf requires good judgement as well as great skill.

TURN PAR 5s INTO A THREE-PART STRATEGY

Many golfers are intimidated by long holes. But a simple change in approach will show you that par 5s are among the easiest holes on the course. The key is to separate a long hole into easily manageable sections: treat the hole as if it is in three parts. The only requirement of your tee shot is that you keep the ball in play. A length of around 180–200 m (195–220 yd) – which for most golfers is achievable with a lofted wood – is more than adequate. Approach your second shot in a similar way: put to the back of your mind all thoughts of hitting the ball as far as possible – instead, focus on position. Keep the ball in play and remember that, on all but the longest par 5, a controlled 180-m (195-yd) second shot will leave you with little more than a short-to-medium iron to the green. A birdie-putt is then one easy step away, and you will have reached such a position without having taken the slightest risk.

PLAN YOUR STRATEGY
Use a course planner to work out how you intend to play the hole. Rethink the challenge of a par 5 as a short series of mini-challenges. Put simply – divide and conquer.

AIM DEAD CENTRE
If, as here, the pin is placed close to a left-hand bunker, ignore the flag and aim for the centre of the green. A long putt is a better prospect than a tough bunker shot.

AVOID "SUCKER" PIN PLACEMENTS

A typical example of a sucker pin placement would be a pin on the right-hand edge of the green closely guarded by a deep bunker to the right. Another might be a pin at the front-edge of a green protected by water. In such situations, you only have to stray off-line by a few paces – not a terrible shot by any means – for the penalty to be severe. Do not be tempted into attacking the pin: whenever you see a sucker pin placement, aim for the centre of the green, giving yourself a comfortable margin for error. If you take this theory to its logical conclusion (hitting every approach shot at the centre of all 18 greens in a round), you might be surprised how well you score, as even slightly stray shots stand a better chance of finishing on the green.

OBSERVE A 10-PACE RULE IN DEEP ROUGH

Most golfers are too ambitious with their shots from deep rough. As a general rule, if you cannot see the ball from 10 paces, you should think about pitching the ball safely into the middle of the fairway, where you will be back in control of your game. This reduces the chances of making a high score on the hole. If, however, you go with a longer club and try to hit the green from a terrible lie, the odds are in favour of a mishit. The ball could go anywhere: if you are lucky, you might end up on the fairway; but, since you have less control over the ball, you could end up in an even worse spot.

A BAD LIE

Consider where your ball lies and, when it is deep rough, only hit a shot that is within your capabilities. Do not risk making matters worse with an over-ambitious recovery shot from the rough. When in doubt, play the simple option.

ADD DISTANCE ON THE ANGLE

Most course planners (course maps that indicate distances between the green and various points on the fairway for each hole) are measured from the middle of the fairway to the centre of the green. If you are in the rough, the angle effectively increases the distance to the centre of the green (as shown on the course planner) by as much as 5 per cent. A shot from 150 m (165 yd), for example, might gain an extra 7.5 m (8 yd). Also check the flag position. If it is central, you can rely on the number in the book. But if the flag is at the front or back of the green, add or subtract distance accordingly.

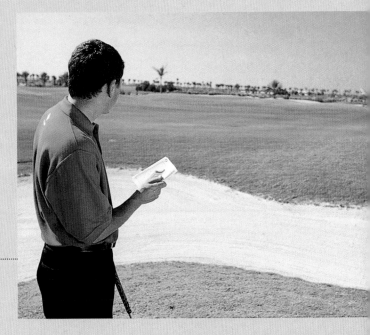

DO YOUR SUMS

Consult the course planner, and make the necessary alterations when working out the distance to the pin. This can make the difference between a short birdie-putt and a potential three-putt.

IMPROVING YOUR MENTAL APPROACH

THERE IS NO DENYING that golf is one of the most mentally challenging games you can play. This is partly due to the fact that you have a lot of time between shots to dwell on what you have just done and what you are about to do. Professionals are acutely aware of this, which is why most tour players consult sports psychologists frequently to encourage constructive, rather than destructive, thought processes. However, most amateurs are reluctant to consider the mental aspect of the game, and this is a grave mistake. If you want better control over your game, you must learn to control your mind.

STICK TO YOUR GAME PLAN

Before a game, it is important to be prepared mentally as well as physically. Contemplate your game plan before you arrive at the course. For example, if you know the course well, you can plan your approach to different greens prior to the round. Decide when you will play defensively (by aiming for the middle of the green) and when you will attack the flag. Obviously certain factors might influence your plan – strong winds, for example, may change your tactics. However, do not let negative factors, such as a bad start, trigger a change in your game plan. Switching to a foolhardy plan of attack in an attempt to redeem a situation generally makes matters worse. Equally, if you have a great start, do not suddenly become overly defensive in your play.

ALL IN THE MIND

It is always wise to have a game plan in your mind, which is easily formulated if you know the course well. Decide, for example, which clubs are "middle of the green" clubs and which are "attack the flag" clubs. Stick to your plan wherever possible.

TREAT EVERY SHOT THE SAME

Golfers tend to build up the importance of certain shots, most commonly the first tee shot or the last few shots in a good round. This is why you generally feel more nervous on the first tee than at any other time during a round: you have put yourself under unnecessary pressure. This is the main reason why some golfers hit poor opening drives.

One of the secrets of successful play is to approach every shot in exactly the same way. If you do so, all of your shots should improve. This is because, mentally, you will not feel under extra pressure, which can lead to tension. Instead, you will feel more confident and relaxed, which all contributes to a better swing.

HAVE FUN BETWEEN SHOTS

Even with the best will in the world, you are not going to be able to maintain 100 per cent concentration for the several hours it takes to play a round of golf. Indeed, it can be quite detrimental to your game if you try to do so. A far better policy is to have a chat and some fun between most shots. This is a good ploy if your last shot was good, and it is especially worthwhile if your last shot was poor because it will help you put the mistake behind you. The only shot that matters, remember, is the next one.

STAY ON AN EVEN KEEL

It can be exciting when something amazing happens in a round, such as chipping-in for a birdie. But, equally, it can be frustrating when you experience some bad luck or hit a poor shot. It is, therefore, always best to keep your emotions on an even keel. Accept the fact that you will hit bad shots and, by the same token, do not become over-excited if you chip-in or hole an impressive putt. If your emotions are under control, the chances are that your game is, too.

PLAY WITH THE BALL
Juggling the ball with a club takes the edge off the seriousness of a round and can help you forget a bad previous hole.

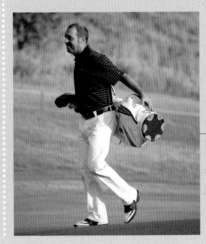

KEEP YOUR HEAD
Everyone reacts in a different way to good or bad luck. However, to play at your best, try to remain unaffected by changes of fortune.

LOSE COUNT OF YOUR SCORE

Never add up your score when you are playing well because, subconsciously, you start thinking ahead and making predictions. "If I can make no worse than a five on each of the last four holes," you might say to yourself, "I will beat my best-ever score." That kind of attitude is rather like drafting your winner's speech while still on the 10th green. It distracts you from the shot in hand and puts undue pressure on your game. Instead of building up this extra stress, try to lose count of your score. To play consistently for the full 18 holes, you must become accustomed to taking the game one shot at a time. It takes practice, but if you focus on each shot as it comes, and stay in the present tense, the future is nearly always brighter. Save adding up your score until the last putt has dropped.

STAY IN THE PRESENT
By all means mark your card after every hole, but do not add up your score as you go and let your mind wander ahead of the game. Such thinking usually ends in disaster. Just focus on one shot, and one hole, at a time.

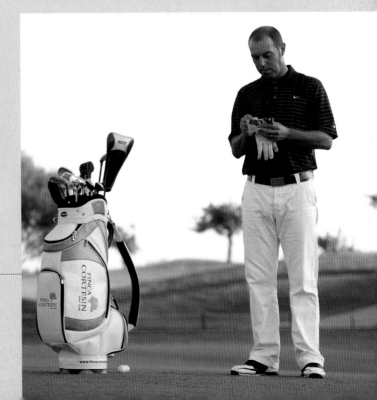

SIMPLIFYING WINTER GOLF

UNLESS YOU are lucky enough to live under sunny skies all year round, there will be several occasions when you must play in adverse conditions. As well as wind and rain, you will probably encounter the inevitably inferior playing surfaces that are part of a round of golf in winter. Grim playing conditions need not ruin your chances of a good score, though: there are certain ways you can alter your strategy and adapt your technique to suit even the roughest circumstances. And no matter how bad the weather and playing surfaces are, it is always as well to remember that the conditions are the same for everyone. Besides, compiling a good round on a nasty day is one of the most satisfying experiences in golf.

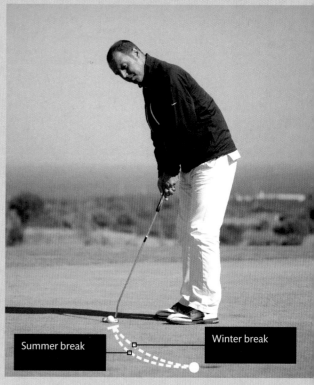

Summer break   Winter break

JUDGING WINTER BREAK
Even on sunny winter days, because putting surfaces are generally more woolly in winter, you have to strike the ball harder than in summer. This means the ball will break less.

ALLOW FOR LESS BREAK ON PUTTS
Because putting surfaces tend to be less closely mown in winter, putts always travel slower than in summer. To compensate for this sluggishness, you have to hit putts more firmly. For this reason, the ball will not take as much break on its way to the hole on winter greens. Even on short putts, the "winter line" and "summer line" will be different. Be aware of this, so that you can make allowances.

SWAP LONG IRONS FOR LOFTED WOODS
Long irons are unforgiving clubs at the best of times, but when the ground conditions are not ideal – a little soggy, perhaps – they become the most demanding clubs in the bag to hit solidly. It is wise to replace a couple of your longest irons with two lofted woods – perhaps a 4-wood and a utility-wood (see pp.327–8). Lofted woods are easier to hit from imperfect lies (either out of the rough or on the fairway) than long irons. This is for several reasons, primarily due to the shape and design of the clubhead. Firstly, the clubhead of a lofted wood will slide more easily through fluffy grass around the ball. Secondly, the sweetspot is larger than on a long iron – slightly off-centre strikes produce acceptable shots. Finally, the centre of gravity is much lower on a lofted wood than it is on a long iron, which makes it easier to get the ball airborne. This produces a longer carry through the air, and on soft ground, the extra "air-time" is very useful.

CLUB CHANGE
In winter conditions it is a good idea to use a lofted wood rather than a long iron whenever possible.

TAKE LESS SAND IN BUNKERS

The sand in bunkers can become much heavier in prolonged spells of wet weather, which calls for a slight change of technique. The main difference is that you should take less sand when it is wet than you would for a splash bunker shot in the dry, as wet sand tends to offer more resistance to the swinging clubhead. As a general rule, you could perhaps halve the distance behind the ball where you would normally strike the sand (see Drill 5 in the "Bunker Play" section, pp.194–5). That should help prevent you leaving the ball well short of the flag. As an alternative, you could experiment with a slightly longer swing. This will enable you to generate more clubhead speed through the hitting area, which will provide an effective solution when the sand is heavy. Try both of these methods in practice and see which one you like best.

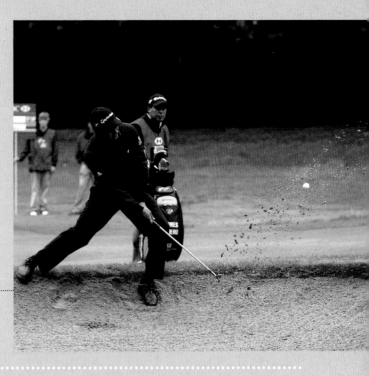

STRIKE ACTION

When sand is wet it becomes much heavier and denser. To compensate, concentrate on either taking less sand at impact or swinging harder, as Andres Romero is doing here.

PITCH IT UP

When the greens are soft and receptive, emulate Lee Westwood and pitch the ball well up to the flag, to ensure that it does not come to rest well short of the flag.

BE BOLD WITH YOUR SHORT SHOTS

Unless the ground is frozen, in winter the greens will be highly receptive to a lofted shot. You can make this work to your advantage. If as you visualize your shot you imagine the ball landing on top of the pin, when you play the shot you will be amazed how often the ball travels the perfect distance. This is because the mental imagery encourages you to be bold when it is all too easy to leave the ball short.

KEY CHECKPOINT

Be smart with your choice of ball

In winter, stopping the ball on soft greens is the least of your troubles. But these very same ground conditions make it harder to generate as much distance off the tee because there is virtually no run on landing. Therefore, if you use a high-spinning, soft-covered ball in summer, in winter it is well worth considering swapping it for a harder, two-piece ball designed more for distance (see the Key Checkpoint on p.131).

MONITOR YOUR PERFORMANCE

FOR AS LONG as you play golf, the tests featured in chapter one of this book will represent a constant and reliable barometer of your ability in every department of the game. Self-assessment is one of the keys to long-term improvement. You should, however, also keep track of your performance during competitive play. While it is easy to judge your success based on your overall score for 18 holes, a detailed breakdown of your results in each department of the game is more revealing. This is certainly also a better method of finding possible ways to lower your scores.

The key areas to examine are as follows: the number of fairways hit in a round; the number of greens hit in "regulation"; the number of successful chip-and-putt saves; the number of successful sand-saves; and your average putts per round. It is probably too time-consuming to take note of such details during a round, but once you have finished, a quick mental analysis of each hole will reveal the exact breakdown of shots. Then compare your results with the tables below. This whole operation takes only a few minutes, and is time well spent, as the data highlights your strengths and weaknesses. Try to keep a file of this information, so that you can monitor performance trends in your game. To become a more complete golfer, you need to work on your weaknesses until there is little difference between your shortcomings and your strengths.

1. DRIVING ACCURACY

Add up the number of par 4s and par 5s on your course, and calculate a percentage figure based on the total number of fairways you hit from the tee. Remember that distance is not the main issue with driving (see p.28). Instead, keeping the ball in play – on the closely mown grass – should be your major consideration. This attitude will help keep you out of trouble.

Results	
FAIRWAYS HIT	RATING
0–30 per cent	Very poor
31–40 per cent	Poor
41–60 per cent	Adequate
61–70 per cent	Good
+71 per cent	Excellent

2. GREENS HIT IN REGULATION

Note how many greens you hit in "regulation" (which means that if you then take the standard two putts to complete the hole, you will achieve par). The number of strokes required to hit a green in regulation are: par 3 – one shot; par 4 – two shots; par 5 – three shots. Obviously, if you hit a green in less than the required number of shots, this also counts as a "hit in regulation".

Results	
GREENS HIT	RATING
0–20 per cent	Very poor
21–40 per cent	Poor
41–60 per cent	Adequate
61–70 per cent	Good
+71 per cent	Excellent

3. CHIP-AND-PUTT SAVES

Every time you miss a green with your approach shot, write down whether you make an "up-and-down" save (a chip and a single putt) or not. This is one area of the game in which good players excel. Increasing your percentage of chip-and-putt saves will have a dramatic effect on your average scores, which will in turn lead to a lower handicap.

Results	
SUCCESS RATE	RATING
0–20 per cent	Very poor
21–40 per cent	Poor
41–60 per cent	Adequate
61–75 per cent	Good
+76 per cent	Excellent

4. SAND-SAVES

Whenever your ball finishes in a greenside bunker, you have the opportunity of a sand-save: a single bunker shot followed by a single putt. Note how often you are successful in sand-save situations. If you have worked through the "Bunker Play" section (see pp.186–231) you should be playing out of a bunker in one shot every time, even if the lie is terrible.

Results	
SUCCESS RATE	RATING
0–10 per cent	Very poor
11–25 per cent	Poor
26–40 per cent	Adequate
41–65 per cent	Good
+66 per cent	Excellent

5. AVERAGE PUTTS PER ROUND

As many as 40 per cent of the shots played in an average round are putts: playing well on the greens can mean a low score. Add up the total number of putts you make during a round. (Note: Be ambitious on the greens, but do not set unrealistic goals. Take heart from the fact that from 2 m [2 yd], the world's best players hole, on average, only about half their putts.)

Results	
PUTTS	RATING
+40	Very poor
39–37	Poor
36–33	Adequate
32–30	Good
-30	Excellent

Only perfect practice makes perfect

One way to improve your results is to note the old adage: "only perfect practice makes perfect". Great players know the importance of this truth, which is one reason why they can put in top performances under severe pressure.

It also explains why most club golfers can hit the ball nicely at the range, but find it difficult to do the same on the course. However, if you treat every practice shot as if it is an important shot in a competition, when faced with a real pressure shot, you will be able to approach it as if it is just another practice shot. The concept of perfect practice is also explored in the "Off the Tee" section (see Drill 1, p.30).

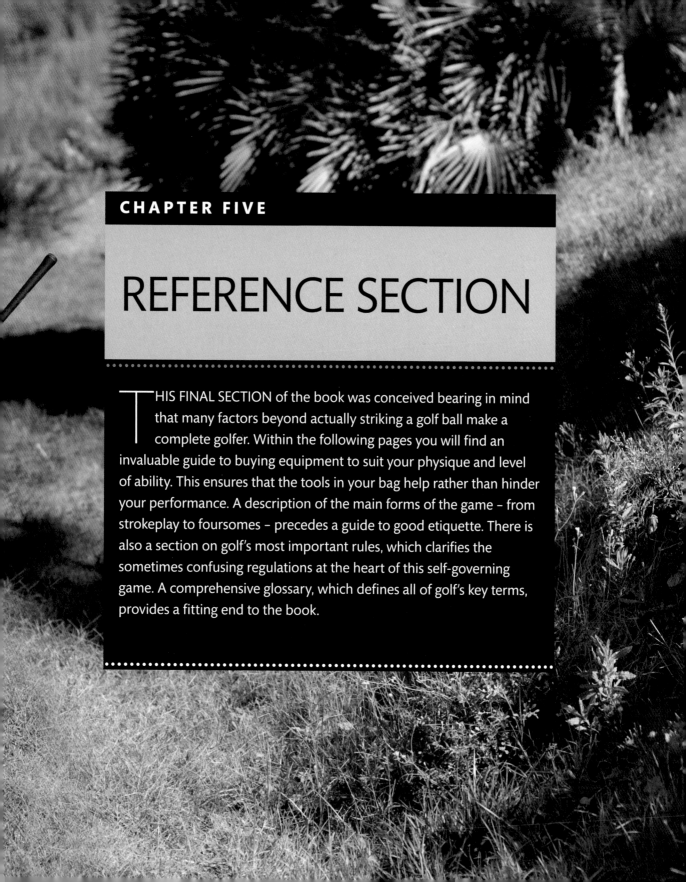

CHAPTER FIVE

REFERENCE SECTION

THIS FINAL SECTION of the book was conceived bearing in mind that many factors beyond actually striking a golf ball make a complete golfer. Within the following pages you will find an invaluable guide to buying equipment to suit your physique and level of ability. This ensures that the tools in your bag help rather than hinder your performance. A description of the main forms of the game – from strokeplay to foursomes – precedes a guide to good etiquette. There is also a section on golf's most important rules, which clarifies the sometimes confusing regulations at the heart of this self-governing game. A comprehensive glossary, which defines all of golf's key terms, provides a fitting end to the book.

BUYING THE RIGHT EQUIPMENT

ENORMOUS ADVANCES IN TECHNOLOGY over recent years have left the consumer spoilt for choice when it comes to club selection. The market has never been more exciting or more confusing. The sheer variety of clubs available, the confusing accompanying jargon, and the advanced construction materials used can sometimes conspire to make it difficult to make the right equipment-buying decisions.

As a result, some golfers stick with the same clubs for years, while others regularly splash out on the latest equipment, picking clubs off the shelf on impulse. Yet in both cases golfers are missing out on the potential benefits of using equipment that is ideally suited to them. While no amount of modern technology can compensate for elementary faults in your swing, it is important that your clubs complement your physique and your swing. Otherwise, your clubs may be holding you back. In this section of the book you will learn how to choose the equipment best suited to you and your style of play.

Make sure that the grip fits your hands

A club's grip tends to be overlooked by many golfers, yet it is the only point of contact between you and the club. Therefore, it makes sense that the grip should suit your hands. Aside from keeping grips in good condition – replacing them when they become shiny or smooth – you also need to make sure that they are the correct size. Perform this simple test. Take a club and hold it in your left hand. Ideally your middle two fingers should lightly touch the fleshy pad at the base of your thumb. If they do not touch at all, or the tips of your fingers dig into your palm, your grips need adjusting. This is a straightforward and inexpensive job that can be done by any club professional.

GRIP SIZE
The correct grip size (left) is very important. If your clubs' grips are too thin (above), it is worth having them altered.

DRIVERS

Selecting a driver was once a straightforward business. Virtually all were made of wood, and the only considerations were price, appearance, and loft. Nowadays metal drivers are the norm, and manufacturers use a huge variety of construction techniques and many different metals to produce clubs they claim offer the ultimate in distance, forgiveness, or both.

When purchasing a driver, it is important to consider the various elements that influence a club's playability. First, the size of the clubhead is an important issue. Big clubheads provide a larger hitting area and are more forgiving to off-centre strikes than small clubheads. Despite these advantages, some golfers still find that smaller clubheads better suit their playing style. The loft on the club is also critical. Powerful ball-strikers can get away with very little loft, as little as seven degrees, whereas less accomplished golfers should not go lower than ten degrees. Do not look at loft in isolation, however, because it is not the only factor that influences the height of your shots. Manufacturers can manipulate the centre of gravity on a club so as to influence ball-flight. Some clubs are designed with a low centre of gravity to help the ball become airborne, which tends to suit

FACE FACTS

Most drivers and lofted woods are made of steel. But titanium, though more expensive, is also popular because it is light, which means that the clubhead can be bigger and thus even more forgiving. Titanium is also harder than steel and so propels the ball faster off the clubface, extending the ball-flight, as well as reducing sidespin.

Shaft flex, material, and length

Do not forget that the shaft of your club is as important as the head. When deciding which shaft is best for you, flex is the first consideration. For men, there are three main flexes: regular, stiff, and extra stiff. The faster you swing and the harder you hit the ball, the stiffer the shaft you need. As a general rule, if the shafts in your set are too flexible, you will tend to hit shots high and with a hook. If the shafts are too stiff, the ball will often fly low and with a slice. The shafts in women's clubs tend to be more flexible, reflecting a generally less powerful swing. But these shafts become progressively stiffer for better players.

Also consider the shaft's material. There are two basic types: steel and graphite. These days, although drivers with steel shafts are still used, most have graphite shafts. For irons, because graphite is a light material, it is favoured by players who struggle to generate speed in their swing, such as seniors. Graphite is also thought to pass on less vibration to the hands and wrists, helping prevent injury. It is common in metal-headed drivers because the lightness means more weight can be placed in the clubhead, which provides greater force at impact. However, steel remains the most popular material for the shaft of irons because of its good all-round performance.

Finally, if you are very tall or have short arms, you might want to have the shafts of your clubs extended by 2–3 cm (¾–1¼ in) so that your posture does not suffer.

N.S PRO TOUR TOURNAMENT SPECIAL 85g type MK-I

Driver with graphite shaft

Driver with steel shaft

the less-accomplished player. Other clubs have a higher centre of gravity, which is better for more advanced players and gives a more penetrating ball-flight. The centre of gravity can even be made bigger, so that there is more mass behind either the heel or toe of the clubhead. This makes the club more forgiving to off-centre strikes. It is also important that the shaft flex is appropriate to your ability (see "Shaft Flex, Material, and Length", above right).

Once you have considered a club's playability, with all clubs it is important that you like their appearance, and the driver is no exception to this rule. If your driver is not pleasing to your eye, you might never pull it out of your bag. And finally, before you step into a shop, establish your spending limit and examine only clubs priced within your budget.

DIFFERENT DRIVERS

With so many drivers on the market, the choice can be confusing. There's always more to these clubs than meets the eye, though, so it pays to do your homework.

Finding the correct lie angle

The angle at which the bottom edge of the club sits on the ground is described as the lie angle. If this is too upright for you, the heel will make contact with the ground first at impact. Conversely, if the lie angle is too flat the toe of the club will strike the ground first at impact. To avoid these problems, check that the bottom edge of the club is level with the ground at address. Then hit a few shots. If the lie angle is correct, the start of the divot-mark will be uniform in shape and depth and pointing straight at the target.

If the lie angle is either too flat or too upright, check your set-up. If this is as it should be, the club professional can adjust the lie angle. Alternatively, you can seek out one of the manufacturers that produce clubs with a range of lie angles.

Correct lie angle

Lie angle too flat

Lie angle too upright

FAIRWAY WOODS

Over the years, lofted woods, or "fairway woods", have developed along the same lines as drivers. This means that these days, the longest clubs in your bag are easier to use, are more forgiving, and can send the ball further than ever. Essentially, you should consider the same factors when buying a fairway wood that you do when purchasing a driver (see pp.326–7). However, the clubhead should be smaller than for a driver because on the fairway it is more difficult to strike the ball out of the centre of the clubface with a big clubhead (this is not a problem on the tee because the ball is teed up). Your main concern when examining a fairway wood should be loft – but bear in mind that you might want to use the club off the tee as well as on the fairway. Given this proviso, a loft of between 15 and 18 degrees strikes a good balance between distance and accuracy.

It is a good idea to introduce a utility wood – a type of fairway wood – to your set. These woods come in a wide range of lofts but the most common utility woods are 5- and 7-woods, which have relatively small and compact heads. This means that utility woods are effective from a variety of lies, so that you can hit the ball from the fairway and from light rough – long irons do not offer this versatility. The other significant benefit of utility woods

Woods: loft and average distance

WOOD NUMBER	LOFT	DISTANCE
Driver	7–11°	220 m (240 yd)
3-wood	15°	200 m (220 yd)
5-wood	21°	175 m (190 yd)

UTILITY WOOD
Compact, shallow-faced clubheads offer versatility from a variety of lies.

is that they make it very easy to get the ball into the air, which means that most golfers will hit their shots further with these clubs than with long irons.

A utility wood can fill a gap in your set. For example, some golfers will carry a 3-wood and a 3-iron, which leaves a big difference in distance between the two clubs. A utility wood with a loft of somewhere between 17 and 23 degrees will bridge the difference nicely.

IRONS
As with drivers, different iron clubs used to be subtle variations of what was basically the same theme. Nowadays, however, manufacturers are in a constant race with one another to come up with the latest innovation. This means that there is a phenomenal variety of iron clubhead designs on the market. However, the key issues when you come to buy are: how much forgiveness do you want, how important is it for you to be able to shape the ball through the air, and do you like the look of the club? In answering these questions you narrow your options, making the buying process that much easier. When it comes to clubhead construction, there are two main types: blades and peripherally weighted irons.

Blades

These clubs, by far the most popular irons up until the late 1970s, have a forged clubhead and a plain shape. Although relatively unforgiving to off-centre strikes, blades produce a purer feel at impact and offer greater scope for shaping the ball through the air. Today, blades are still favoured by traditionalists and some professionals and accomplished amateurs.

Peripherally weighted irons

Also known as "cavity backs", peripherally weighted irons often have cast rather than forged clubheads and are designed to offer maximum forgiveness to off-centre hits. This is because they have more weight at the extremities of the clubhead. Such clubs were originally seen as game-improvement devices, and they did not offer the pure feel or shotmaking potential of blades. They were considered of most use to average golfers and were thought the antithesis of the bladed iron. That is not the case today, however. In addition to peripherally weighted cast clubs, there are now many "in-between" peripherally weighted irons available, which offer some of the benefits of bladed irons yet are still forgiving to off-centre strikes. Some of these irons, especially those used by many of today's professionals, are even designed to look very much like a blade – at least from the player's-eye view.

BLADE
Providing the purest feel at impact, blades make it much easier to shape shots at will through the air.

PERIPHERALLY WEIGHTED IRON
Peripherally weighted irons are more forgiving to off-centre strikes but do not make it so easy to shape shots.

Irons: loft and average distance

IRON NUMBER	LOFT	DISTANCE
2-iron	18°	190 m (210 yd)
3-iron	22°	175 m (190 yd)
4-iron	26°	165 m (180 yd)
5-iron	30°	155 m (170 yd)
6-iron	34°	145 m (160 yd)
7-iron	38°	135 m (150 yd)
8-iron	42°	130 m (140 yd)
9-iron	44°	120 m (130 yd)

Bounce angle

SAND WEDGES
SAND WEDGES
Clubs with lots of bounce (left) work best in soft, powdery sand; less bounce is appropriate for coarser, heavier textured sand.

Wedges: loft and distance

WEDGE TYPE	LOFT	DISTANCE
Pitching Wedge	46°	100 m (110 yd)
Standard Sand Wedge	56°	75 m (82 yd)
Lob Wedge	60°	55 m (60 yd)

WEDGES

There is a massive choice of wedges on offer. When buying a wedge or wedges, you should consider loft, the degree of bounce (the roundness and breadth of the flange at the bottom of the wedge), and clubhead materials.

The standard pitching wedge has 46 degrees of loft. The most lofted wedge, commonly known as a lob wedge, has 60 degrees, or even as much as 62 degrees. You should have at least three clubs within these parameters, as this offers you maximum versatility in your short game. The bounce angle is just as important as loft. The degree of bounce you select will depend on the kind of shots you wish to play. For fairway shots, less bounce is desirable (no more than 5 degrees) because the clubhead sits almost flush to the ground behind the ball, promoting a clean strike. From most types of sand and from soft ground and rough, however, you need more bounce (somewhere between 10 and 14 degrees) to stop the clubhead digging into the turf or sand rather than making solid contact with the back of the ball.

As for clubhead material, steel is the standard and most preferred metal for wedge clubheads. However, if you want even greater levels of control you might consider beryllium-copper, which has a softer feel at impact.

PUTTERS

Since as many as 40 per cent of the shots played in an average round are putts, it is virtually impossible to exaggerate the importance of using a putter with which you feel confident. As with putting technique, choosing a putter is open to greater personal interpretation than any other club. Putters can have standard-length or long handles, and there are three main types of putterhead (peripherally weighted, mallet-headed, and centre-shafted), but within these styles there is an unbelievable degree of variation in design, colour, and feel. The best idea is simply to try out as many putters as you can, and choose one that feels right to you.

Peripherally weighted putters are constructed using the same principle employed in peripherally weighted irons (see p.329): the weight is positioned across the clubface to minimize performance loss caused by off-centre strikes.

A mallet-headed putter has a semi-circular head. This putter offers the same benefits as a peripherally weighted putter, only in a different package. This is probably the most distinctive of the three designs.

Centre-shafted putters are plain in shape and, arguably, less forgiving with off-centre hits than a peripherally weighted club. For this reason, centre-shafted putters are best suited

TAKE YOUR PICK
There are hundreds of putters on the market, but they all come in three basic designs; peripherally weighted or mallet-headed (right), and centre-shafted (not shown).

Mallet-headed putter

INSERT PUTTER
There are many types of insert available in putters; from soft to relatively hard, but they all share one goal – to improve the feedback of the ball on the putterface on impact.

to accomplished golfers, who can consistently produce strikes from the centre of the putterface.

Putterface inserts
Golf club manufacturers have responded to golfers' quest for maximum feel on the greens by introducing the concept of face-inserts in putters. Some inserts are

Use the ball type that suits your game

Once you have purchased the perfect set of clubs, do not forget about balls: the type of ball you play is a reflection not only of your ability but also your priorities in the game. The following guide to the three main types of ball will help you make an informed choice.

THE CONTROL BALL
If you want maximum feel and spin when you play short shots, a control ball, which will usually have a cover made of high performance urethane, or another artificial compound with the same playing characteristics, is your best bet. This soft cover allows for good feel on and around the greens. The inner construction is also designed to produce greater levels of spin, which further enhances your control for all shots. The downsides to this ball type are that you will lose some distance on long shots, the soft cover is prone to scuffing (although the covers are more durable than they were 10–15 years ago), and these balls are generally more expensive than the other types.

THE DISTANCE BALL
All manufacturers produce balls designed for maximum distance. These balls, which feel very hard off the clubface, offer the most distance of all the ball types. They

are characterized by a distinctive "clicky" sound made at impact and are almost indestructible. However, distance balls offer less control: so around the greens, do not expect lots of backspin on your pitch shots and chips.

THE COMPROMISE
Some balls offer a "happy medium" between control and distance. While they cannot offer the feel of a control ball or the length of a distance ball (they are not designed solely for one purpose), they do provide some of the advantages of both. Compromise balls feature an outer layer that provides some spin yet is still durable. In many respects these are the perfect balls for winter golf – giving you a decent distance for your money and, since the greens are generally soft, all the control you need from short range.

made from relatively soft rubber compounds, while others are built up from complex mixtures of metals.

Despite the variety of colours and materials used, the idea behind these inserts is essentially the same: to promote a soft feel off the putterface in order to enhance control and give the ball a smooth roll.

The benefits of a fat grip
Some professionals have jumbo-fat grips fitted to their putters. These fill the hands more than a conventional grip and reduce excessive wrist action during the stroke. You might want to experiment with a fat grip.

Peripherally weighted putter

LONG PUTTER
Although few amateurs currently use the long putter, the fact that several tour pros can be seen wielding it effectively may eventually make it more universally popular.

TYPES OF PLAY AND HANDICAPS

S O FAR, this book has covered almost every conceivable aspect of how to play golf and of what equipment to use. Now is an appropriate time to examine the multitude of competitive and friendly formats of the game, each of which has its own challenges and excitements. The most popular types of play seen on courses all over the world are discussed, as are a few that are sadly not played often enough. Additionally, a full and clear explanation is given of how handicaps work with each format, both in terms of playing against the course and against your opponents.

If you play the same type of game every time you set foot on a course, you risk missing out on one of golf's greatest attractions: variety. When you arrange your next round with friends, why not spice things up by trying out a new format? You will not only enjoy the change but also learn from it.

STROKEPLAY

Most professional and amateur tournaments take place under the format known as strokeplay. In this form of the game you simply record your score for each hole, and add up the total at the end of the round. The person with the lowest score wins.

The total number of shots taken in strokeplay is known as the "gross score". In a tour event, this is the score that counts because professional players do not have a handicap. But at club level, each player's handicap is deducted from the gross figure to produce a "net score", which in most amateur events decides the winner.

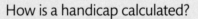

How is a handicap calculated?

Handicaps allow golfers of different abilities to compete on equal terms. Gaining your first handicap is a straightforward process that involves playing usually three rounds on the same course. You then combine the scores and divide by three to arrive at a figure relative to the standard scratch score (SSS) of the course. For example, if you play three rounds and score 86, 91, and 84, these figures are then totalled to make 261. This number is divided by three (which makes 87). If the SSS of the course is 70, then you will be given a handicap of 17. The maximum handicap for men is 28; for women the upper limit is 36. Your handicap is then adjusted every time you play in a strokeplay competition. There are three possible scenarios. Firstly, you can shoot a score better than your handicap, which means your handicap will be lowered. Secondly, you can shoot a score the same as, or one–three strokes above, your handicap. This places you in a "buffer zone", wherein your handicap does not move up or down. This zone allows for a minor dip in form, which does not warrant an increase in your handicap. Finally, you can shoot a score more than three shots above your handicap, which places you beyond the buffer zone. In this situation, your handicap will go up.

STABLEFORD

This format works on the principle of awarding points for scores gained on each hole. An albatross is worth five points, an eagle four points, a birdie three points, a par two points, a bogey one point, and anything worse than a bogey scores no points at all. The person with the highest score at the end of the round wins.

Most stableford competitions offer competitors the full handicap allowance, so that if your handicap is 12 you are "given" a stroke on each of the holes with a stroke index of between 1 and 12. This means that you deduct one stroke from your

ADAPTABLE PLAYER
For the last 20 years Bernhard Langer has been one of Europe's finest players – a master of both strokeplay and matchplay.

score on each of these 12 holes: a par, for example, counts as a birdie, which gives you three points instead of two. Stroke indexes are indicated on all score cards, and, broadly speaking, reflect the degree of difficulty of each hole. The hardest hole on the course has a stroke index of 1 and the easiest has a stroke index of 18.

MATCHPLAY SINGLES
This format involves head-to-head competition, one against one. Individual holes are won, lost, or halved (whereby each player scores the same), and every hole contributes to the state of play of the match. For example, the player who wins the first hole is "one-up". If that player wins the next hole, he or she goes "two-up", and if he or she loses the next, the player is back to "one-up". If a hole is halved, the match score stays the same. The match is decided when a player is "up" by more holes than there are holes left to play. For example, if a player is four-up with three holes to play, this is known as victory by four and three. In the event of the match being all square after 18 holes, a sudden death play-off ensues.

The golfer with the lowest handicap gives strokes to his or her opponent, based on three-quarters of the difference between the two handicaps. For example, if Player A has a handicap of 4 and Player B has a handicap of 16, three-quarters of the difference (12) is 8. Therefore, Player B receives a stroke from his or her opponent on each of the holes with a stroke index of between 1 and 8. This means that on each of the "stroke holes", one shot will be deducted

from Player B's score. Therefore, a four will count as a three, a five will count as a four, and so on.

FOURBALL BETTERBALL
This is similar to matchplay singles, only the game is played in pairs. Each player in the two pairings plays his or her own ball and the lowest score from each pair on each hole is the one that counts. The method of keeping score, and how the handicaps work, is the same as in matchplay singles. Fourball betterball can also be applied to the stableford format but seldom to strokeplay.

FOURSOMES
This is another game played in pairs, but in this format each pairing shares just one ball. One player in each pair tees off on the odd-numbered holes, the other on the even-numbered holes. Thereafter, alternate shots are played with the same ball until the hole is completed. This format can be applied to matchplay, strokeplay, or stableford.

In matchplay foursomes, the pair with the lowest combined handicap give shots to the other two players based on three-eighths of the difference. For example, if Team A has a combined handicap of 10 and Team B has a combined handicap of 26, the difference is 16. Since three-eighths of 16 is 6, Team B receives a stroke on holes with a stroke index between 1 and 6.

GREENSOMES
This is a great variation on the foursomes format, the difference being that both golfers in each pair tee off

RYDER CUP
The Ryder Cup is one of the few professional tournaments played in the foursome format. Here, Ian Poulter and Justin Rose are reading a putt.

and then select the more favourable of the two drives. Then, alternate shots are played as in foursomes.

The handicap calculations work in exactly the same way as with foursomes. Greensomes is also a popular stableford format.

BOGEY
This almost-forgotten format is essentially a game against par. The course is your opponent, and the scoring system is based on holes won, lost, or halved (as in matchplay). The only difference is that the game is not over until the last hole has been completed. The ultimate aim when playing the bogey format is to finish as many holes "up" on the course was possible.

As you play, you receive shots from the course, most commonly based on three-quarters of your handicap allowance. If you play with a handicap of 8, for example, the course gives you six shots. You receive these shots on the holes that have a stroke index between 1 and 6.

THE IMPORTANCE OF GOOD ETIQUETTE

THE TERM "ETIQUETTE" can bring to mind images of stuffiness and an overly regimented code of behaviour. This is a misconception, however, because following good etiquette helps ensure that everyone on the course enjoys their round.

This section highlights the main principles of good etiquette. These are as easy to understand as they are to perform and in time should become second nature. It is as well to remember that in striving to become a more complete golfer, good etiquette is just as relevant as the very act of striking the ball. In the eyes of many golfers, it may even be the more important half of the equation. There are two key areas of etiquette: how to look after the course and behaviour on the course.

DIVOT-MARKS
If you take a divot, always place the turf back in its hole and tread it down. If you do this, the grass should recover quickly, and the damage to the course will be negligible.

LOOKING AFTER THE COURSE
Even the finest courses are less enjoyable to play if they are in poor condition. You can play your part by ensuring that your impact on the course is as minimal as possible. The following guidelines will ensure that you always look after the playing surfaces in the correct way.

Leave the tee in good shape
While you will not usually take a divot on par-4 or par-5 tees (where you will most likely be using a wood), if you take a divot on a par-3 tee, use the sand-and-soil mix provided to fill the divot-mark. If there is no sand-and-soil mix, simply place the divot back in its hole.

Replace divots in the fairway
It is extremely frustrating when your ball comes to rest in an old divot-mark after a perfectly good shot (see p.299). To avoid such misfortune is not the only reason you should replace divots, however. A divot that is immediately placed back in its hole soon repairs itself because the roots usually find their way back into the ground. But if a divot is not replaced, it leaves an ugly scar, making the course look scrappy, and it is harder for the greenkeeper to repair the divot-mark. Therefore, before leaving the scene of every fairway shot, place the divot back in its hole, and tread it down firmly with the sole of your shoe.

Leave no trace in the sand
In the section on bunker play, there is a discussion of the importance of raking

COVER YOUR TRACKS
If you do not rake up your marks in the sand, there is a chance that someone in a group behind could have to play out of one of your footprints. This annoying situation makes the bunker shot much more difficult.

GENTLY DOES IT
Never hurl the flag across the green: this can damage the putting surface. Instead, place it carefully on the ground, well away from the line of play.

over your footprints in the sand after you have played a shot (see the Key Checkpoint on p.203). It is worth reiterating this point because there is scarcely a more depressing moment in a round than when you walk up to a bunker only to find your ball resting in a deep footprint. No one deserves this fate, no matter how awful the stroke was that put the ball there in the first place. Therefore, once you have played your bunker shot, use the rake provided to smooth the sand. If there is no rake, use the back of your sand wedge and do the best you can. Remember to cover your footprints as well as the trough left by the clubhead splashing through the sand. Raking a bunker only takes a few moments, yet this act of consideration can make all the difference to those playing behind you.

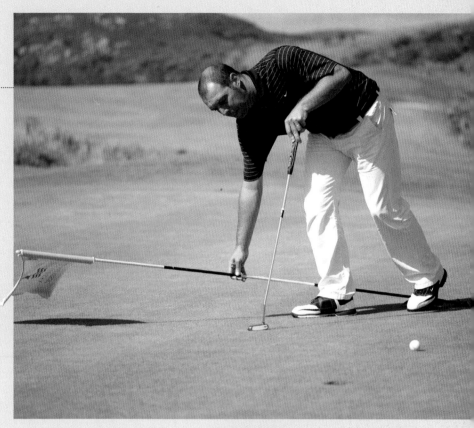

Repair pitch-marks on the green
Pitch-marks on the green are unsightly and can deflect a ball on its way to the hole. Not every shot played on to a green will leave a pitch-mark, but those that do should be repaired the moment you set foot on the green. You can use a pitch-mark repairer, which is designed specifically for the job, or alternatively a wooden tee-peg will suffice (plastic ones bend). The procedure is simple and takes only a few seconds. Stick the pointed end of your tee-peg, or the fork of your pitch-mark repairer, into the ground and gently ease the turf up. This will level the indentation. The pitch-mark will then "heal" within 24 hours, whereas an untended pitch-mark can take weeks to recover completely. A green dotted with pitch-marks is no fun to putt on.

Be careful with the flag
It is amazing how many golfers are careless when it comes to placing the flag on the green. Do not throw it across the green, as this is likely to cause serious damage to the putting surface. Instead, lower it gently to the ground. It is also worth noting that if you hit a putt and the ball strikes a flag lying on the green, you receive a two-shot penalty. Therefore, it makes sense to place the flag well out of harm's way, ideally on the apron of the green. What you can and cannot do on the green is covered in more detail on pp.342–3.

REPAIR JOB
On receptive greens, the ball often leaves a pitch-mark when it lands. Make sure that you repair these indentations immediately, either using a wooden tee-peg, or a pitch-mark repairer.

HOW TO BEHAVE ON THE COURSE

While looking after the course is an essential requirement of good etiquette, your on-course behaviour is equally important. Inconsiderate conduct during a round can take the shine off even the sunniest of days. However, if you adhere to the advice given below, you will not be guilty of ruining other players' enjoyment.

Wait your turn

Honour on the tee – who plays first – is secured by the golfer with the lowest score on the previous hole. On the first tee, honour is decided by lots or the toss of a coin. Elsewhere on the hole, the golfer furthest from the hole plays first. Only on the green might this order change. For example, in a strokeplay event you can elect to continue to putt out after your initial approach putt, but you must first make your intentions clear to your playing partners. This option will almost certainly not be open to you in a matchplay competition. You can ask, but as there is rarely anything for your opponent to gain by letting you hole-out, your request will probably be denied.

Out of sight, out of mind

It is very easy to be distracted by movement in your peripheral vision when you are about to play a shot. After being distracted in this way, it is sometimes difficult to regain concentration. Therefore, when your opponent is about to play, make sure that you stay out of the player's line of vision as much as possible. On the tee, the best place to stand while you are waiting is 45 degrees behind and to the right of the golfer; and remain at least four or five paces away. Do not make practice swings or talk: stand still and be quiet. On the fairway, be mindful of a player's line of sight to the target, and try to stay out of the way. On the green, never stand on an extension of another player's putt (that is, right behind the hole) – this can be extremely distracting.

DANGER ZONE

Before you play a shot, be aware of the positions of your fellow golfers. While they should know the correct place to stand, some players, especially beginners, might be unaware of the correct etiquette. This is a potentially dangerous situation: a quick check all around you will help avoid nasty accidents.

Be a good timekeeper

While golf need not be a race, neither should it be a crawl. Slow play is incredibly tiresome – do your best to keep play moving along without undue delay. There are several measures you should adopt. To begin with, if you fear your ball might be lost, play a provisional ball (see p.339). This way, if the original ball is in fact lost, you do not have to waste time walking all the way back to the site of the stroke that resulted in the lost ball to play another ball. If the ball you feared lost is not sighted straight away and there is a group behind you, immediately call them through (rather than waiting until the obligatory five minutes' searching time is up). If your ball disappears into the rough, watch where it comes to rest and try to "spot mark" it with a distinguishing feature, such as a tree that is along the same line. On the green, before you begin putting, leave your golf bag on the side of the green closest to the next tee, so that you can easily collect it on your way to the next hole. Do not mark your card on the green, as this can hold up the players behind you. Instead, it is better to do this on the next tee while waiting your turn to play. Also, always keep an eye on the group in front. If you start falling behind, take steps to catch up. And finally, walk briskly between shots.

Get ready while you are waiting
It is shocking how much time is wasted by golfers unprepared to play when it is their turn. To ensure that you are not

caught out, always be aware of the order of play, and go through some of your preparations while others are playing their shots (providing you do not distract them). For example, make up your mind which club you are going to hit, and start picturing the shot in your mind's eye. On the green, if you are not the first to putt, set about reading your line as you are waiting your turn (but be careful not to walk over the line of another golfer's putt). Although these measures probably only save 10 or 20 seconds on each occasion, this really does add up to a significant amount of time over the duration of an entire round.

Always shout "fore!"
Tragically, people have been killed and seriously injured as a result of being struck by a golf ball. With this in mind, if you hit a wayward shot that you think

might endanger others, shout "fore!" loudly and without hesitation. Do not be shy – it is better to be safe than sorry. Also, be certain that the group ahead of you is out of range before you hit your shot. Again, err on the side of caution.

Be a good searcher
Anyone who has played golf will know how grim it can be searching for a ball; you may also be familiar with the anxiety that sets in when this happens during an important competition. At such times your playing partners should assist in the search – make sure that you do the same for them. Do not leave a golfer forlornly looking for a ball by him- or herself; instead, help out. If you do so, when you next lose a ball, there is more chance that your playing partners will help you out, too.

Be careful where you tread
On the green, be aware of where your playing partners' balls have come to rest and avoid treading on the line of their putts. On a soft putting surface your feet can leave marks, albeit temporarily, but these may affect the smooth roll of a ball. Even on a firm green it is courteous to avoid treading on the line of another golfer's putt. Bear this in mind before you march around the green looking at your line and before you stride up to the hole to putt out. If you are unsure whether or not, in adopting your normal putting stance, you will stand on another player's line, it is best to wait before putting out. Many a short putt has been missed by impatient golfers awkwardly straddling the line of another golfer's putt to complete a hole.

MARKING THE CARD
The next tee is the best place to mark your card, rather than on the previous green. This way you will not unnecessarily hold up the group of golfers playing behind you.

THE GOLDEN RULES OF GOLF

GOLF HAS MANY more rules than most other sports, but this reflects the nature of the game. After all, there is much more scope for incident on a 40-ha (100-acre) plot of varied and tree-lined landscape than there is on the relatively sanitized environment of, for example, a snooker table, tennis court, or football pitch.

Sadly, there is a great deal of ignorance of the rules at amateur level, which is worrying but ultimately not surprising. The rule book itself is a heavily worded and, at times, complex work. Indeed, there is even a supplementary rule book, Decisions on the Rules of Golf, which covers bizarre occurrences that require clarification. With such unappealing material on offer, the rules can take some learning. This section should change all that, however. It will provide you with a basic understanding of the main rules and will therefore allow you to play the game as it is meant to be played. It should also enhance your enjoyment of the game and save you from the misery of unnecessary penalty shots or even disqualification. Besides, the following pages should also help you realize that the rules do not exist solely to punish you. Instead, with a thorough understanding of the rules, you will find that they can work in your favour, too.

ON THE TEE
Excess baggage
Before you hit your first shot of the day, it is worth checking the number of clubs in your bag. The maximum allowed is 14, and you are penalized if you carry more than that on to the course. In a matchplay competition you will have to deduct one hole for every hole played with the extra clubs, up to a maximum of two holes. This means that if you discover on the 3rd tee that you have extra clubs and you have already lost the first two holes, you will suddenly find yourself four down. In a strokeplay competition you are penalized two strokes for each hole played with the extra clubs, up to maximum of four strokes. It does not matter how many extra clubs you have in your bag – one or ten – the penalty is the same.

Playing out of turn
In a strokeplay event, if you play out of turn there is no penalty as such, but to do this is poor etiquette (see p.336). In a matchplay competition, on the other hand, if you tee off first when it is not your honour, your opponent has the right to cancel that stroke and ask you to play again.

Outer limits
The teeing area is as wide as indicated by the tee markers and two club-lengths deep, creating a rectangular shape within which you must tee your ball. You cannot move the two tee markers, but you can stand either side of them, providing the ball is teed up

AWARENESS ON THE TEE
You should always pay attention on the tee, as a courtesy to your partners and to ensure that you observe the correct order of play.

within the designated area. As discussed in the "Strategy Off the Tee" section (see pp.314–5), utilizing the full width of the teeing ground, and therefore gaining the best angle of attack, can increase your margin for error or give you a better line into the flag.

If you play from outside the limits of the teeing area, the penalty varies depending on the type of game you are playing. In a strokeplay event you incur a two-stroke penalty and are required to replay the stroke. This is known as playing "three off the tee" (your stroke off the tee counts as your third). In matchplay there is no penalty as such, but your opponent has the right to ask you to play the shot again. The likelihood of this happening probably depends on the quality of your tee shot. If you have played a poor stroke into the trees, for example, it is safe to assume that you will not be given another chance.

Accidental nudge
If, when you address the ball, you accidentally nudge it off the tee-peg with the clubhead, there is no penalty. You simply place the ball back on the tee-peg and start again.

Provisional ball
If you suspect that the ball may be lost from your tee shot, it is advisable to play what is known as a provisional ball (see "Trouble Off the Tee", top right). You must, however, state your intentions to your playing partners or your opponent. Once you have hit your provisional ball, you can begin searching for the first ball. But you are only allowed five minutes in which to find it, starting from the moment you begin looking (not from when you leave the tee). If you cannot find the ball within five minutes, you must declare it lost, add two shots to your score, and

Trouble off the tee
If you lose your ball off the tee (below), or hit your tee shot out-of-bounds (bottom), use the illustrations below to help you work out the correct procedure to follow and the appropriate penalty to add to your score.

PLAYING A PROVISIONAL BALL

1 Your first shot lands in deep rough, and you fear that it might be lost.

2 To save time, you should play a provisional ball. If you cannot find your original ball within five minutes, you must continue playing with the provisional ball and add two penalty strokes to your score.

3 Because of the penalty strokes, your next shot is therefore your fourth.

HITTING A SHOT OUT-OF-BOUNDS

1 Your tee shot is wildly off line, and the ball disappears out-of-bounds.

2 You must play another shot from the tee.

3 Assuming this tee shot stays "in bounds", the shot counts as your third.

continue playing with your provisional ball. This means that if you were to lose your tee shot, your second shot with a provisional ball would count as your fourth. If you find the first ball, though, you may play it without penalty and you can then simply pick up the provisional ball. (Note: the procedure outlined above for playing a provisional ball is the same if you fear you might have lost your ball as the result of a wayward fairway shot.)

Out-of-bounds
An area of the course on which play is permanently not permitted (as defined by local rules) is described as "out-of-bounds". If you hit a tee shot out-of-bounds (see "Trouble Off the Tee", above), you must replay the stroke from the tee and this counts as your third. This is known as a stroke-and-distance penalty. If you hit that drive out-of-bounds, you will be playing "five off the tee". (Note: the penalty is the same if you hit a fairway shot out-of-bounds.)

STRIKING THE BALL

A stroke is defined as the forward momentum of the club made with the intention of fairly striking at and moving the ball. It is useful to recall this description when considering what to do, for example, if you play an air shot. In this situation some believe that because the ball was not hit, the attempt to hit it does not count as a stroke. This is not correct because the intention of striking the ball must be taken into account. A legal strike of the ball also requires a backswing: you cannot scoop or push a ball towards the target. You may be tempted to do so if, for example, your backswing is restricted by a fence or tree – but if you succumb to this urge you will incur a two-stroke penalty.

HAZARDS AND UNPLAYABLE LIES

Bunkers

As mentioned in the "Bunker Play" section, the number one rule in sand is to hover the clubhead above the surface, as touching the sand before playing a shot incurs a one-shot penalty (see the Key Checkpoint on p.209). There are, however, finer

DO NOT TOUCH THE SAND

You must not ground your club in a hazard. In a bunker, the clubhead must not touch the sand either at address or in your backswing.

points to consider with bunker play. For example, if the clubhead touches the sand in your backswing, you are penalized just as you would be at address. Equally, you are not allowed to make a practice swing that comes into contact with the sand – but by all means make one that makes contact only with fresh air. (Note: the drills in the "Bunker Play" section that involved drawing lines in the sand are only suitable for practice. You cannot mark the sand during a proper round.)

The unplayable lie

In the chapter on shotmaking there is a section that describes three escape shots from trees (see pp.300–1). However, if you decide that such shots are too risky (for example in a competition), or that the lie is "unplayable", you could opt for a penalty drop instead (see "How To Take a Penalty Drop", below). When deciding whether to play or not, only you can decide if a lie is unplayable: it is your choice alone.

How to take a penalty drop

The rules of golf are very strict regarding the exact procedure to follow when taking a penalty drop. First of all, you must signal your intentions to one of your playing partners or your opponent, as it is essential that another player is aware of your intentions. As you make the drop, stand upright with your arm extended in front of you at shoulder height, then let the ball fall out of your hand and drop to the ground.

You are not allowed to influence the ball's flight in any way, for example by spinning the ball in your fingers or casting it in a particular direction. Just let gravity take its course. If the ball comes to rest nearer the hole, you must re-drop. If this happens again, you are permitted to place the ball on any lie you like, so long as you choose a position within two club-lengths of your originally identified dropping spot.

MARK THE SPOT

If you have an unplayable lie, and feel that taking a drop from two club-lengths away is your best option, mark out this distance with two woods. (You can also drop from behind the ball on an extension of the ball-to-target line, or you can replay the offending shot.)

DROPPING THE BALL

With your arm fully extended at shoulder height, let the ball fall naturally from your hand – do not attempt to influence the outcome of the drop.

If you feel that the lie is unplayable, you have three options for a penalty drop.

First, you can drop a ball within two club-lengths of where your original ball came to rest (so long as you choose a spot that is not closer to the hole). Measure two club-lengths using a couple of woods (the longest clubs in your bag), and mark this spot with a tee-peg before you pick up your ball. Second, you can choose to go back to the spot from where you played the stroke that got you into trouble and take a drop from as near to the original site as you can remember. This is known as a stroke-and-distance penalty. Third, you can imagine a line between the ball and the flag, walk back on an extension of that line, and then drop your ball. There is no limit as to how far back you can go. Each of these three options incurs a penalty of one stroke.

Water hazards

There are two types of water hazard on a golf course: "water hazards" (marked with a yellow stake or a yellow painted line) and "lateral water hazards" (indicated by red stakes or a red painted line). Whenever your ball finishes in water it is important to identify which of the two hazards you are dealing with, as the procedures for each vary slightly.

Free drops

There are many situations when you are entitled to a free drop, also known as "free relief", such as when the ground is under repair (see p.344), when you come across "casual" water (see p.343), or when you encounter certain immovable obstructions (see p.344). The most important point to remember is that although a free drop does not incur a penalty, you are allowed only one club-length's relief. Also bear in mind that the relief does not take effect from the position of the ball, but from the point where the obstruction or abnormal ground condition ceases to cause a problem.

DROP ZONE
Tiger Woods takes a free drop from a pop-up sprinkler, an immovable obstruction that would have interfered with his stance and swing.

What to do in a water hazard

You have three options if your ball lands in a water hazard, which is identified by a yellow painted line or yellow stakes.

1 You may play the ball in the water – without incurring a penalty. However, as you address the ball, the club must not touch the water. This is a very risky shot.

2 A safer option is to drop the ball on an imaginary line that runs from the target through the point at which the ball first crossed the edge of the water hazard. You may go back as far from the target as you like. The penalty, however, is one stroke.

3 A further option is to play another ball from where the original shot was played (one-stroke penalty).

Dropping line

Water hazard · Ball position

Crossing point

Ball flight

With a simple water hazard (marked yellow) you have three options (see "What To Do in a Water Hazard", p.341). First, you can play the ball as it lies, without penalty. This is only possible in very shallow water, and even then is not recommended because such a shot usually ends in disaster. Second, you can identify an imaginary line between the flag and where your ball first crossed the edge of the water hazard, then walk back and drop the ball on an extension of that line (as with an unplayable lie, see p.341). The third option is to return to the spot where you played the shot that ended up in water (this is a stroke-and-distance penalty). These last two options incur a one-stroke penalty.

With a lateral water hazard you can choose from the three alternatives outlined above, or you can drop a ball two club-lengths either from where the ball first crossed the edge of the water hazard or from a similar spot on the opposite side of the water (see "What To Do in a Lateral Water Hazard", below). Again, this incurs a one-stroke penalty. Remember, as with all drops, that you cannot give yourself a lie nearer to the hole.

Playing the wrong ball
It is against the rules to play a stroke with a ball that is not your own. In matchplay the penalty is the immediate loss of the hole, while in strokeplay you receive a two-shot penalty and must take your next shot from where you played the wrong ball. In strokeplay, if you fail to correct your mistake before teeing off at the next hole, you are disqualified from the competition.

ON THE GREEN
What you can do on the green
If you want to clean your ball before putting, mark the ball by placing a coin or ball-marker behind the ball before lifting it away. If the ball is damaged, you can replace it with another, providing there is agreement from your fellow competitor or opponent. If your ball-marker interferes with the line of a fellow competitor's putt, use your putterhead to measure as far to the side as is necessary and re-mark (see "Moving the Marker", p.343). Make sure that you do not forget to put the marker back in its original position before you replace the ball.

Regarding obstructions on the line of your putt, you can repair pitch-marks and old hole-plugs but not spike marks. You can brush aside leaves, twigs, and loose sand, providing you use your hand or the putterhead.

What you cannot do on the green
Being close to the hole does not mean you are entirely safe from penalty. The key points to remember in order to avoid breaking the rules on the green are as follows. First, do not touch the line of the putt, unless you are brushing aside loose impediments (see "Impediments and Obstructions", p.344), repairing a pitch-mark or old hole-plug, or measuring distance to

What to do in a lateral water hazard

If your ball lands in a lateral water hazard, indicated by a red painted line or red stakes, you may choose any of the three options listed in "What To Do in a Water Hazard" (see p.341) or you may prefer one of the two alternatives discussed below. Both possibilities incur a one-stroke penalty.

1 | You may take a drop two club-lengths from where the ball first crossed the edge of the water. You must not give yourself a lie closer to the hole.

2 | If Option 1 is not practical, you may drop a ball as described above, except on the other side of the hazard.

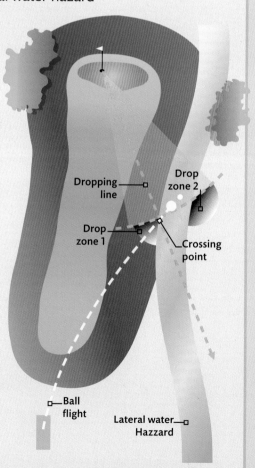

Dropping line
Drop zone 2
Drop zone 1
Crossing point
Ball flight
Lateral water Hazzard

Moving the marker

You should move your marker if it is on the line of another player's putt or if it interferes with a player's stroke or stance. The procedure outlined below will show you the correct way to do this.

POSITION THE CLUB

If your playing partner asks you to move your ball-marker out of the line of his or her putt, begin by carefully placing the toe of your putterhead so that it sits next to the marker.

MOVE THE MARKER
Pick up the marker and position it behind the heel of your putterhead. You may move several putterhead-lengths away if neccessary.

determine whose putt should be played first. Second, do not test the putting surface by rolling a ball along the green. Third, do not hit your putt while another ball is in motion. And finally, do not brush aside early-morning dew or frost (neither of which are "loose impediments") from the line of your putt (this is a common infringement).

Flagstick misdemeanours

When your ball is on the green, you have only two options regarding the flagstick. If you are a long way from the hole you will probably choose to have it attended (so that you can see where the hole is). In this situation the flag must be pulled out before the ball goes in the hole. Failure to do this incurs a two-stroke penalty. However, if you decide to have the flagstick taken out, make sure that it is left well out of the way, as there is a two-stroke penalty if your ball hits it. From off the green you have three options. You can have the flag out (two-stroke penalty if your ball hits it), left in (no

CASUAL WATER

A player and Rules Official attempt to positively identify a ball that was buried in the heavy rough surrounding a bunker, a procedure that is quite within the rules.

penalty if the ball strikes it), or you can choose to have it attended (two-stroke penalty).

ABNORMAL GROUND CONDITIONS

Casual water

One of the oldest rules in golf is that you must play the ball as it lies, but there are exceptional circumstances

that override this principle. One such situation is if your ball lands in casual water – a temporary accumulation of water (often found after heavy rain). This is a free-drop scenario (see "Free Drops", p.341), and whenever it is practical to do so, you must mark the original position of the ball, identify the nearest point of relief (where the water ceases to become an obstruction to either your stance or the lie of the ball), mark that spot with a tee-peg, and drop within one club-length of the tee-peg in any direction (so long as you do not end up closer to the hole).

The procedure is slightly different if the casual water is in a bunker. You must identify the nearest dry patch on which to drop the ball, but that spot must be within the confines of the bunker. If the bunker is completely waterlogged, you must either drop the ball into the shallowest area of water or drop it outside the bunker and incur a one-stroke penalty. This is one of the harshest rules in golf.

Ground under repair

Any portion of the course that would be damaged if played on, for example a patch of newly planted grass, can be declared "ground under repair". Such areas are encircled by a white line, and often have the letters "GUR" painted alongside. If your ball lands inside the white line, measure one club-length from the point where the ground under repair no longer interferes with either your stance or the ball, and take your drop from there.

Plugged ball

When a ball plugs in its own pitch-mark on a closely mown area of grass, you are allowed a free drop. You

LOOSE IMPEDIMENTS

A natural object, such as this pinecone, is classed as a loose impediment and may be shifted, provided the ball does not move.

simply mark the position of the ball, lift it, clean it if necessary, and drop it as close as possible to where it became plugged. If a ball plugs in its own pitch-mark in the rough, the Rules of Golf do not permit a free drop. However, during winter months, when plugged balls are most common, golf clubs often introduce what are known as "Winter Rules", which allow free relief in the rough. It is usually stipulated that you may not clean your ball, as you can if your ball becomes plugged on a closely mown part of the course.

IMPEDIMENTS AND OBSTRUCTIONS

Loose impediments

Moveable natural objects – leaves, twigs, branches, stones, and so on – are described as loose impediments. Providing the object is not growing and is not solidly embedded in the ground, you are allowed to move it without penalty. However, you will be penalized one shot if the ball moves as you clear the object away (unless you are on the green).

You cannot move loose impediments in a hazard. The one exception to this rule is that you can move stones from around the ball in a bunker (for safety reasons).

Finally, sand and loose soil are defined as loose impediments on the green, but not off the green. Make sure you remember this if you are putting from the apron of the green, which is technically not part of the green.

Immovable obstructions

Obstructions are defined as artificial objects; typical immovable obstructions include fixed sprinkler

heads around greens (see "Obstructing Objects", left) and the concrete tee boxes to the side of a teeing area that provide information about the hole. If such an obstruction interferes with either your stance or your intended swing, you are entitled to free relief. Since the obstruction is immovable, you can move your ball (no nearer the hole) within one club-length from the spot where the obstruction no longer interferes with your stance or swing. You are not allowed relief, however, if the obstruction is merely in the flightpath of your next shot.

Movable obstructions

Empty cans and bunker rakes are common examples of movable obstructions. If your ball comes to rest touching a movable obstruction or in such close proximity to the obstruction that it interferes with your stance or swing, you are allowed to move the obstruction. Before you do so, it is wise to mark the position of your ball with a tee-peg, so that if the ball moves during the process of lifting away the obstruction you can simply place the ball back on its original spot, without penalty.

Obstructing objects

There are many different types of object that you might encounter on your journey from the tee to the green. The rules relating to these differ according to the type of object in question. A commonly encountered object is an immovable obstruction, which is a fixed, artificial object. If your ball comes to rest near such an obstruction and your stance or swing is impeded, you are allowed free relief.

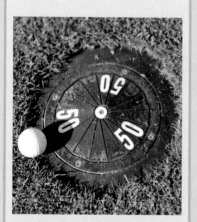

IMMOVABLE OBSTRUCTION
As a fixed sprinkler head may impede your stance or swing, you are allowed to take a free drop.

LOST BALL
Be very careful when searching for your ball in long grass; if you kick it or tread on it, even accidentally, you will be penalized one stroke.

DEFLECTED BALLS
Ball deflected while in motion
If your ball is deflected while in motion, the correct procedure varies according to the cause of the deflection. If your ball hits something natural, such as a tree, you must play the ball from where it comes to rest. The same is true if your ball hits an "outside agency", examples of which include greenkeeper's equipment – such as a mower – or a spectator.

If an animal intercepts your ball while it is in motion, you must replace the ball on the spot from where it was first taken. Although this may be short of where your shot might have finished, if the ball was heading towards a hazard or the rough, this rule can work in your favour. If an animal steals your ball on the green while you are putting, you can replay the stroke without penalty.

If your moving ball hits a ball at rest, you must play your ball from wherever it finishes. On the green, if your putt strikes a ball at rest, you are penalized two strokes and the struck ball should be replaced in its original

position. Always ask a ball to be marked, even if you think there is only a remote chance of hitting it.

Stationary ball deflected or moved
If your ball, while at rest, is moved by an outside agency, such as an animal, there is no need to panic. Simply replace the ball as close as possible to the spot from where it was moved (there is no penalty). Even if the ball disappears forever (if, for example, a crow flies off with it – which is not as unusual as you might think), you can take another ball from your bag, place it where the original was, and proceed without penalty.

The rules are not so benevolent if a ball is moved by you (for example, if you kick the ball while searching for it in deep rough), your caddie, your partner, or any piece of equipment belonging to you or your partner. In this situation there is a one-stroke penalty, and you must replace the ball in its original position. However, there are exceptions to this rule. You are not penalized if, so long as you return the ball to its original position, your ball is moved during the process of:
- measuring putts on a green to determine the playing order
- repairing a pitch-mark on the green
- moving an obstruction (see "Movable Obstructions", p.344), such as a bunker rake, out of the way
- searching for a ball in a hazard, such as a bunker
- brushing aside loose impediments, such as leaves or sand, on the green
- moving a ball that is interfering with play
- lifting, placing, or replacing a ball during the course of taking free relief.

BUNKER DISTRACTION
A bunker rake is classed as a moveable obstruction and can be moved so that it does not interfere with your stance or swing.

GLOSSARY

ADDRESS
An alternative word used to describe a golfer's set-up.

AIR SHOT
A stroke whereby the clubhead fails to make contact with the ball.

ALBATROSS
A score of three under par on one hole.

APPROACH SHOT
A stroke played with the intention of hitting the green.

APRON OF THE GREEN
The closely mown area of grass between the rough and the putting surface.

BARE LIE
A situation in which the ball is sitting on a patch of ground with very little or no grass on it at all.

BIRDIE
A score of one under par on one hole.

BLADE
A forged iron clubhead thought to offer superior feel off the clubface, but is less forgiving to off-centre strikes. Also the bottom edge of an iron.

BOGEY
A score of one over par on one hole. Also a matchplay competition played against the par of the course.

BORROW
Another word for break.

BOUNCE
The wide flange at the base of a sand wedge.

BREAK
The deviation left or right made by a ball rolling along a green due to slopes on the putting surface.

CARRY
The distance a ball flies through the air.

CAVITY BACK
An iron with the back of the head hollowed out, which positions weight around the perimeter of the clubhead. This increases the mass behind off-centre strikes.

CLOSED STANCE
An address position in which the golfer's alignment is to the right of the target.

CLUBBING DOWN
A situation in which a golfer takes a more-lofted club, for example an 8-iron instead of a 7-iron.

CLUBBING UP
A situation in which a golfer takes a less-lofted club, for example a 5-iron instead of a 6-iron.

COLLAR OF ROUGH
The area of grass where the apron of the green joins the rough.

COURSE PLANNER
A booklet with a diagram of each hole that shows the distinguishing features of the hole, as well as the distances from various points between the tee and the green.

DISTANCE CHART
Another term for course planner.

DIVOT
The turf dislodged at impact while playing a shot.

DIVOT-MARK
The hole in the ground left as a result of a divot being taken.

DOGLEG
A hole, either a par 4 or par 5 (but never a par 3), where the fairway bends from left-to-right or from right-to-left at some point between the tee and the green.

DORMIE
The state of play in a matchplay competition when a player is up by as many holes as there are left to play in the round. For example, four-up with four holes to play is described as "dormie four".

DOUBLE BOGEY
A score of two over par on one hole.

DOUBLE EAGLE
Another word used to describe an albatross.

DRAW
A shot in which the ball moves from right-to-left through the air, due to sidespin imparted at impact.

DRIVER
The longest club in the bag, designed for hitting tee shots.

EAGLE
A score of two under par on one hole.

FADE
When the ball moves from left-to-right through the air, due to sidespin imparted at impact.

FAIRWAY
The closely mown area of grass bordered on either side by longer grass (rough).

FELLOW COMPETITOR
A person with whom you play in a strokeplay competition.

FOURBALL BETTERBALL
A competition played in pairs, in which the best score of the two partners on each hole counts.

FOURSOMES
A game of pairs in which two golfers share the same ball, one teeing off on odd-numbered holes, the other on even-numbered holes. After the tee shot the pair play alternate shots.

FRINGE
Another word for the apron of the green.

GAP WEDGE
A club designed to bridge a gap in terms of loft, usually between a sand wedge and pitching wedge.

GREEN
The putting surface. (The hole is located on the green.)

GREENSOMES
A type of play in which partners both tee off on each hole. They then select the more favourable of the two balls and play alternate shots with the same ball until the hole is completed.

GRIP
The rubber handle at the top of a club. Also, both hands positioned on the club's grip are referred to as the grip.

GROUNDING THE CLUB
Resting the clubhead on the ground behind the ball at address.

HALVED
In a matchplay competition, if opponents register the same score on a hole, the hole is said to be "halved".

HANDICAP
A figure that reflects a golfer's ability relative to the par of the course.

HEAVY
A shot in which the clubhead strikes the ground before the ball.

HEEL
The area of the clubface nearest to the shaft of the club.

HOLE
The hole itself (which is located on the green). Also a general term for describing the area between the teeing ground and the green, for example: "the first hole".

HOLING OUT
The actual process of getting the ball into the hole.

HOOK
A shot in which the ball moves right-to-left through the air due to sidespin imparted at impact. An exaggerated version of a draw.

HOSEL
The part of the clubhead into which the shaft is secured.

LAYING UP
Playing a shot short of the green, through choice or necessity.

LIE
Where the ball comes to rest on the course. Also the angle at which the bottom edge of the clubhead sits relative to the shaft.

LINKS COURSE
A golf course by the sea.

LOFT
The angle at which the clubface sits relative to perpendicular. This determines the ball's trajectory.

LOOSE IMPEDIMENT
A term used in the Rules of Golf to describe a movable natural object, such as a leaf or twig, interfering with the line of play.

MATCHPLAY
A game played between single opponents or pairs in which holes are won, lost, or halved.

OBSTRUCTION
A term from the Rules of Golf to describe an artificial object that might interfere with play, such as a fixed sprinkler head (an immovable obstruction) or empty can (a moveable obstruction).

OPEN STANCE
An address position in which the golfer's alignment is to the left of the target.

OPPONENT
A person whom you play against in a matchplay situation.

OUT-OF-BOUNDS
A designated area of a golf course where play is permanently not permitted. The penalty for hitting a ball out-of-bounds is stroke and distance.

PAR
The standard score for a hole, based on the number of shots an accomplished player would normally take to complete the hole. Also a score equal to the par on a hole.

PAR OF THE COURSE
The total of the pars of all 18 holes.

PAR 3
A hole that should be completed in three strokes. To achieve par, usually the green should be hit in one stroke, followed by two putts.

PAR 4
A medium-length hole, which should be completed in four strokes. To achieve par, the green should be hit in two strokes.

PAR 5
A long hole, which should be completed in five strokes. To achieve par, usually the green should be hit in three strokes.

PERIPHERAL WEIGHTING
The principle of distributing the mass of a clubhead around its edges to allow for a degree of forgiveness for off-centre strikes.

PGA
The Professional Golfers' Association, which looks after the interests of professional golfers in the UK. Each country has its own PGA, such as the Australian PGA.

PIVOT
The coiling and uncoiling of the upper body in the swing, combined with the correct weight transfer.

PLAYING PARTNER
A person with whom you team up in a game played in pairs, such as foursomes.

POSTURE
The overall position of the body and legs in the set-up.

PREFERRED LIES
A local rule often introduced during the winter months when ground conditions are usually poor. The rule permits golfers to move their ball on to a more favourable lie, so long as this is within 15 cm (6 in) of the spot where the ball originally came to rest. The rule usually only applies on closely mown areas of grass, such as the fairway or the apron of the green.

PULL
A shot in which the ball starts left of target and continues to fly in that direction.

PUSH
A shot in which the ball starts right of target and continues to fly in that direction.

READING A PUTT
The process of studying the line of a putt to identify possible breaks that might occur as the ball moves towards the hole.

RELEASING THE CLUB
A phrase describing how the right hand rolls over the left through impact, indicating a powerful and free swing of the clubhead.

ROUGH
The thicker grass either side of the fairway and around most greens. The rough is designed to penalize wayward shots: it is more difficult to play from than the closely mown grass of the fairway.

ROYAL & ANCIENT
The governing body for amateur golf all over the world, except in the US. The Royal & Ancient, commonly referred to as the R&A, administers the official Rules of Golf.

RUN
The portion of a ball's journey from the moment the ball first hits the ground to the point where it eventually comes to rest. More lofted clubs produce less run; less-lofted clubs, such as the driver and long irons, tend to generate more run.

SCRATCH
A handicap of zero.

SET-UP
The position you adopt before striking the ball, including your grip, aim, stance, and posture. Also known as the address.

SHAFT
The part of a club between the grip and the clubhead.

SHANK
A shot in which the ball is struck from the hosel of the club, causing the ball to fly sharply to the right of the target.

SKY
A tee shot played with either a driver or lofted wood in which the top edge of the clubhead strikes the bottom of the ball, which flies steeply upwards.

SLICE
A shot in which the ball moves from left-to-right through the air as a result of sidespin imparted at impact. An exaggerated version of a fade.

SPLASH SHOT
A bunker shot in which the clubhead strikes the sand behind the ball, and a wave of sand propels the ball out of the bunker.

STABLEFORD
A type of play in which points are awarded according to the score relative to par on each hole. The golfer with the most points after 18 holes is the winner.

STANCE
The width your feet are apart at address, and the position of the ball relative to your feet.

STROKE AND DISTANCE
A penalty in which the golfer must return to the spot from which the last stroke was played (conceding the distance gained) and add one stroke to their score for that hole.

STROKEPLAY
A type of play in which each competitor records his or her score for each hole. The golfer with the lowest total is the winner.

SWEET SPOT
The centremost portion of the clubface, where the majority of the clubhead's mass is located.

TEE
A common abbreviation, referring to either a tee-peg or the teeing ground itself.

TEE BOX
Another term used to describe the teeing ground.

TEEING AREA
The part of the teeing ground from which golfers must hit tee shots. The teeing area is two club-lengths deep and its width is defined by two tee markers.

TEEING GROUND
The whole area of closely mown grass on which the designated teeing area is situated.

TEE-PEG
The implement on which a golfball sits during the process of hitting a tee shot.

THIN
A shot during which the bottom edge of the clubhead strikes on or above the equator of the ball, causing it to fly on an uncharacteristically low trajectory (or even along the ground).

TOE
The area of the clubface furthest from the shaft of the club.

TOUR EVENT
A professional tournament usually played over four rounds, in which the golfer with the lowest 72-hole score is the winner.

TRAJECTORY
The arc on which the ball flies through the air. Higher-numbered irons, which have more loft, propel the ball on a higher trajectory. Lower-numbered irons, which have less loft, send the ball on a lower trajectory.

TRIPLE BOGEY
A score of three over par on one hole.

USGA
The US equivalent of the Royal & Ancient.

USPGA
The United States Professional Golfers' Association. An organisation that looks after the interests of professional golfers in the US.

UTILITY WOOD
A lofted metal-wood, such as a 7-wood, that features a small clubhead. Utility woods are designed for advancement shots from the fairway and light rough.

WEIGHT TRANSFER
The process whereby the bodyweight moves from one foot to the other during the process of swinging a club.

WINTER RULES
Local rules introduced by a golf club's committee during winter to allow preferred lies on closely mown areas of grass.

INDEX

A

accidents, avoiding 336, 337
address position
    bunker play 230, 231
    chipping 184
    iron play 71, 104, 111
    pitching 146
    putting 238, 239, 240, 250-1, 278
    tee shots 36, 54, 64, 65
aim, improving 20-1, 42, 257, 296
air shot and intention to strike 340
Aoki, Isao 220

B

backspin
    bunker play 222-3
    and pitching 134-5, 143, 147
    reduction, iron play 145
backspin, chipping
    and choice of club and ball 164
    on landing 154
    and loft 173
    rough shots 170
backswing
    and legal strike 340
    restricted 301, 340
backswing, bunker play
    on an upslope 211
    and followthrough, matching 202-3
    long, and short strokes 221
    perfect 230
    and sideslope lies 214-5
    upright plane of 220
backswing, chipping
    and body rotation 151
    and clockface drill 162-3
    and grip lag between downswing 151
    length and deceleration 162-3, 169
    perfect 184, 185
backswing, iron play
    adding resistance to 101
    and downswing, pausing between 88
    downswing speed matching 85
    and shanked iron shot 285
    squeezing elbows stay connected 92-3
    steep angle shots from rough 289
    straight left arm, problems with 95
    "thumbs up" position 98
backswing, pitching
    angle of attack 114, 115, 120-1, 143
    arm-swing, body-turn balance 129

avoiding too much 145
    forcing club upwards 129, 285
    length and distance matching 138-9, 142-3
    perfect 146
    and relaxed wrists 111
    shortening and stance 109, 121
    and swing plane 116-7
    and wrist hinge 115, 116-7, 143
backswing, putting 242-3, 260-1 278, 279
backswing, tee shots
    arc and skied drive 46-7, 49, 286
    body rotation 45-7, 49, 59, 60
    choking down on driver 38-9
    controlling length of 47, 50
    creating box at top of 58
    and direction 49
    flexed right knee 47
    grounded left heel 48
    left shoulder behind ball 60-1
    lifted left heel 50-1
    pausing at top of 42
    perfect 64
    and power 288
ball
    animals, intercepted by 345
    buried 218-9
    choice of 164, 331
    choice, and pitching 131, 135, 331
    cleaning before putting 342
    deflected 345
    early days 9
    high and low trajectory 145
    identification and heavy rough 343
    juggling with club 319
    lost 337, 345
    penalty for playing wrong 342
    playing wrong 342
    position in early days 9
    running speed on green 258-9
    searching, assisting in 337
    topping 287
    types 131, 164, 321, 331
    winter play choice 321
ball position
    bunker play, above feet 214-5
    bunker play, below feet 216-7
    chipping, perfect 153, 154
    curving shots, above feet practice 99
    on downslopes 294
    iron play, and good 70
    putting 238, 246, 278, 279
    rough shots 289
    tee shots 35
    on upslopes 295

ball-then-sand contact 205, 226, 340
ball-then-turf contact 63, 75, 153, 154, 167, 185, 284
Ballesteros, Seve 220
bare lie shot 298
baseball
    grip 18
    swing 46
body-turn practice 49, 132-3
bogey play 333
bucket drill, and accuracy 123
bull's-eye at back of hole 247
bunker play 186-7
    address 230, 231
    backswing see backswing, bunker play
    ball above feet 214-5
    ball below feet 216-7
    ball-then-sand contact 205, 226, 340
    buried ball 218-9
    and casual water 343
    chipping over 164, 170
    choking down 204, 205, 214, 220, 225
    clubface open 18, 191, 193, 208, 221, 224, 230, 231
    clubhead acceleration 196
    distance variation 200-1
    downslope 209, 212-3
    downswing, perfect 231
    fear of 187
    intermediate shots 206-7
    line in sand to focus 192-5, 215, 222
    long-range shots 204-5
    9-iron practice 229
    obstructions, loose 344, 345
    perfect 230-1
    performance monitoring 323
    pitching over 122
    pitching wedge see pitching wedge
    practice with a variety of clubs and shots 227-9
    pre-shot routine 312-3
    punch-and-spin shot 226, 340
    putting from sand 225
    raking over tracks 203, 334-5
    right-hand action, and throwing stone 196
    right-handed swings 189
    sand focus 197, 226, 231, 321
    and sand, touching 340
    sand wedge see sand wedge
    set-up organization 188, 190
    shallow cut for extra spin 222-3
    short strokes 221
    sound of good 190-1
    stance 188, 195, 208, 221, 231

swing length, and distance 198-9, 200-1, 321
    target staggering 209
    upslope 210-1, 212
    and winter conditions 321

C

Casey, Paul 146-7
casual water 341, 343
catcher, pitching to imaginary 122
cavity backs 329
century on the green 275
chipping 148-9
    accuracy improvement (umbrella drill) 158
    address 184
    and angle of attack, correcting 154
    backspin see backspin, chipping
    backswing see backswing, chipping
    ball position 153, 154
    ball-then-turf contact 153, 154, 167, 185, 284
    bellied wedge shot from collar of rough 176-7
    body motion, and extended club 152
    chip-and-runs 164, 185
    circle round green 175
    club choice 156-7, 161, 167, 169, 178
    contests 172-3
    downslope practice 166
    downward strike 154, 185
    fairway strategies 316-7
    flop shot 170
    free swing, and clipping tee-peg 155
    and green reading 160, 179
    green sloping up 171
    grip, weak, and open face 174
    hard surface practice 167
    and heavy contact 154, 155, 284
    and impact position 150, 153
    landing errors 169
    loft 156-7, 165, 171, 173, 175, 182-3, 185, 320, 321
    mini-hook shot 181
    and obstructions 344
    perfect 184-5
    performance monitoring 322-3
    pitching wedge see pitching wedge
    pre-shot routine 312-3
    putting technique 178-9, 180, 182
    rehearse, look and hit drill 159
    from rough 157, 170, 176-7, 180, 183, 317

set-up organization 150, 167, 182
shaft rocking, body and arms together 164
stance 150, 182, 185
sucker pin placement 316
swing path monitoring 108, 151, 153, 161, 169, 284
toe-poke from collar of rough 180
upslope 165, 171
visualization 156–7, 175
as warm-up 311
in winter conditions 320
choking down on grip 38–9, 117, 178, 182, 204, 205, 214, 220, 225, 297
Christine, Jim 82–3
clockface drill, and chipping 162–3
club
and "carry" and "roll" 161
choice, chipping 156–7, 161, 167, 169, 178
choice, iron play 59, 67, 68–9
club-down, downslopes 294
club-up, bunker play 225
club-up, upslopes 295
extended 152
juggling balls with 319
length and trajectory variations 144–5
"middle of green" 84
penalties for excess of 338
release, and swing 27, 94, 140
shaft flex, material and length 327
shaft rocking, body and arms together 164
tee shots, using different 59
clubhead
acceleration, bunker play 196
hosel strike and shanked shot 285
coaching role 10–11
compass drill 252–3
compromise ball 131, 164, 331
concentration, maintaining 243, 269
confidence building 247–9, 252–3, 272–3, 274, 277
control ball 131, 164, 331
Couples, Fred 48, 103
course
care of 334
ground under repair 341, 344
planner, use of 317
crosswinds 303
curving shots 99

D
"dead-hands" technique 176–7
distance
ball (type) 131, 164, 321
checking personal 103

control, and swing arc 110
forearms touching to improve release 53
judgement, pitching 108, 110, 113, 119, 126–7, 161
judgement, putting 258–9
loss and skied drive 286
tee shots, on the run 62–3
variation methods, bunker play 200–1
distraction, keeping out of sight 336
divot marks 75, 84, 143
existing and tee shot aim 42
playing out of 299
and replacement 334
scooping motion to avoid 119
and swing information 118–21, 143, 291
dogleg fairways 314
downslope
bunker play from 209, 212–3
over-shooting on 294
putts 271, 273
downswing
bunker play, perfect 231
and flexed right knee 47
and slicing 282
downswing, iron play
and backswing, pausing between 88
backswing speed matching 85
"getting ahead of the ball" 89
"late hit" 95
staying square in the takeaway 90–1
downswing, pitching
and ball position 119
controlled aggression 124–5, 136, 139
gradual acceleration in 138–9, 142–3
and open stance 109
path and angle of attack 114, 118–9
perfect 146–7
and weight transfer 119
draw shot 306, 314
drivers, choices 326–7

E
Els, Ernie 18, 48, 60, 103
equipment 327–31
see also balls
escape shots 300–1, 340
etiquette 334–8

F
fade shot 307, 314
fairway strategies 316–7
fairway woods 81, 328
Faldo, Nick 10, 18, 55, 243, 257
fear
of bunker play 187
of long holes 316

50 per cent rule and tee height 32
flag
go-for-the-flag range 84
hitting from off-green 182
taking care with 335
flop shot 170
football drill, and release 94
"fore!", shouting 337
fourball betterball play 333
foursomes 333
free drop 341, 344
freezing, avoiding 114, 274
Furyk, Jim 276

G
game play 308–9
fairway and rough strategy 316–7
mental approach 318–9
off the tee strategy 314–5
performance monitoring 322–3
pre-shot routine 312–3
warm-up 310–1
winter golf 320–1
gap wedge 125
geometry of good shots 143, 237
"getting ahead of the ball" 89
green
ball running speed on 258–9
and chip shots 148–9
flag see flag
flat part, aiming for 172
hole width 247
obstructions 342, 343, 344
pitch-marks, repairing 335
playing from circle round 175
reading 24, 160, 179, 254–5, 277, 278
rules 342–3
sloping 145, 171, 254–6, 277
see also putting
greensomes 333
grip
baseball 18
before aim 20
checking 18–19
and chipping 150, 166
choking down 38–9, 117, 178, 182, 204, 205, 214, 220, 225, 297
closing clubface at address 62–3
crossing hands style 276
in early days 9
interlocking 18
jumbo-fat 331
left-handed players 18
loosening for free-flowing shot 111
overlapping (Vardon) 9, 18
putting 176, 178, 234–5, 275, 276, 278
reverse overlap 234–5, 276

strengthening 40
tee-peg in, as guide 289

H
Hagen, Walter 197
hand and arm rotation 98
handicap calculation 332
Haney, Hank 11
hard surface practice 167
Harmon, Butch 10
Harrington, Padraig 276
head position
iron play, movement up or down 87
movement and weight shift 86
putting, head down 245, 249
and tee shots 36, 59, 65
heavy contact
chipping 154, 155, 284
and deep divot-mark 118
heel
grounded 48
lifted left 50–1
missing, by addressing off the heel 54
hitters 61
Hogan, Ben 10, 18
hooking 41, 181, 283
"hot" ball flight and ball above feet 297
hovering club
bunker play 209, 225, 340
pitching, for rough shots 137
putter for smooth stroke 272–3
on rough chips 183

I
impact position
and chipping 150, 153
pitching, pre-setting 134–5
putterface alignment at 241, 246
interlocking grip 18
intermediate
bunker shots 206–7
swing, tee shots 46
target and direction finding 74–5
iron play 66–7
address 71, 104, 111
backspin reduction 145
backswing see backswing, iron play
ball positions 70
choosing correct iron 59, 67, 68–9
control and power balance 80
curving shots 99
downswing see downswing, iron play
elbows stay connected 92–3
fairway strategies 316–7
feet together shots 96–7, 120
freeze-frame right moves 78–9
hand and arm rotation 98

head movement up or down 87
head movement and weight shift 86
intermediate target 74–5
knee flexing and swing resistance 101
launch angle and trajectory 102–3
loft 100, 304
long holes, intimidated by 316
obstructions 344
perfect 104–5
performance monitoring 84, 322–3
pitching see pitching
posture 104
practice swings, copying 81
pre-shot routine 312–3
range-finding with every iron 68–9
release improvement, football drill 94
rope exercise to improve swing 82–3
rough play strategies 289, 299, 317
shadow, learning from 85
solid strikes and left-eye focus 89
squeezing shots 100
stance 23, 104
videoing set-up and swing 76–7
and weight distribution 25
in winter conditions 320
irons 328–9
and par-3 holes, tee shots 63
Irwin, Hale 97

J
Jacobs, John 10
Jacobsen, Freddie 230–1
Jones, Bobby 9, 10, 85, 200
jumbo-fat grip 331

K
Karlsson, Robert 278–9
Kim, Anthony 101
knee
flexed 24, 47, 101
left, fanned out 9
knockdown-punch shot 305

L
Lane, Barry 184–5
Langer, Bernhard 137, 332
"late hit" 95
Leadbetter, David 10, 55
left-handed players 12, 18
loft
and backspin 173
chipping 156–7, 165, 171, 173, 175, 182–3, 185, 320, 321
iron play 100, 304

pitching 123, 125, 126–7
tee shots 39
and upslopes 295
long shots
bunker play 204–5
intimidated by 316
landing 169
putting 266–7
lost balls 337, 339, 345
Love, Davis 60, 81

M
McIlroy, Rory 64–5
marker, moving 342, 343
matchplay singles 333, 336
mental approach 318–9
Mickelson, Phil 124
mistakes, learning from 94
Montgomerie, Colin 275
Morris, Tom 8, 9

N
Nelson, Byron 9–10
Nicklaus, Jack 10, 20, 51, 114, 312
Norman, Greg 20, 182

O
obstructions 300, 341, 342, 343, 344, 345
high shots to clear 145, 160
on-course behaviour 336–7
order of play, awareness of 337
out-of-bounds tee shot 339
outer limit, and tee shots 338–9
overlapping (Vardon) grip 9, 18

P
Palmer, Arnold 265
par-3 holes, teeing up correctly 63
Park, Mungo 9
Pelz, Dave 182
penalty drops 300, 340
perfect
bunker play 230–1
chipping 184–5
iron play 104–5
pitching 146–7
putting 246, 249, 278–9
tee shots 64–5
performance monitoring 84, 322–3
peripherally weighted irons 329
pitching 106–7
accuracy 107, 123, 140
address 146
backspin 134–5, 143, 147
backswing see backswing, pitching
body-turn practice 132–3
catcher, imaginary 122
distance judging 108, 110, 113, 119, 126–7, 161
divot-marks and swing

information 118–21, 143, 291
downswing see downswing, pitching
hovering club for rough shots 137
impact position, pre-setting 134–5
loft 123, 125, 126–7
multiple-target drill 141
obstructions 145, 160
perfect 146–7
pre-shot routine 312–3
speed limit, personal 112–3
stance 109, 121, 143, 146–7
swing, freeing up 136
swing length matching 126–7
swing path 130–1
swing, right-armed 27, 140
weight transfer 119
windy conditions 144
and wrist hinge 146
pitching wedge 151, 154, 330
bellied wedge shot 176–7
different kinds of 125, 128
green sloping upwards 171
on hard-packed sand 208
intermediate bunker shots 206–7
metal compound head 135
and plugged lie 218–9
practice 229
shots, different 128, 144–5
when to use 106
see also sand wedge; wedge play, types of 332–3
Player, Gary 114, 265
playing out of turn 338
plugged ball and free drop 344
plugged lie 218–9, 231, 344
positive thinking 177
posture
checking 24–5
iron play 104
putting 176, 236–7
tee shots 52–3, 64, 287
three-step technique 24
and topping the ball 287
see also stance; weight distribution
Poulter, Ian 278
practice nets 37
pre-shot routine 312–3
Price, Nick 10
problem shots 298–9
pull shot 291
punch-and-spin shot 226, 340
punching the ball low 305
push shot 290
putt line, straddling another 337
putter 330–1
centre-shafted 330–1
jumbo-fat grips 331
long 275, 331
mallet-headed 330

peripherally weighted 330, 331
putterface alignment 239–41, 246, 276, 279
putterface inserts 331
sweet spot 244, 245
toe, and fast putts 271, 273
toe-poke with 180
putting 232–3
address position 238, 239, 240, 250–1, 278
backswing, matching to distance 242–3, 260–1, 278, 279
ball position 238, 246, 278, 279
ball running speed 258–9
brush forward to check aim 257
bull's-eye at back of hole 247
century on the green 275
close-range, and precision 271
crossing hands style 276
downhill 271, 273
fast putts 271, 273
flowing stroke with one hand 270
and green see green
grip 176, 178, 234–5, 275, 276, 278
head down for perfect strike 245, 249, 279
holing-out skills and compass drill 252–3
hovering for smooth 272–3
and lag 241, 264, 276, 278
listen, don't look 249
long-range test 266–7
moving marker 342, 343
obstructions 342, 344
pace and line experiments 277
perfect 246, 249, 278–9
performance monitoring 323
pre-shot routine 312–3
putter sweet spot 244, 245
putterface alignment check 239–41, 246, 276, 279
from sand 225
short putts 274
stance 176, 236–7, 278–9
straight putt, treating every putt as 256
swing path 237, 241
technique, and chipping 178–9, 180, 182
three-putt, avoiding 258–9, 262, 266–7
up-and-down putts 262–3
visualization 268–9
wall, stroke practice against 246
weight distribution 237
and wind play 303
in winter conditions 320
wrist action, excess 264–5, 270, 278, 279

Q R

Quiros, Alvaro 61, 103
raking over bunker 203, 334–5
range-finding with every iron 68–9
reverse overlap grip 234–5, 276
rhythm
  swing and balance 103, 105
  and timing, tee shots 33, 35, 45
right-hand action, and throwing
  stone 196
Robertson, Allen 9
rope exercise to improve swing
  82–3
rough
  and ball position 289
  bellied wedge shot from collar
    of 176–7
  chipping from 157, 170,
    176–7, 180, 183, 317
  ball identification 343
  iron play 289, 299, 317
  strategy 316–7
  thick 299
round-the-clock drill 138–9,
  142–3
rules of golf 338–45

S

sand wedge 125, 298, 330
  bounce 191, 208
  and downslope 166
  and right-handed swings 189
  and varying bounce 226
  see also pitching wedge; wedge
Sarazen, Gene 191, 226
scoring, losing count of 319
set-up organization
  bunker play 188, 190
  chipping 150, 167, 182
  iron play, videoing 76–7
shadow, learning from 85
"shaking hands with the target"
  56–7, 65
shanked iron shot 285
shaping shots 306–7
short shots
  bunker play 221
  landing 169, 173
  putts, and watching hands 274
shotmaking
  escape shots 300–1, 340
  high and low shots 304–5
  problem shots, tackling 298–9
  shaping shots 306–7
  sloping lies 214–5, 294–7
  wind play 302–3, 305
sideslopes 214–5, 295
sidespin, and iron play 306–7
skied drive 46–7, 49, 286
slicing 282
  and 4 o'clock on the ball 43
  ways to avoid 40, 43, 45, 49,
    282
sloping lies 214–5, 294–7
Snead, Sam 111

speed limit, personal 112–3
Stableford play 332–3
stance
  and ball above feet 296, 297
  bunker play 188, 195, 208,
    221, 231
  checking 22–3
  chipping 150, 182, 185
  consistency 32
  distance between grip and
    thigh 25
  on downslopes 294
  in early days 9
  iron play 23, 104
  left knee fanned out 9
  in modern game 9
  pitching 109, 121, 143, 146–7
  putting 176, 236–7, 278–9
  and shoulder alignment 23
  tee shots 23, 31, 32, 287, 288
  3-cm rule 23
  on upslopes 295
  see also posture; weight
    distribution
stationary ball deflected 345
stretching exercises 310
stroke-and-distance penalty 339
strokeplay 332, 333
"suck back" 145
sucker pin placement 316
swing
  and club release 27, 94, 140
  and curving shots 99
  divot-marks, information from
    118–21, 143, 291
  feet together shots 96–7, 120
  followthrough 27, 47
  free, and clipping tee-peg 155
  freeing up 136
  length, and distance variation
    198–9, 200–1, 321
  length matching 126–7
  overswing 48
  path 27, 65, 99, 120–1, 130–1,
    230–1, 237, 241, 283
  path, chipping 105, 108, 151,
    153, 161, 169, 284
  rhythm and balance 103, 105
  right-armed 27, 140
  right-handed, bunker play 189
  rope exercise 82–3
  shadow, learning from 85
  sloping lies 296
  straight-armed 95, 300
  "trigger" to avoid freezing 114
  zones 9, 10, 26–7
swingers 60

T

target
  drill, multiple 141
  practice, chipping 168–9
  staggering, bunker play 209
tee shots 28–9
  accidental nudge 339

addressing 36, 54, 64, 65
backswing see backswing, tee
  shots
choking down on driver 38–9
clubs, using different 59
distance on the run 62–3
downswing, perfect 65
drivers, choice of 326–7
first of the day 314
forearms touching 53
hitting too hard 40, 65
and hooking 41, 283
and knee, flexing of right 47
loft 39
mental approach 318
obstructions 344
out-of-bounds threat 314–5,
  339
and outer limit 338–9
par-3 holes 63
penalties for excess of clubs
  338
perfect 64–5
posture 52–3, 64, 287
power loss 288
power shots 52–3, 56–7, 65
practice, and iron play 59
practice nets, hitting back of 37
practice time, importance
  of 30
pre-shot routine 312–3, 314
resistance, adding 48
rhythm and timing 33, 35, 45
"shaking hands with the target"
  56–7, 65
skied drive 286
slicing 40, 43, 45, 49, 282
stance 23, 31, 32, 287, 288
straight line down on ball 44
strategy 314–5
takeaway, keeping it all
  together 55
tee height and 50 per cent
  rule 32
tee, leaving in good shape 334
tee pegs, corridor of 34
"three off the tee" penalty 339
and wedge practice 35
weight distribution 25, 36, 46,
  48–9, 51, 288
wind play 62–3, 302
tension release 33, 136
Texas Wedge shot 157
3-cm rule 23
"three off the tee" penalty 339
"thumbs up" position 98
timekeeping 336–7
toe-poke 180
trees
  ball in cluster of 301, 340
  branches and launch angle
    102–3
Trevino, Lee 111

U

umbrella drill, chipping 158
upslope
  bunker play 210–1, 212
  chipping 165, 171
  club-up, 295
  stance 295
utility woods 328

V

Vardon, Harry 9, 18, 45
videoing set-up 76–7
visualization
  club loft 156–7, 175
  hitting to smaller target 268–9
  target practice 168–9, 175

W

waggling 40
waiting your turn 336
wall, stroke practice against 246
warm-up routine 310–1
water hazards 341–2
Watson, Tom 51, 162
wedge 330
  bellied shot from collar of
    rough 176–7
  gap wedge 125
  practice, and tee shots 35
  Texas Wedge shot 157
  see also pitching wedge; sand
    wedge
weight distribution
  chipping 150
  iron play 25
  putting 237
  sloping lies 294, 295, 296
  swing zones 27
  tee shots 25, 36, 46, 48–9,
    51, 288
  thick rough 299
  wood play 25
  see also posture; stance
wet grass 157
wind play 62–3, 302–3, 305
winter golf 320–1, 344
wood play 290–1
  fairway woods 81, 328
  and slicing 282
  3-wood and distance when
    teeing 39
  utility woods 328
  and weight distribution 25
wooden-shafted clubs 9, 10
Woods, Tiger 10, 11, 48, 104–5,
  125, 182, 341
Wright, Mickey 138
wrist action
  and pitching 146
  putting 264–5, 270, 278, 279
  and tee shots 58
wrong ball penalty 342

Z

Zoeller, Fuzzy 54

ACKNOWLEDGMENTS

THANKS FROM THE AUTHOR

In time-honoured fashion there are many people to whom I would like to express my thanks for their tremendously valuable contributions to this book; although unlike an Oscar winner's speech, I'll keep it brief.

First and foremost, well done to our models, all of whom toiled in the heat of the Spanish sun – thank you Carlos Dominguez Moreno, Julio Fernàndez Gõmez, Charlotte Grundberg, and Carlos Mena Quero. And to photographer Gerard Brown who did such a wonderful job of capturing the many hundreds of images required for this book, and under such a tight deadline. Thanks also to his support team on the photoshoot in Spain, ably marshalled by Nigel Wright. We could not have found a better location for photography than southern Spain and our thanks go to three wonderful golf clubs – El Chaparral, Finca Cortesin, and Alcaidesa – for kindly playing host to our team.

My sincere thanks also go to Managing Editor Stephanie Farrow, the book's editor Richard Gilbert, and the design team led by Phil Gamble. No one puts a book together better than the extremely talented and capable staff at Dorling Kindersley.

Finally, thanks to my Dad for introducing me to golf all those years ago. It certainly has been a life-enhancing experience!

THANKS FROM THE PUBLISHER

Dorling Kindersley would like to thank the following people for their help in the preparation of this book: Vishaal Mistry for design assistance; Martin Copeland, Jenny Baskaya, and Emma Shepherd for picture research; and Margaret McCormack for indexing.

PICTURE CREDITS

The publisher would like to thank the following for their kind permission to reproduce their photographs:

(Key: a-above; b-below/bottom; c-centre; l-left; r-right; t-top)

6–7 Getty Images. 8 Getty Images: (b); Hulton Archive (t). 9 Getty Images: Hulton Archive. 10 Getty Images: (b); Hulton Archive (t). 11 Getty Images: (t) (b). 16–7 Corbis: Randy Faris. 37 Getty Images: David Madison. 60 Getty Images: (bl). 61 Getty Images: US PGA TOUR (br). 64 Visions in Golf: (cl) (c) (cr). 64–5 Visions in Golf: (t). 65 Visions in Golf: (cr). 104 Visions in Golf: (cl) (c) (cr). 104–5 Visions in Golf: (t). 105 Visions in Golf: (cr). 146 Visions in Golf: (cl) (c) (cr). 146–7 Visions in Golf: (t). 147 Visions in Golf: (cr). 184 Visions in Golf: (cl) (c) (cr). 184–5 Visions in Golf: (t). 185 Visions in Golf: (cr). 191 Getty Images: Dave Cannon (br). 226 Getty Images: Dave Cannon (bl). 230 Visions in Golf: (cl) (c) (cr). 230–1 Visions in Golf: (t). 231 Visions in Golf: (cr). 243 Corbis: Paul Velasco; Gallo Images (br). 275 Getty Images: (br). 278 Visions in Golf: (cl) (c) (cr). 278–9 Visions in Golf: (t). 279 Visions in Golf: (cr) (cl/inset). 289 Getty Images: Dave Cannon (tr) (cl). 302 Getty Images: Dave Cannon (cl) (bl) (br). 316 Getty Images: Dave Cannon (cra) (bl). 317 Getty Images: Dave Cannon (br). 321 Getty Images: (bl) (tr). 328 Getty Images: Dave Cannon (cl) (bl) (clb). 331 Callaway Golf (br) . 332 Getty Images: US PGA TOUR. 333 Getty Images. 341 Getty Images: (bl). 343 Getty Images: Sports Illustrated (b). 345 Getty Images: (t).

All other images © Dorling Kindersley

For further information see:
www.dkimages.com

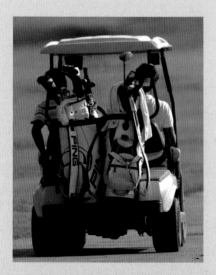